PRAISE FOR *GREAT COMMUNICATION SECRETS OF GREAT LEADERS*

"Baldoni's *Great Communication Secrets of Great Leaders* is a veritable handbook of tips, secrets, and procedures for leading like the great ones. Armed with this book, you can develop a strong leadership message, deliver it powerfully, and keep it evergreen."

—Nick Morgan, editor, *Harvard Management Communication Letter*, and founder, Public Words

"*Great Communication Secrets of Great Leaders* describes how to plan and deliver messages that get results. This remarkable book covers everything that drives successful communication, from the basic concepts that set the stage to the smallest details that make the biggest difference. Drawing on the author's years of experience as a practitioner and teacher of executive communication, it stresses the importance of leaders planning their messages and sustaining them over time. By featuring examples from a wide range of outstanding leadership communicators, *Great Communication Secrets of Great Leaders* brings the lessons of leadership communications to life in a clear and compelling way. For those who want to make a difference in an organization or those helping others to do so, I highly recommend this book."

—Chuck Snearly, director, Stakeholder Communications, Ford Motor Company

"WOW! *Great Communication Secrets of Great Leaders* is a wonderful journey from Appomattox to Calcutta, from Britain's finest hour to America's darkest day. John Baldoni gives us 1000 practical and actionable leadership lessons as he introduces us to dozens of famous and not-so-famous leaders. As you travel you will learn how to develop, deliver, and sustain your leadership message. Soon you're back home, realizing the most important leadership journey is inside your own heart. John is a great tour guide. My advice: take the trip! Now!"

—Boyd Clarke, CEO, tompeterscompany

"In the day and age of 'me first' and the spin speeches of politicians, the nation is crying out for leaders of character, for those who can communicate a purpose, who can 'walk the talk.' John Baldoni does this in *Great Communication Secrets of Great Leaders*. It's an enjoyable, easy-to-read book that is educational yet entertaining. Whether you are a student, a seasoned executive, a military leader, or a sports leader, this book should be your guide to better communication. It will provide you with a solid foundation."

—Donald E. Vandergriff, U.S. Army, editor of *Spirit, Blood and Treasure: The American Cost of Battle in the 21st Century*, and author of *Path to Victory: America's Army and the Revolution in Human Affairs*

"Staying connected with key stakeholders is a 'must have' for leaders at all levels. Thanks to John Baldoni for giving us an engaging and very practical set of guidelines for what leaders must do to build trust and achieve results that matter through effective communication. Kudos for a great contribution that will be useful for anyone interested in learning more about what it takes to lead in today's tumultuous world."

—Stew Friedman, practice professor, The Wharton School, former director, Leadership Development Center, Ford Motor Company, coauthor, *Work and Family—Allies or Enemies?*

"Baldoni bridges the 'Grand Canyon' between leaders who *want* to connect with their people and leaders who actually *do*. His leadership communication lessons are straight from the University of the Streets … they are insightful, practical, and actionable."

—Jim Haudan, president and CEO, Root Learning® Inc.

"If you want to be a great leader, you must study great leaders. John Baldoni offers excellent insight from some of the world's biggest difference-makers. I enjoyed it and I learned from it."

—Lloyd H. Carr, head football coach, University of Michigan

GREAT COMMUNICATION SECRETS OF GREAT LEADERS

ALSO BY JOHN BALDONI

Personal Leadership, Taking Control of Your Work Life

180 Ways to Walk the Leadership Talk

180 Ways to Walk the Motivation Talk (coauthored with Eric Harvey)

GREAT COMMUNICATION SECRETS OF GREAT LEADERS

John Baldoni

McGraw-Hill

New York Chicago San Francisco Lisbon London Madrid Mexico City Milan New Delhi San Juan Seoul Singapore Sydney Toronto

The McGraw-Hill Companies

22 23 24 25 26 27 28 29 LHN 22 21 20 19 18 17

ISBN 0-07-141496-7

McGraw-Hill books are available at special quantity discounts to use as premiums and sales promotions, or for use in corporate training programs. For more information, please write to the Director of Special Sales, Professional Publishing, McGraw-Hill, Two Penn Plaza, New York, NY 10121-2298. Or contact your local bookstore.

Library of Congress Cataloging-in-Publication Data

Baldoni, John.
Great communication secrets of great leaders / by John Baldoni.
p. cm.
ISBN 0-07-141496-7 (pbk)
1. 3. 3.
4. Title.
002 CIP

To Paul and Annie

Contents

Acknowledgments

This book represents the union of the two sides of my professional career—communications and leadership. As a result, this book reflects the sum of the experiences I have had in working to help men and women become better communicators and better leaders.

The people who have contributed to this book are many. I want to thank some special people at Ford Motor Company. Anne Marie Gattari allowed me to implement many of the ideas in this book, and Chuck Snearly provided me with insights into keeping leadership messages alive and fresh.

On the professional side, I want to thank Dan Denison and Bill Neale of Denison Consulting for their insights into how communications shapes culture. Stew Friedman of Wharton School pushed me to stretch my boundaries as a communicator. Stephen J. Gill provided valuable advice on the research and evaluation components of leadership communications. Peter Moorcroft was very helpful in shaping my thinking about the role of leadership communications in large organizations. Mark Linder of Ogilvy & Mather not only taught me about the power of brand, but also opened some doors, for which I am grateful. Nick Morgan, editor of the *Harvard Management Communications Letter*, deserves very special thanks for publishing some of this book's key concepts in article form.

I want to thank my writer colleagues, Chuck Dapoz and Chris Merlo, for their support and suggestions as well as their challenges to my concepts. Jeff Herman, my agent, believed in this book and made the connections that brought it to fruition. And my editor, Barry Neville, helped bring the final edit to completion. The book is better for his assistance. Janice Race and Alice Manning provided the copyediting this book needed.

On the home front, my wife, Gail Campanella, remained a constant source of support, eagerly reviewing the manuscript and doing essential administrative tasks. She also allowed me the freedom to work the extra hours that were needed to produce this book. I am forever grateful.

Prologue

If I went back to college again, I'd concentrate on two areas: learning to write and to speak before an audience. Nothing in life is more important than the ability to communicate effectively.

Gerald R. Ford

It could have been worse, much worse, but—fortunately for the nation—the bloodiest conflict in American history ended not with rancor and bitterness but with two men, the military leaders of their respective causes, sitting together at a small table in a rural courthouse. One was dressed in his resplendent gray uniform, his last one; the other wore a mud-splattered blue cavalryman's field coat. Their conversation was quiet. The victor recalled his meeting with the vanquished, 16 years his senior, during the Mexican War, in which both men had served. The older man said that he could not recall their meeting, but he appreciated the younger man's mention of it. After more discussion of their service in Mexico, the surrender terms were drafted. The terms were generous. Officers could keep their side arms, cavalrymen their horses. It was planting season, and if the nation were ever to heal, it would have to begin to renew itself sooner rather than later. And in this way, General Ulysses S. Grant accepted the surrender of General Robert E. Lee at Appomattox Courthouse, Virginia, on April 9, 1865. Later that day, another Union general, the oft-wounded, valorous Joshua Chamberlain, a hero of Gettysburg, accepted the surrender of Lee's forces with grace and dignity, ordering his men to salute their foe as they strode past to deposit their rifles. The significance of these acts—an amalgam of words, gestures, and symbols—was fundamental to the healing of a nation that had been "torn asunder."[1]

Sadly, the war was not yet completely over. Fighting continued sporadically but lethally throughout the South. Then came word of Abraham Lincoln's assassination, and many wondered how the South would react. Passions ran high in both North and South. With Lincoln dead, the voices of Northerners seeking retribution grew louder, and many in the South were willing to fight on. One officer said to Lee, "You have only to blow the bugle," and the troops would rally. Lee had returned to a devastated and destitute Richmond; he was sick of war and desperately wanted peace. At the end of April, the New York Herald *requested an interview; Lee had remained pub-*

licly silent since Appomattox. This gave Lee the opportunity he had been waiting for. Not only could he repudiate the killing of Lincoln, he could also issue a call to his fellow Southern generals to lay down their arms and avoid a protracted guerrilla war that could not have been won, but would have prolonged the bloodshed. Upon learning of Lee's wishes, the Confederate generals followed his example and surrendered. This savage war was hastened to a final denouement through the leadership messages of a general who at his surrender had given up his power but not the authority of his leadership communications. It was a profound moment, one in which words begat actions that created understanding and achieved inspired results.[2]

A leader can use words to accomplish much. Words by themselves are bits of information. Words backed by the leader's character, conviction, and personal example have the power to communicate: to inform, to exhort, to cheer, to heal, or to inspire.

Speaking out loud, the most self-evident form of communications, is probably the easiest thing any leader can do. Most people who are in supervisory positions have the ability to speak. The ability to speak, however, is not the same thing as the ability to communicate. Communications is a two-way process that involves both speaking and listening, and also checking for understanding. This is not easy. The ability to communicate is the leader's most effective tool. The capacity to construct a message, address it to another, listen for feedback, process that feedback, and continue to communicate in ways that are understood is one of the hardest things a leader will have to do. But it can be done. And it can be done by anyone who is willing to invest the time and effort to do it.

THREE THINGS

Great Communication Secrets of Great Leaders is about three big leadership ideas (see Figure P-1):

- *Developing the leadership message*—what you want to say and do
- *Delivering the leadership message*—getting the message across, verbally, mentally, and metaphorically
- *Sustaining the leadership message*—keeping the message alive and fresh and meaningful

FIGURE P-1 Leadership Messages

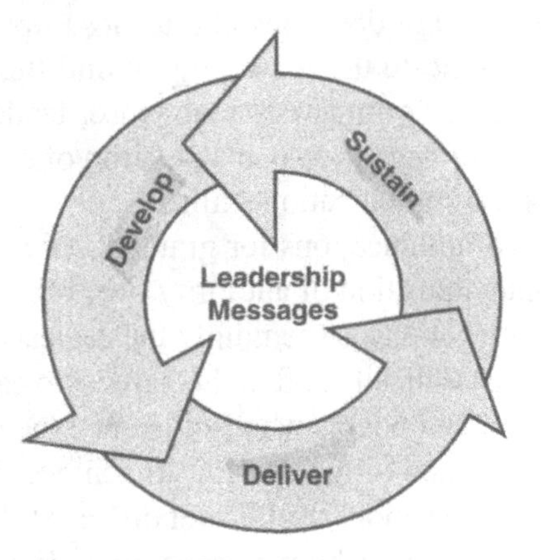

While each of these ideas is distinct, they form a cycle. There are no boundaries at which one begins and another ends. Effective leaders are always developing, delivering, and sustaining their leadership messages as part of their regular communications. The secret to good communications is to do it every day. Leaders who communicate regularly and frequently, both in good times and in bad, will improve organizational and individual performance, get results, and create a successful enterprise. And with each passing year, it seems, the imperative for good communications grows stronger.

A FAILURE TO COMMUNICATE

The chief reason that CEOs fail to achieve their aims is not lack of vision, lack of ambition, or even lack of desire. No, according to a *Fortune* magazine article, the chief reason leaders fail is lack of execution.[3] Three years later, *Fortune* explored why corporations fail. Of the ten reasons cited, four ("see no evil, dysfunctional board, fearing the boss, [and] dangerous culture") can be attributed to a failure of another sort—a failure of communications.[4]

Further affirmation of communications as a leadership attribute comes from presidential historian Robert Dallek. He describes five key factors of a successful presidency: "vision, pragmatism, consensus-building, charisma, and trustworthiness."[5] Four of these factors depend heavily upon an ability to communicate on multiple levels. Presidents, like all leaders, need to be able to describe where they are going (vision), persuade people to come along with them (consensus), connect on a personal level (charisma), and demonstrate credibility, i.e., do what they say they will do (trust). Even pragmatism depends on communications. Leaders need to describe the options facing an organization and make tough decisions about those options. It is then their responsibility to communicate the reasoning behind their decisions and the results of those decisions. So in a very real sense, leadership effectiveness, both for presidents and for anyone else in a position of authority, depends to a high degree upon good communication skills.

It is easy to take communications for granted. After all, anyone who has the ability to climb into a position of authority over others can communicate, right? Wrong. Communications is seemingly the easiest of leadership behaviors, but experience tells us that it is often the hardest to carry out consistently. How often do we hear about bosses who fail to set expectations, fail to listen to what people tell them, and in the end fail to achieve the results they were hired to achieve? Communications itself is not difficult. Verbal expression and listening to others are common human behaviors. The reason people find communications difficult is that it takes so much commitment. Often leaders are so busy doing all the other important things related to managing systems and people that they simply run out of time and thus do not communicate effectively. And that's the reason so many leaders fail at communications. Communications requires discipline, thought, perseverance, and the willingness to do it again and again every day.

Effective leadership, both personal and corporate, is effective communications. Leaders and employees need to be in synch throughout the decision-making and implementation process. Leaders and employees need to understand one another. Leaders and employees also need to be able to exchange ideas in an open and honest way. These things can occur only through communications, in particular through what I refer to in this book as *leadership communications*.

Great Communication Secrets of Great Leaders is the result of more than 20 years of helping leaders at all levels communicate their messages in ways that reflect their own viewpoints as well as those of the organizations for which they work. Just as there is no single way to lead, there is no single way to communicate—in fact, there are countless ways. What matters most is the willingness to do it, with a consistent message, a constancy of purpose, and a frequency of performance. In other words, leaders communicate all the time and do it willingly in order to convey their goals, gain support for those goals, and demonstrate concern for all who follow them.

MANY LEADERS, MANY STYLES

Examples of leadership communication form the context and heritage of our culture, past and present. These include

- Winston Churchill becoming prime minister of Great Britain in May 1940. Churchill rallied a nation under siege, inspiring hope and the will to persevere until victory over fascism was achieved.
- Mother Teresa gaining support for her mission to the "poorest of the poor" through her prayers, writing, and public appearances.
- George C. Marshall speaking to Congress on the need for military preparedness. He mobilized our armed forces to defeat fascism and later to rebuild a broken Europe.
- Katherine Graham providing leadership at the *Washington Post.* Graham's steady hand on the helm enabled the paper to face down a president and to weather a crippling strike and become a preeminent publishing power.
- Bill Veeck promoting baseball both as a game and as entertainment. Veeck's promotional outlook stemmed from his values of storytelling, listening to his constituents, and giving back to the fans.
- Rosabeth Moss Kanter demonstrating the role of effective communications during transformational change. Kanter's writings have provided a roadmap for two generations of managers seeking to cope with and embrace the changes that have swept the management landscape.
- Oprah Winfrey using her own personal stories to make connections with others in ways that dispel prejudice and illuminate and celebrate life.
- Rudy Giuliani taking command at the site of the World Trade Center collapse. He served as the lighting rod for both the grieving and the rebuilding of New York City in the wake of September 11.
- Shelly Lazarus demonstrating a leadership role in advertising management. She exemplifies how women can lead their companies as well as their industries and still lead fulfilled personal lives.
- Peter Drucker writing on the role of management. He invigorated the role of management by providing insight and direction.

What all these leaders have in common is a commitment to a cause larger than themselves. Each of them is using communications to further the leadership message through words and deeds. Each understands that leadership communications binds leader to followers in a partnership that is founded in mutual benefit and cemented by trust.

Leaders need to do more than just stand up and speak. They need to integrate communications into everything they do as leaders so that their communications, both oral and written, emerge from who they are as leaders and within the appropriate cultural context. Leaders who fail in communications will fail to achieve their organizational aims.

THE IMPORTANCE OF LEADERSHIP COMMUNICATIONS

Great Communication Secrets of Great Leaders shows how to develop and deliver the leadership message: how to develop it for organizationwide communications, create strong e-communications, and connect with the winning presentation. The book features a multipart communications planner, complete with illustrations, that provides advice and examples on how to craft a powerful presentation, deliver it with style, and create a lasting relationship. This book contains four sections:

- *Part I* deals with developing the leadership message, which is defined as a communication from the leader that covers a key organizational or business issue and is rooted in the cultural values of the organization. Examples of leadership messages include vision and mission statements, calls for transformational change, and calls to action. The main purpose of a leadership message is to build trust. The effectiveness of the leadership communication depends upon how it is communicated and in what manner it is disseminated—all-employee meetings, face-to-face, video, or email. Developing the message includes planning and proper selection of communication channels. Part I also traces the development of the message by tracking the evolution of a topic from its inception through the stages of an outline, draft, revision, and visualization.
- *Part II* covers the delivery of the leadership message. The leader must take what is in the message and proclaim it to the outside world. The leader must know the audience and what it expects to hear. An understanding of audience perception is essential to success at the podium. Connecting to the audience through voice and movement is necessary to underscore intention.
- *Part III* involves sustaining the leadership message. The work is not complete when the presentation is over; communications is an ongoing process. Essential to communications is ensuring continuous feedback. Leaders need to iterate and reiterate their messages in ways that con-

nect beyond words. An element of this connection involves coaching. Coaching is really leadership communication on an individual level. Leaders use their ability to communicate to develop their people to the next level of performance, both for the job they are in now and for the future.

- *Appendix A* is the "putting it all together" section. It includes Summary Notes, reiteration of key points; Action Steps, or suggestions for demonstrating leadership through communications; and the Leadership Communications Action Planner, a practical guide to communicating leadership messages and behaviors in the workplace.

Intercut throughout *Great Communication Secrets of Great Leaders* are real-life examples of how leaders have used communications to amplify their leadership. Written in the style of vignettes, these stories, gleaned from history, business, and sports, illustrate key principles of leadership communication. Each story concludes with a dot-point summary of the leadership message.

NO MYSTERY, JUST PRACTICE

Great Communication Secrets of Great Leaders takes the mystery out of communications. These four sections give the leader a complete picture of what it takes to develop, deliver, and sustain a leadership message. The secret is to adopt a leadership perspective, to learn how to craft the message and how to deliver it convincingly so that the message sticks. The ultimate goal of communications is to address immediate concerns and issues, and to open the door to future dialogue, discovery, and engagement. *Great Communication Secrets of Great Leaders* can help you push that door open so that your ideas and those of others can flow freely back and forth.

Good luck and best wishes.

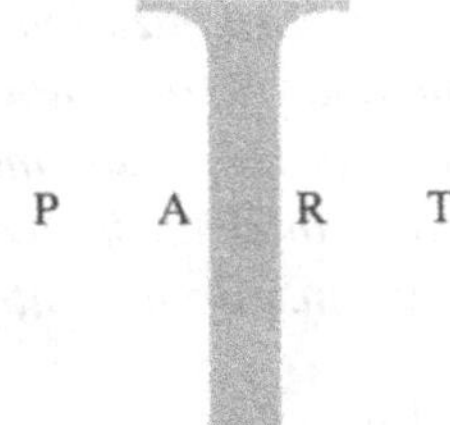

Developing the Leadership Message

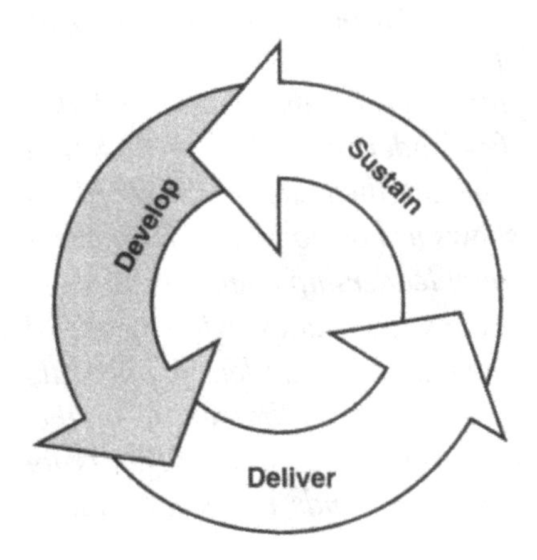

COMMUNICATION IS THE GLUE that holds organizations together; it is the chief means by which people relate to one another. The aim of organizational communications is to ensure that everyone understands both the external and internal issues facing the organization and what individuals must do to contribute to the organization's success.

Communications belongs to everyone in the organization; it is not a functional responsibility limited to marketing, public relations, or human resources. Communications must become a core competency—the responsibility of everyone within the organization.

A key element of organizational communications is the messages from the leader that we call leadership communications. The chapters in Part I will show you how to develop your own leadership point of view, which you can develop into your leadership message.

At the end of each chapter are vignettes of exemplary leadership communicators. Frequently they focus on a specific moment in time when the leader used his or her communications skills to convey a leadership message in a manner that affected the vision or mission of an organization and resulted in a positive outcome.

This collection is by no means definitive. In fact, a good argument could be made that every successful leader is at heart an effective leadership communicator. The leaders presented come from all walks of life. The single unifying thread is that they all have a personal leadership style that is rooted in communications as a means of accomplishing their vision, mission, and goals as a leader for the good of their organization and for themselves as contributors to the organization.

It is worth noting that not all of the leaders included in these vignettes are world-class orators—few leaders are. All of them, however, do have an exceptional ability to communicate their ideas with words and to listen with their hearts. Each of them shows us how to lead in thoughts, words, and deeds, and in that, all are exceptional leadership communicators.

Each of the vignettes concludes with Leadership Communications Lessons that are designed to help you identify particular leadership communication strengths. You will notice that many of the lesson points occur repeatedly—with new examples, of course. This is for good reason. Good leadership communications depends upon constancy, consistency, and frequency.

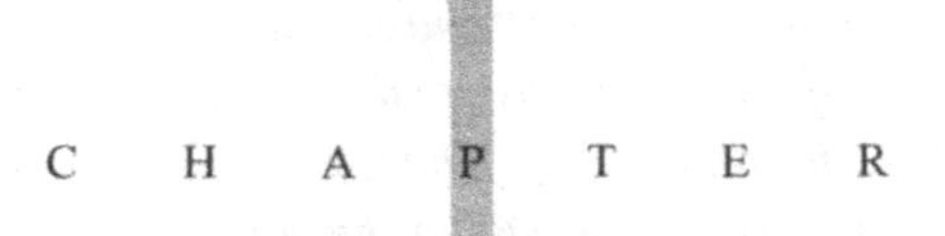

Of all the talents bestowed upon men, none is so precious as the gift of oratory.

Winston Churchill

WHAT IS LEADERSHIP COMMUNICATIONS?

THE COMPANY IS A BONA FIDE SUCCESS. Its stock price is climbing. Market analysts are praising the management team. Morale is high. For a brief, shining moment, it seems that the company can do no wrong.

Then it all comes apart. Perhaps it's a new product failure, a defection of a senior leader to a competitor, or a market reversal, but suddenly the only people calling on the company are members of the media looking to find out what went wrong.

When this happens, and it seems to happen in the cycle of any successful enterprise, the company's leaders have two choices when it comes to communications: They can say nothing and hope the story just goes away, or they can speak out and work out their issues with input from key stakeholders.

Invariably companies make the wrong choice—in the face of bad news, they hibernate rather than proclaim. Worse, senior managers huddle quietly among themselves rather than speak even to employees. When this happens, communication does continue. Communication, like nature, abhors a vacuum. In the absence of word from the leader, people will create their own messages, typically in the form of rumor, innuendo, and gossip. The net result is a compounding of difficulties: Employees who could be part of the solution instead become part of the problem. Why? Because they are uninformed—worse, they are ill informed. The leader needs to get out front and tell the truth, instead of letting people draw their own conclusions. When you leave employees to draw their own conclusions without providing the proper message, they will draw the opposite conclusion from the one you want them to draw. They will automatically assume the worst, when perhaps the problem is not so grave, if it is addressed in time.

Have you ever heard something that sounds right but does not feel right? For example, when the boss says, "Our people are this company's most valuable resource," you groan because you know it's a cliché. You also know better. The boss rules by fear and looks over your shoulder constantly. Your coworkers are frustrated at their inability to make decisions. Your subordinates are fearful of losing their jobs. And the bean counters are making noises about impending job cuts. And this from a company where people are important! Could it be that there is a disconnect between the speaker and the message? Exactly! The words are not consistent with the boss's behaviors. As a result, what sounds well and good comes across as phony and false. This is an example of a situation where speaker and message do not intersect; there is a lack of credibility.

Effective messages are built upon trust. Trust is not something that we freely grant our leaders; we expect them to earn it. How? By demonstrating leadership in thought, word, and deed. Credible leaders are those who by their actions and behaviors demonstrate that they have the best interests of the organization at heart. They are the type of bosses who view themselves as supporters; they want their people to succeed, and they provide them with the help they need in order to achieve. These bosses know that they will be judged by the accomplishments of the individuals or teams who report to them, and that is why they invest so heavily in those individuals or teams.

When a leader makes a commitment to the success of individuals in order to achieve organizational goals, that leader is well on the way to earning trust. All of the leader's specific actions, such as articulating the vision, setting expectations, determining plans, and allowing for frequent feedback, are further ways of demonstrating trust.

The message emerging from a leader whom we trust is said to be a *leadership message*. Such a message is rooted in the character of the individual as well as his or her place within the organization. The leadership message is essential to the health of the organization because it stems from one of the core leadership behaviors—communications. Of all leadership behaviors, the ability to communicate may be the most important. Communications lays the foundation for leading others.

WHAT IS LEADERSHIP COMMUNICATIONS?

Leadership communications consists of those messages from a leader that are rooted in the values and culture of an organization and are of significant importance to key stakeholders, e.g., employees, customers, strategic partners, shareholders, and the media. These messages affect the vision, mission, and transformation of an organization. The chief intention of a leadership message is to build trust between the leader and her or his constituency. Traits of leadership communications (shown in Figure 1-1) reflect:

- *Significance.* Messages are about big issues that reflect the present and future of the organization (e.g., people, performance, products, and services).
- *Values.* Messages reflect vision, mission, and culture.
- *Consistency.* Messages exemplify stated values and behaviors.
- *Cadence.* Messages occur with regularity and frequency.

In its simplest form, leadership communication is communication that flows from the leadership perspective. It is grounded in the character of the leader as well as the values of the organization. It is an expression of culture as well as an indicator of the climate, e.g., openness, integrity, and honesty.

FIGURE 1-1 Leadership Communications Model

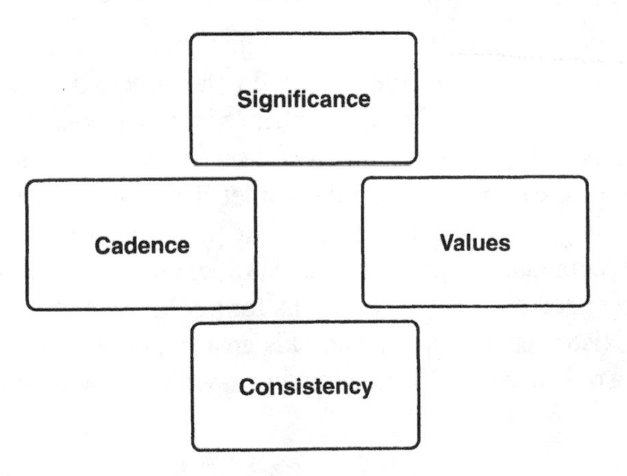

PURPOSE OF LEADERSHIP COMMUNICATIONS

There are many types of leadership communications. Each of them emerges from a leadership action that is communicated from the point of view of the leader—i.e., doing what is beneficial for the organization and the people in it. Leadership communications are designed to engage the listener, gain commitment, and ultimately create a bond of trust between leader and follower. They also do something more: They drive results, enabling leader and follower to work together more efficiently because they understand the issues and know what has to be done to accomplish their goals.

Specifically, leadership messages do one or more of the following:

- *Affirm organizational vision and mission.* These messages let people know where the organization is headed and what it stands for. General George C. Marshall lived and breathed the core values of the U.S. Army. His penchant for preparation prepared the nation for fighting the conflict it did not want to fight—World War II. By giving detailed briefings to Congress, developing a cadre of superior officers, revamping military training, and supporting President Franklin Roosevelt, Marshall mobilized the armed forces to go overseas and defeat the tyrannical powers of the Axis. And later, as secretary of defense, he helped Europe recover economically, socially, and politically through a comprehensive aid program that eventually bore his name, the Marshall Plan.
- *Drive transformational initiatives, e.g., change!* These messages get people prepared to do things differently and give the reasons why. Rich Teerlink, former CEO of Harley-Davidson, spent much of his time at the helm enkindling a passion for the company among dealers, owners, and employees. Part of this passion was rooted in the need to transform Harley from an old-line manufacturer into a modern enterprise in which employees shared in the voice and the vision.
- *Issue a call to action.* These messages galvanize people to rally behind an initiative. They tell people what to do and how to do it. Rudy Giuliani, as mayor of New York City, inherited a city whose citizenry accepted as fact that high crime, social service failures, and city hall ineptitude were part of the social contract. Through a combination of daily meetings with city agencies, public proclamations, and holding people accountable, Giuliani reduced crime, reinvigorated social agencies, and raised citizens' expectations for public servants' performance. Giuliani also prepared himself and his government for prompt response to the horrible events of September 11, in which New York City served

as a proud example of civic and individual and collective heroism, stoicism, and eventual healing.

- *Reinforce organizational capability.* These messages underscore the company's strengths and are designed to make people feel good about the organization for which they work. Katherine Graham, publisher of the *Washington Post*, relied upon the people in her organization to build a world-class news organization. Her public comments in the face of the publication of the Pentagon Papers, the Watergate investigations, and nasty labor struggles at the paper demonstrated her undying commitment to the paper.
- *Create an environment in which motivation can occur.* These messages provide reasons why things are done and create a path of success for people to follow. They also describe the benefits of success, e.g., a more competitive organization, more opportunities for promotion, or increased compensation. Joe Torre, manager of the New York Yankees and winner of four World Series in his tenure, believes that everyone on the team has a role to play. His quiet demeanor, coupled with supportive words and actions, has created an environment in which players feel that they can achieve and strive to do so.
- *Promote a product or service (and affirm its link to the organization's vision, mission, and values).* These messages place what the organization produces within the mission, culture, and values of the organization; e.g., we create products that improve people's lives. Shelly Lazarus, the CEO of Ogilvy & Mather, a leading advertising agency, makes her living using communications to promote the virtues of internationally known brands like IBM and Ford Motor Company. She applies the same commitment to promoting her agency's brand as a place where exceptionally talented people can succeed.

EXAMPLES OF LEADERSHIP MESSAGES

The style of leadership messages varies according to their purpose. Here are some examples:

VISION

Our challenge is to complete this project by year's end. When the project is complete, we will have the exciting new product our customers have been asking for. This product will enable them to work more efficiently, and it will enable us to grow our business profitably.

TRANSFORMATION

The challenges in the market dictate that we do things differently—internally in the way we operate and externally in the way we serve our customers. The changes we are calling for will not be easy, but they will be necessary. Yet we must learn to embrace change. Instead of viewing change as something to be feared, we must leverage its power and capitalize on the new opportunities it will bring us.

CALLS TO ACTION

The days ahead will call for critical thinking and timely action. We need all of us to pull together as a team. I am asking each of you for your support as we go forward together in our quest to create a better future for us and for future generations.

EXPECTATION

I view my leadership role as one of supporting our team. I expect everyone on our team to support our collective objectives and work cooperatively with one another. I expect people on our team to think and problem-solve for themselves. When you encounter obstacles that you cannot resolve, I expect you to bring them to my attention. If you stonewall and hide problems, you will be asked to leave the project.

COACHING

Your enthusiasm for this job is admirable. I would like to make a few suggestions for ways in which you might improve your performance.

RECOGNITION

You have done an outstanding job on this project. I want you to know how important your contributions are to our team. Bravo. Well done!

You can probably think of many more examples yourself. These are just for starters. The importance of leadership communications is the seminal role it plays in enabling the leader to succeed.

ENABLING LISTENING

Communications, as Peter Drucker has written, is less about information than it is about facilitating kinship within the culture.[1] Employees must feel that they have a stake in the organization and its outcome. The ownership stake is initiated, nurtured, augmented, tested, and fulfilled through leadership communications. It is absolutely critical for the leader to facilitate two-way communications, specifically allowing feedback in the form of ideas, suggestions, and even dissent. Too often communications within organizations is interpreted as being one-way from the top, that is, information is disseminated in neat packages like commercial messages. In fact, leaders would do well to emulate one aspect of the advertising process, and that is the relentless search for information in the form of consumer research. Advertisers want to know what you think of the message. Leaders can do the same. It's called listening.

REITERATING LEADERSHIP

Communicating the leadership message over and over again in many different circumstances lets employees come to a better understanding of what the leader wants, what the organization needs, and how they fit into the picture. In time, leader and followers form a solidarity that is rooted in mutual respect. When that occurs, leader and followers can pursue organizational goals united in purpose and bonded in mutual trust.

The chief aim of organizational communications is to ensure that everyone understands both the external and internal issues facing the organization and what individuals must do to contribute to the organization's success. Communications belongs to everyone in the organization; it is not a functional responsibility limited to marketing, public relations, or human resources. Communications must become a core competency—the responsibility of everyone within the organization. Toward this end, management must establish a climate that ensures that employees feel free to express their ideas and concerns. At the same time, management must be clear in its expectations for individuals, teams, and the organization. Management must also structure its communications in ways that are meaningful and in keeping with the culture of the organization.

Communications Planner: The Leadership Message

Leadership communications emerge from organizational culture and values as well as from the values of the leader. Their ultimate aim is to build, or continue to build, a relationship between leader and follower.

As you think about your communications, take a quick assessment of your organizational culture and its values. Culture is often referred to as the way an organization behaves, i.e., its attitudes, beliefs, actions, and value system.

1. How would you describe the culture in your organization?
2. What are the core values of your organization?

3. What are your core values?
4. Are your values and those of your organization in harmony? If so, how? If not, why not?
5. How can you use your communications to strengthen your leadership role?
6. Pick one thing you can do in the next week to improve your communications.
7. How would you like people to remember you as a leader?

WINSTON CHURCHILL—THE LION WHO ROARED FOR HIS PEOPLE

Winston Churchill wrote this about becoming prime minister in May 1940 during what some have called Britain's darkest hour:

> As I went to bed at about 3 a.m., I was conscious of a profound sense of relief. At last I had the authority to give directions over the whole scene. I felt as if I were walking with destiny, and that all my past life had been but a preparation of this hour and for this trial. . . . I thought I knew a good deal about it all, and I was sure I should not fail.[2]

Soon enough, Churchill would refer to this period, in which Britain, her skies defended by men in their twenties and her people bloodied, battered, and bruised by nightly bombardments, stood alone against Nazi Germany, as her "finest hour." It was a phrase that historians would later use to describe his performance as leader.

How did he do it? His own words just cited give a good indication. He knew a "good deal": His two stints as First Lord of the Admiralty, plus his time as minister, had given him insight into how the military and government must coordinate their efforts. He had the "authority to give directions": He had led men in battle, in government service, and in Parliament. He was one with "destiny": As a historian and an avid reader, he measured himself against the legacies of great leaders in wartime. He was confident: "I was sure I should not fail." As historian Geoffrey Best amply illustrates in his one-volume meta-biography, Churchill had been preparing for this challenge for his entire life: as soldier, parliamentarian, minister, historian, and journalist.

A NATURAL COMMUNICATOR

What Churchill's words do not say, but imply, is this: He was a born communicator. He knew how to describe a scene, present a point of view, and tell a good story. He also, as his biographer Geoffrey Best writes, put his audience at the center of the action. During his speeches and broadcasts of the war years, he positioned the British people at the center of the world; he spoke to them as actors on the world stage.[3] By so doing, he made them feel a sense of importance—or, as we would say today in management, encouraged them to take a position of ownership of the issue. When this occurs, people have a sense of their own destiny; during any great event, such as a war, people may feel a sense of insignificance, a sense that they have no ability to affect the outcome. Churchill's speeches counteracted that sentiment as he spoke again and again of the individual contributions of the British people at home or abroad.

Churchill made certain that his message got through. His speeches in Parliament were of course widely covered. And when he took to the airwaves, people stopped what they were doing, whether at home or at work, to listen. He courted the press barons of his day, in particular Lord Beaverbrook, making him a member of his Cabinet.

Churchill also made frequent use of memos, or, in his parlance, "minutes." Reading samples of them, one gets the feeling that he was totally immersed in the activity, quick with suggestions or requests for follow-up.[4] His memo writing enabled him to use his pen when he did not have the luxury of face-to-face communication. These memos also documented what occurred and what follow-up actions resulted. Again and again, Churchill insisted on written communications for precisely this reason: He wanted to be in the loop on important decisions.[5]

BRUTAL HONESTY

Churchill was direct and straight with his people. He did not hide the dangers that faced the island kingdom in the dark days of 1940. As he told the House of Commons in his first speech after becoming prime minister,

> I would say to the House, as I said to those who have joined this government: "I have nothing to offer but blood, toil, tears, and sweat."
>
> We have before us an ordeal of the most grievous kind. We have before us many, many long months of struggle and of suffering. You ask, what is our policy? I can say: "It is to wage war, by sea, by land, and air, and with all our might and with all the strength that God can give us."[6]

Ever the realist, Churchill knew that he could not simply deliver a challenge. He had to sketch his vision of the end—a note of inspiration in a time of desperation.

> You ask, what is our aim? I can answer with one word: It is victory, victory at all costs, victory in spite of all terror, victory, however long and

> hard the road may be; for without victory, there is no survival. Let that be realized; no survival for the British Empire, no survival for all that the British Empire has stood for . . . and I say, "come then, let us go forward together with our united strength."[7]

With that speech, which is brief by Churchillian standards, he rallied Parliament, which had not been favorably disposed toward him. As he closed, he, along with the House, was in tears. This speech was also the beginning of the metaphysical union between Churchill and the British people that would endure throughout the war. As philosopher Isaiah Berlin essayed,

> The Prime Minister was able to impose his imagination and his will upon his countrymen . . . precisely because he appeared to them larger and nobler than life and lifted them to an abnormal height in a moment of crisis. [In doing so] it did turn a number of inhabitants of the British Isles out of their normal selves [and capable of heroism].[8]

"FLYING VISITS"

One way in which Churchill maintained unity with his people was by meeting and mingling with them. From his earliest days, he had had a love of action. As prime minister, he took it upon himself to make frequent "flying visits" to the front in North Africa or Europe, to America to press British interests with the Roosevelt administration, and even to Moscow and Yalta to negotiate Soviet support during the war and stem Soviet aggression in the postwar era. Another kind of flying visit was to his own people. He visited the London Docklands area, which was heavily bombed during the Blitz, and even risked his own life when he stayed until nightfall and was caught in the middle of a raid. Never lacking in courage, Churchill believed it was important that he both see the damage firsthand and be seen as a leader who was one with his people.

LEADERSHIP QUERY

One of the methods Churchill used to exert a measure of control, which also helped him to come to grips with issues, was interrogation. Military analyst Eliot Cohen writes that Churchill did not just ask a question and then forget it; he followed up with "a relentless querying of their assumptions and arguments, not just once but in successive iterations of a debate."[9] While at times this drove his generals and aides crazy, it did keep Churchill informed and his direct reports on their toes. Churchill, unlike other wartime leaders, was both a former military officer and a historian. So while his questions may have irritated his generals and aides, and while at times he did go too far, Churchill's breadth of knowledge lent him a greater degree of credibility in military matters.

One story among many illustrates Churchill's insight as well as his willingness to ferret out answers. Upon learning that regimental patches (a form of military insignia) were no longer being issued to British troops, Churchill investigated. The Army Office said that it was cooperating with the Board of Trade, which had forbidden the patches as an unnecessary use of cloth. In reality, the Board of Trade had no problem with the patches; the Army was making excuses for its "wildly unpopular decision." The real issue, as Churchill understood, was not a patch of cloth; it was esprit de corps. British Tommies identified with their regiments; to deprive them of this distinction would adversely affect morale. The regimental patches returned.[10]

Unlike lesser leaders, Churchill expected his generals to disagree with him. He did not want yes men; he wanted commanders who could think and plan for themselves.[11] And this is why he had such fractious relationships with his chiefs of staff. By repeatedly questioning their decision making, Churchill assured himself, and by extension the British people, that their military strategies were sound. Mistakes were made, of course, but Cohen believes that Churchill's hands-on approach, chiefly by virtue of his communications, was the proper course.[12]

LEADERSHIP OF PRAGMATISM

Churchill was a pragmatist. He was elected to Parliament as a member of the Liberal party, and he was a minister in David Lloyd George's cabinets before and during the First World War. When the fortunes of the Liberals declined, he declared for the Conservatives, his father's party, and in the late 1920s became chancellor of the exchequer, again something his father had been. His party switch was opportunistic, of course, but it was born of his need to be in the thick of the action, to be of service, to be doing something of value and merit. As a result of his opportunism, he was widely disliked throughout his career by those of his own class as well as by party loyalists. As his biographers point out, it was his service as prime minister that endeared him to the people. Prior to that, all too often he had been regarded more as a busybody, an opportunist, and a self-promoter.

Contrary to his image as a tough leader, Churchill was repeatedly kind to his adversaries once he had defeated them. He kept his predecessor, Neville Chamberlain, whom he had criticized for his appeasement strategy in dealing with Hitler, in his War Cabinet. In part this was due to the fact that most Conservatives favored Chamberlain over Churchill; nonetheless, Churchill was generous to his political enemies after the battle was won—something his adversaries were not throughout his long career in politics. (When Chamberlain died in November 1940, Churchill gave a eulogy for him in the House of Commons.)[13]

Churchill put his own perspective on his wartime leadership when he said to the House of Commons in 1954, "It was a nation and race dwelling all around the globe that had the lion heart. I had the luck to be called upon to give the roar."[14] Never have the forces of freedom been blessed with such a roar!

Leadership Communications Lessons

Give people ownership of their own destiny. Make your stakeholders feel that they are at the center of the issue. Dramatize their role in the events. Give them ownership of their destiny. Churchill's wartime messages echoed this theme again and again.

Be consistent and repetitious. Never be afraid to repeat your leadership message over and over again. Churchill had railed against Hitler and Nazism for years prior to the outbreak of the war. When Germany did attack Poland, Churchill looked prescient.

Lead from the front. Go to the front lines. Churchill did this to great effect all through his career, not simply during the war but all during his service in government.

Be curious. Ask questions. Look for answers. Churchill surrounded himself with people smarter than himself from whom he could learn.

Publicize your message. Tell your story to people through the media. As a journalist and historian, Churchill knew how to craft a story. During the war, he practically collaborated with Lord Beaverbrook, a press baron, to convey his point of view to his people and the world.

Be honest. Tell it straight. Churchill was brutally honest in his wartime speeches; he let his people know the ordeal they would have to face if they were to be victorious.

Live your message. Churchill embodied the spirit of the British people in their darkest days. He was emboldened by the terrible odds.

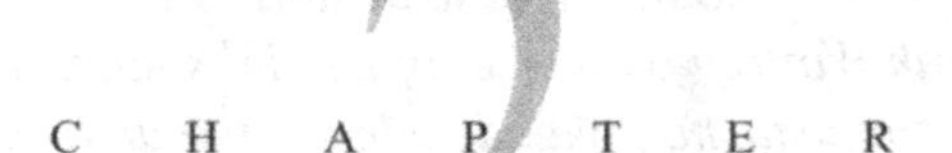

C H A P T E R 2

So what ties us together? We're tied together by our belief in political democracy. We're tied together by our belief in religious freedom. We're tied together by our belief in capitalism. . . . We're tied together because we respect human life. We're tied together because we respect the rule of law. Those are the group of ideas that make us Americans.

Rudy Giuliani

WHO ARE YOU . . . AND WHY ARE YOU TALKING TO ME?

THERE IS A STRIKING MOMENT IN THE MOVIE PATTON *where George C. Scott speaks stirringly, almost poetically, about the warrior culture and the sacrifice it takes to be a soldier. In that instant, you can catch a glimpse of what it means to be a leader speaking to a group of followers. Here is Patton, the archetype of the American general, expounding on his theory of the warrior in history. He is confident, purposeful, and very direct. In short, he is a man who knows who he is and why he is speaking. That is the moment of awareness that every leadership speaker should strive to achieve.*

Switch to another scene: Oprah Winfrey on the set of her TV studio. She alternates between calmness and enthusiasm, joy and sadness, fun and seriousness. Ms. Winfrey is a world away from a fictionalized George Patton, but she is every bit as dynamic and in control as he was—and maybe more so. She is a speaker who possesses the moment of awareness. She knows who she is and what her message is.

Patton and Winfrey are not unique. Every good leader-presenter possesses a high degree of self-awareness mixed with self-understanding of his or her role as a communicator. To many, the following questions may seem obvious, but until the framework for speaking is defined, the message cannot be clear. In this chapter, we will explore two concepts:

- Who are you as a leadership communicator (e.g., a presenter, a coach, or something else)?
- Why are you speaking to me?

DISCOVERING WHO YOU ARE AS A LEADERSHIP COMMUNICATOR

Creating a leadership message is about having a point of view. It is the perspective that you bring to the subject material as a leader within the organization. Your perspective on the issue emerges from your role within the organization as well as the content of your leadership character, i.e., what you stand for.

It is important to note, however, that a leader's speaking style on the stump in front of an audience can differ somewhat from that leader's private side. Some of the most dynamic leaders may be quiet and shy off stage. They reserve their passion for the stage and the audience, rather like actors do. Likewise, some leaders who are lively and funny one on one are absolute duds on stage. This occurs because they have been unable to capture their private persona or are unwilling to share it with others in a public forum.

As a leadership communicator, you will be called upon to make your messages public. Why? Because that's how you lead. When a leader keeps everything inside, people are left to their own devices to try and figure out what the leader may, or may not, want. This is a failure of communications and a failure of leadership.

FIGURE 2-1 Types of Leadership Communicators

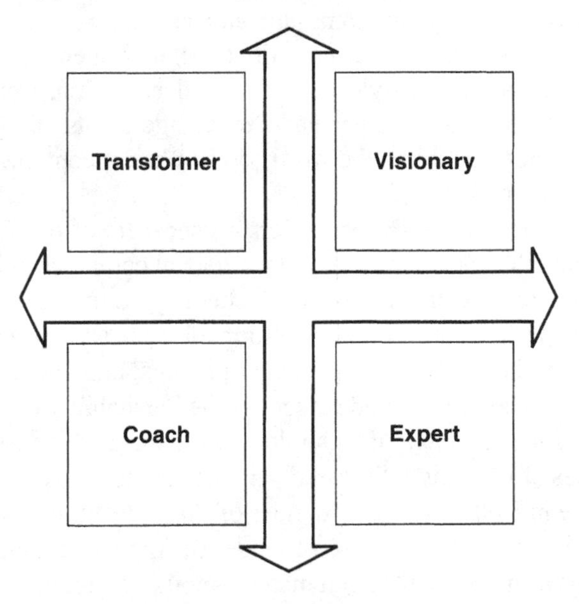

FOUR TYPES OF LEADERSHIP COMMUNICATORS

The role that you, as a leader-presenter, play in public is up to you. As a general rule, the closer you are on stage to what you are in private, the more meaningful and believable your presentation will be.

We offer four models of leadership presentation (see Figure 2-1).

THE EXPERT

The first type of leadership communicator is the *expert*, or the keeper of the mission. The expert holds to the organization's mission—what the organization is and how it conducts business. Experts base their decision making on facts and their relationship to the business environment—how the company can anticipate and capitalize on market opportunities.

Colin Powell is an excellent example of the expert who understands the mission and what it takes to fulfill it. As one who was raised in the military as a soldier and then as a military aide to politicians, Powell knows his subject matter. When you listen to him speak, he presents his point of view as a matter of fact; in other words, he is abiding by the mission.

Corporate leaders, too, can be experts. They also keep close tabs on their human resources, always evaluating whether they have the right people doing the jobs and what they need to do to develop the next generation of leaders.

THE VISIONARY

The second type of leadership communicator is what we call the *visionary*. Visionaries are those leaders whose ardent belief in their cause outweighs their words. Their speaking style comes from deep within, from their inner core values. Their mission is to persuade, to change points of view. And their leadership does not stop when the words do. Rather, it continues in the conduct of their daily lives.

One of the most impassioned leadership speakers of our times is Steve Jobs. A pioneer in the development of the personal computer, Jobs is a highly vocal advocate for the integration of technology into one's lifestyle. An accomplished speaker, Jobs knows how to involve the audience, how to tell a story, how to use language to draw mental pictures, and, most convincingly, how to use his passion to persuade others of the inevitability of his cause.

Jobs mixes the language of technology with a gee-whiz fascination with the possibilities of what digitally based personalized technologies can deliver. His experience in Hollywood as a founder of Pixar, an animation house, coupled with his iconic stature as the co-founder of Apple Computer, lends Jobs a stature that few in his industry can match. Another secret to Jobs's ability to sell his message is his willingness to intertwine his personal destiny with that of Apple. Thus, his message becomes larger than life and has more of an opportunity of being heard, not simply by dedicated users of Apple computers, but also by the mainstream media.

In our context, the visionary has a passion that supercedes spoken words. The message itself is always in what the speaker says—as it is with the expert—but what gives it power is the leader's conviction concerning the cause. The visionary as a leader-presenter is consumed with passion. He or she believes in the cause and wants others to embrace it.

THE COACH

The third type of leadership communicator is a combination of the previous two—part visionary and part expert. We call this type of leader the *coach*. The coach is a collaborator, the one who is called upon by virtue of her or his expertise in a particular subject. Coaches are those who change organizations one person at a time. They look for the unique way to communicate to an individual by discovering what motivates that person, e.g., more money, advancement, or prestige. Once the coach learns the motivational point, he or she can leverage it to help the person succeed.

More and more management, and by extension leadership, involves coaching. Why? Leaders are evaluated on the results of their people. It is up to the leader to enable the team to succeed. Success depends upon communication, as the leader must determine what people need and how the leader can deliver it.

Leader-coaches must adjust their focus throughout the day to address the needs of individuals as well as the needs of the team. The model of the successful sports coach is an apt example. Vince Lombardi was a coach who was able to communicate to players one at a time; his players say that he got them to play better because he raised their expectations of themselves. In other words, he elevated their own perceptions of their abilities and in so doing enabled them to play better.

When Lombardi addressed the entire team, he leveraged the raised expectations to the entire team. But he did more: He provided a firm foundation. How? By teaching. Having begun his coaching career as a high school teacher, Lombardi continued his teaching of the fundamentals. His teaching gave the team a framework upon which they could apply their individual and collective talents.

THE TRANSFORMER

The fourth type of leadership communicator is again one part visionary, another part expert, but this individual leans toward the visionary. He or she is the *transformer*: The mission is to persuade—to change minds. Transformers also are one part visionary. They know where they want to take their people, and they apply their selling skills to convince people to come along with them. The transformer as a leader-presenter is one who has both the information and the conviction to persuade the listener to her or his point of view.

Think of a successful salesperson. Think of the words that come to mind when you think of such an individual: knowledgeable, personable, willing to take questions, patient, and persistent. All of these are qualities that salespeople—and presenters who want to persuade others—need to have in abundance.

A good example of a transformer is Mother Teresa. As a sister working in the slums of Calcutta, she brought food, rudimentary medical assistance, and hope to the street people. Realizing strength in numbers, she founded a missionary order to carry out her good intentions. Their continual presence in Calcutta reminds the rest of the world of its obligation to those less fortunate. As word of her work spread throughout the world, she became a willing participant in "selling the mission" to those who could be of assistance. She badgered popes, princes, presidents, and celebrities, all in the name of her mission. She communicated her zeal for her mission through her writing and her public appearances. Her example reminds us of what it takes to make a difference.

Keep in mind that your leadership communication style may vary from situation to situation. One day you may need to be the expert, adhering to the organizational mission. Other times, you may act as the coach, willing to advise, but careful to let the audience make up its own mind. And still other times, you may be communicating in all four modes, depending upon the situation.

DISCOVER WHY YOU ARE SPEAKING

Once you know who you are as a leader-presenter (visionary, expert, coach, or transformer), it is necessary for you to determine *why* you are speaking.

- *Is it to explain?* The most common purpose of a presentation is to convey information as a means of explanation. We see examples of the explanation presentation at press conferences as well as in corporate boardrooms.
- *Is it to overcome objections?* Not everyone will believe everything you say! That may be hard to believe, but it's true. When people do not believe him or her, the presenter must shift into the "overcoming objections" mode. Sometimes the entire presentation can be structured around this idea; at other times, it may be necessary to prepare a brief in advance covering how to deal with questions.
- *Is it to sell/persuade?* Are you convinced that what you are offering the audience is good for them? Then you become the pitchman. Sometimes the presenter is actually selling a product; other times, the presenter is selling a better way of doing things.
- *Is it to celebrate?* Milestones are meant to be marked. When this occurs, the presenter serves as a chief celebrant. Often it is customary to thank the audience for their participation and cite specific examples of achievement.
- *Is it to entertain?* Do you know someone who is about to retire? Very often friends and associates hold a dinner and invite folks close to the individual to say a few words, often in the spirit of lighthearted fun.

These are only a few of the reasons why we make presentations. Unlike presentation styles, purposes can be mixed within the same presentation. For example, you can begin with an explanation and close in a selling mode. This happens quite frequently and enables the presenter to lead the audience from one point to another.

WHO AND WHY LEAD TO WHAT

Knowing *who* you are as a leadership communicator and *why* you are speaking will make the next step—determining *what* you will say—that much easier. It is often tempting to skip these first steps, but that is a mistake that could lead you to overlook the needs of the audience as well as important attributes of your message.

So, whether you are the expert explaining an issue or a transformer selling change, you need to know *who* you are and *why* you are there if you expect people to believe *what* you have to say.

Communications Planner: Discovering the Leadership Communicator Within

Discovering your purpose and style as a leadership communicator is essential to getting your message across in ways that enable it to be understood. As we have mentioned, your approach may vary from situation to situation. In order to provide clarity, here are a series of questions you can ask yourself in the interest of sharpening your focus as a leadership communicator. The answers to these questions will prepare you to begin the development of your message, which we discuss in the next chapter.

Getting to Know Yourself as a Leadership Communicator

1. How does the audience know you?
2. Do you or your organization have a prior connection to this audience? Explain.
3. What type of presenter appeals most to this audience?
   - Expert
   - Visionary
   - Coach
   - Tranformer

Identifying Your Purpose as a Leadership Communicator

1. What does the audience expect you to say?
2. What changes have occurred recently that may affect your message?
3. How receptive is the audience to what you have to say? Explain.

4. Check the purpose of the presentation as you see it now. *(Select no more than 2 boxes.)*
   - Explain
   - Sell/preach
   - Overcome objections
   - Entertain
   - Celebrate

RUDY GIULIANI—LEADING WITH HOPE

For a few hours on that terrible day, he was the de facto leader of the nation as the president and vice president were kept from public view by the Secret Service. His city had been brazenly attacked, and he was at ground zero coordinating with fire, police, and rescue personnel, all the while standing in the media spotlight deftly fielding questions and parceling out information as best he could. His performance, in the apparent absence of national leadership, made him stand out, and as a result, the entire nation stood shoulder to shoulder with him—Rudy Giuliani, mayor of New York.

RUDY EVERYWHERE

Giuliani believed that it was his duty to be visible. "I was there. I was the mayor of New York. My whole approach as mayor was to be there and be in charge. If I had not gone on TV, it would have been worse for the city." There were rumors that the mayor had been killed during the collapse of the first tower. That made his public visibility all the more vital.[1]

As the grim reality of the loss of nearly three thousand people became apparent in the collapse of the World Trade Center on September 11, and as the hours dragged into days and finally into weeks, Giuliani, or Rudy more aptly, seemed to be everywhere—meeting with state and federal officials, grieving with the families of fallen firefighters, huddling with prominent city businessmen, and of course maintaining vigil at Ground Zero with fire, police, and rescue people. Later, he appeared at ball games and even on *Saturday Night Live.*

We can discern much about Rudy Giuliani's leadership communications by examining his farewell address, delivered in St. Paul's Chapel, a small church near the World Trade Center that served as a food and rest shelter for rescue personnel. Giuliani opens with an acknowledgement of his people and their unique capacity to inspire.

> [P]eople will ask me where do I get my strength? Well, it's really simple. . . . [M]y strength and energy comes entirely from the people of New York

> and it comes from a place like this, St. Paul's Chapel. This is a House of God and it's one of the homes of our republic.[2]

As an Italian American, Giuliani feels the presence of those who made sacrifices for him. He speaks lovingly of his grandfather, Rodolfo, who came to America with $20 in his pocket. "So how did he do it? . . . [He and other immigrants] were able to do it because they kept thinking about this idea in their head, this idea of America . . . land of the free and the home of the brave."

He continues with a tribute to his Uncle Rudy, a New York City policeman who served in the Pacific during World War II and was nearly killed. He concludes this mention with an acknowledgement of how his uncle also risked his life on his last day of service as a cop to save someone who was about to commit suicide by leaping from the Brooklyn Bridge. What Giuliani has done is to link himself, his family, and all of America's immigrants to the culture and values of America.

Having established his roots, Giuliani launches into a recapitulation of his record as mayor. He prefaces his record by mentioning a cover of *Time* magazine in 1990 that called New York "The Rotting Apple." As Giuliani says, "I felt that my job as mayor was to turn around the city. Because I believed rightly or wrongly that we had one last chance to do that, to really turn it around in the opposite direction."

Despite some initial hostility, Giuliani did turn around the fortunes of the city, and in the process reduced crime, increased jobs, and solidified the business base. He was named *Time* magazine's "Person of the Year" for his efforts in leading the city during its darkest days post-September 11. Giuliani the fighter emerges when he speaks of victory in America's battle against terrorism:

> I know we won because I saw within hours the reaction of first, the people of New York City, then the people of the United States of America. I saw within the first hours the three firefighters who lifted the American flag high, within hours of the attack when it was still life-threatening to be there.

His victory theme is echoed, this time with levity, in his mention of the crowds along the West Side Highway, a liberal stronghold. "And when they cheered for President Bush who none of them had voted for I knew for sure that we had won." As he concludes, Giuliani issues a call to action:

> [W]e have an obligation to the people who did die to make sure of two things about which there can be no compromise: Their families need to be protected just as if they had been alive; and second, this place has to be sanctified . . . [so that] anybody who comes here immediately . . . feel[s] the great power and strength and emotion of what it means to be an American.

Giuliani's final words are those of the Gettysburg Address. By concluding with these remarks, Giuliani seeks to place the suffering of New York into the panorama of the American people's enduring legacy of sacrifice for ideals larger than themselves.

LEAVING OFFICE

There was one hiccup. For a few weeks, amid intense speculation—will he or won't he?—reminiscent of another Giuliani, he wondered in public, but chiefly through aides, if he shouldn't stay on as mayor past the end of his term or, better yet, try to get permission to run for another term despite term limits. Better judgment prevailed, and he extinguished the speculation. He left office as planned on January 1. And when the new mayor, Michael Bloomberg, a millionaire financier, took office, Rudy was beside him, in Times Square and at City Hall, symbolically handing over the reins. It was fitting and graceful, almost noble.

LEADERSHIP—THE BOOK

Giuliani's personal account of how he responded to the attack on the World Trade Center is a primer on leadership communications. Again and again throughout his detailed account in his book, *Leadership*, he writes of the importance of communications. He was insistent about getting the media involved and provided them with direct access to him. He even went so far as to conduct live on-the-spot interviews as he walked away from Ground Zero en route to a makeshift command center. The command center, too, was an example of coordinated on-site communications between fire, police, rescue, and government personnel. Face to face or phone to phone, communications are essential in responding to a crisis. As is remaining calm, something that Giuliani speaks about frequently; even if the world around you is going to hell, as it was with the World Trade Center, leaders need to project a sense of calmness.[3]

Curiously, his account contains a near litany of the names of people he encountered on that fateful day. Mentioning these people reflects more than a politician's gift for names; it is a clue to his communications psyche. Good leaders know that actions do not occur because you want them to; they are the result of the actions of others. And if you want people to keep working for you, it is important for you to acknowledge who they are, what they do, and how well they are doing it. Giuliani is a master at this.[4]

In *Leadership,* Giuliani offers some pithy insights into communicating as a leader. Not surprisingly, given his strong character, Giuliani believes, as do other leaders, that communications begins with a value system and therefore needs to be articulated as "strong beliefs." In line with this, Giuliani believes in “direct” and “unfiltered” communications; throughout his career, he has been front and center on media platforms setting forth his views in plain and simple language.[5]

Giuliani is very particular about his choice of words. A blunt speaker, Giuliani is fond of plain talk and is not above telling his constituents what they “should” or “should not” do. Exhortations are not viewed kindly, but they form Giuliani’s character as a communicator and over the years have lent him the credibility he needs in order to lead. A case in point was his deliberate choice of the word *Mafia* as a U.S. attorney general during his first indictment against organized crime in 1983. Until then, government officials had not wanted to use the word for fear of alienating the 20 million Americans of Italian heritage. Giuliani continued to use the term, explaining that the Mafia represents a tiny minority of Italians. “Ultimately, ‘Mafia’ says only that Italians and Italian Americans are human beings. Once we acknowledge that, we take much of the mystique out of it.” He also understands the “symbolic weight” of words. As mayor, his administration “changed the name on every ‘Welfare Office’ to ‘Job Center.’ ”[6]

In another chapter, “Reflect, then Decide,” Giuliani speaks of the necessity of leaders listening to opposing viewpoints: “Make it clear [prior to a decision’s being made] you’ll entertain changing your mind even on cut and dried issues.” By hearing dissent, the leader exposes him- or herself to an alternative view as well as to new sources of information. After gathering the information, Giuliani advocates reflection, which is really a dialogue with one’s self. This process prepares the leader to make an informed decision based on facts, opinion, and personal conviction.[7]

THE FUTURE

Whatever the future brings Giuliani, he will be forever linked with his heroic performance under fire as he at first commanded, then grieved, then cheered, and always, but always, fought to bring his City back to a sense of if not normalcy, at least, what passes for it as New Yorkers return to their lives. And like one of his heroes, Winston Churchill, Giuliani has elevated the suffering of his City to heroic status as a means of giving the people who live there a sense of hope, of mission, and of determination.

Leadership Communications Lessons

Lead from the front. Go to where you can do the most good. From the moment the Towers were struck, Giuliani was front and center, helping to coordinate, command, and commandeer state and federal assistance.

Be seen as the leader. Get out of the bunker. Let people know what you are doing. In the wake of September 11, Giuliani was everywhere; he used his public persona to console, grieve with, and inspire his ravaged city.

Elevate the status of sacrifice. Give meaning to the sacrifice of others. Giuliani repeatedly cited the heroism of the New York City firefighters who, as the Towers were crumbling, went in as others were coming out.

Show the human side. Do not be afraid to show emotion. We witnessed Giuliani shedding tears as well as embracing the widows and orphans of victims lost in the Towers' collapse.

Give in to levity. It's okay to laugh in the face of tragedy; it is an appropriate human response. Giuliani's appearance on *Saturday Night Life* sanctioned the right to laugh, to experience joy once again.

Live your message. Giuliani symbolized the spirit of the people of New York. His emotions were their emotions; his actions were their actions; his humanity was their humanity.

CHAPTER 3

I consider it the role of the head of a newspaper to be bi-partisan and to bring journalists together with people from government. . . . I fear unspoken anger. Especially, people who may disagree on politics must still be able to communicate, and it's crucial for all of us in the press to listen to all sides.

Katherine Graham

DEVELOPING THE LEADERSHIP MESSAGE

"AND THAT, LADIES AND GENTLEMEN, is why we are gathered here tonight."

With that statement, the audience explodes in applause, and the speaker steps back from the lectern for a moment and beams. It is the rousing conclusion to a crafted piece of oratory. The speaker and audience seem as one—but wait a minute. There in the back row, one person turns to another and says, "Nice words, but what the heck was he saying?"

Whoa!

Unfortunately, this little back-row interrogatory happens all too often. We like the speaker. We like the words. We even like the response from the audience, but when we step back metaphorically, as the speaker does physically, we are left with an empty feeling.

Why is this? How can this be? Everyone liked the presentation.

There's a simple reason: There was no message to the speech. The speaker certainly had his style and his purpose for being clear, but there was a disconnect between the speaker and the audience. Why? The purpose of the leadership message was unclear. Unfortunately, this situation occurs all too often, both on the public stage and on the corporate stage—or, frankly, even in the church basement during a fundraising planning session.

The same thing occurs in one-on-one meetings. For example, the boss calls you into his office. He starts talking about the business. He asks you how you are doing, but before you can respond, he's off talking about other people in the department. He eventually focuses on you and asks how things are going for you. As you begin to speak, the phone rings. He answers it, then holds up his hand and says, "Hey, nice of you to drop by. Could we continue this conversation next week?" You mumble something as you walk out of the office shaking your head. *What was that little talk all about?*

Just as the speaker in the introductory vignette was unclear about his message, the boss was unclear about his. Leaders cannot afford to be unclear; clarity of purpose extends to communications. If the leader cannot express a coherent point of view, the department, the team, and individuals are left adrift in a sea of uncertainty. As hard as we work on who we are and why we are there, we sometimes forget the "What is my message?" part.

ESTABLISHING CREDIBILITY

The purpose of leadership communications, as pointed out in Chapter 1, is to build (or establish) trust between leader and follower. This trust is essential to a leader's credibility. Lyndon Johnson lost the trust of the American people over his conduct of the Vietnam War. His accomplishments in civil rights legislation and the war on poverty were overshadowed by his refusal to be straight with the American people, or even with himself, over the issues involved in Vietnam. The accounting firm Arthur Andersen suffered an enormous lack of credibility in the wake of its faulty auditing. Its lack of accountability (no pun intended) destroyed the company and cast a harsh light on other major accounting firms that were beset with their own scandals. The financial markets, too, reverberated as investors wondered if they could trust the financial statements of any company.

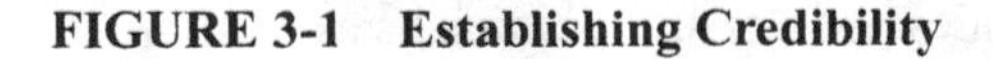

FIGURE 3-1 Establishing Credibility

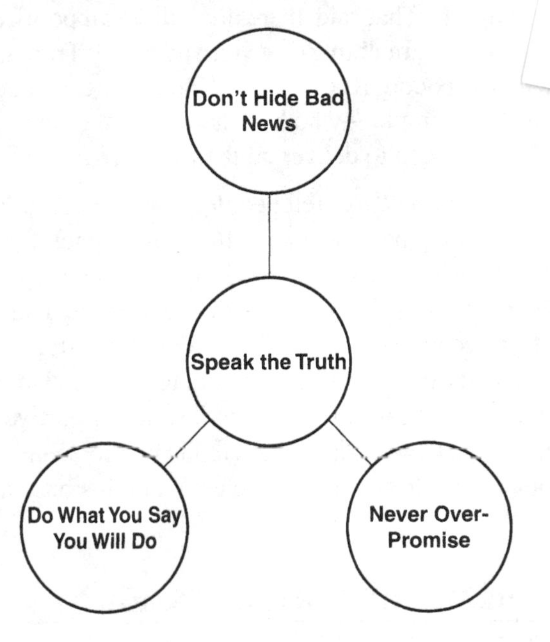

Credibility is a leader's currency. With it he or she is solvent; without it he or she is bankrupt. Communications reinforces a leader's credibility. How can a leader establish credibility (see Figure 3-1)?[1]

- *Speak the truth.* Tell people what the facts are. Be straight with people. The "open book" management style (where employees are free to look at management finances and policies) works because it shares information across all levels. The approach fosters a greater sense of responsibility. Zingerman's, a thriving community of food-related businesses in Ann Arbor, Michigan, employs the open book style with great success. As a result, Zingerman's owners have created a sense of shared ownership as well as an esprit de corps for the entire enterprise.
- *Don't hide bad news.* We live in an era of transparency: People want to see inside an organization. With the multiplicity of information channels that are available, bad news always becomes known, so it behooves management to be candid right from the start. Winston Churchill did not shirk from telling the British people how dire the odds were in May 1940 as Britain stood alone against the Nazi war machine. And there was no wide-scale panic. People are capable of accepting the truth if you are honest with them.
- *Never overpromise.* Do not make promises that you cannot keep. Politicians seem never to learn this lesson. Campaign promises are not

promises at all; they are platitudes. As a result, politicians as a group have little credibility. That said, there are individual political leaders in both major parties—Franklin Roosevelt and Harry Truman among the Democrats and Theodore Roosevelt and Ronald Reagan among the Republicans, for example—who have a great deal of credibility. Why? Because they were seen to deliver on their promises.

- *Do what you say you will do.* Tell people what you are going to do, and then do it. Tom Brady became the starting quarterback for the New England Patriots when the starter was injured. To everyone's surprise, he led his team to a series of victories that landed the team in the Super Bowl. Brady, a second-year man, never gave the rah-rah speech; he let his actions on and off the field do the talking for him. He was focused and clear in his signal calling in the huddle and supportive on the sidelines. Off the field, he was disciplined in his workouts and in his comments to the media. He simply said he would do his best, and he did.

UNCOVERING THE MEANING OF THE MESSAGE

The message is the most important part of the presentation or the one-to-one chat. It is the core upon which the entire presentation or conversation depends. Think of the message as the 30-second "take-away thought" that you want people to remember. The message is not the same as the content of the presentation or conversation; it is the reason for the speaking. If you will indulge a simple analogy, consider the presentation or conversation as a piece of chocolate candy. The content is the chocolate surrounding the creamy center. The creamy center (or the cherry, if you prefer) is the message—the heart of what you are saying.

What are you trying to do? Why are you speaking to this group or this individual? Do you wish to explain a hot topic? Do you need to sell them on a new process? Do you wish to impart a need for change? Or do you just want them to have some laughs? Each of these purposes is valid. Your challenge as a leader is to decide what you want to do, and do it.

If you work for an organization of any size, you quickly become accustomed to presentations. Politicians make them. Celebrities make them. Entertainers make their living off them. The most successful leaders are those whose message you can sum up quickly in a sentence or so.

- We know where we are headed and why.
- We are an organization that puts people first.
- We must change the way we do business.

That sentiment is the beginning of the message. It is not the message itself; rather, it is the flavor of the message. Returning to our chocolate analogy, it is the difference between raspberry and orange fillings, or between strawberry and vanilla. All of these fillings may be creamy, but the flavor varies. As a rule of thumb, the more precise and concise you are about your message, the more precise and concise your presentation will be.

CREATING THE LEADERSHIP MESSAGE

Now we're getting to the filling. What do you want people to remember? Is it fluffy and light? Chewy and rich? Nutty and scrumptious? You as the presenter need to make certain that your message is clear and unambiguous.

Here are some examples of leadership messages.

- *Our company is going to be number one in its market by this time next year.*
- *We are a company that attributes its success to the contributions of its employees, so every employee will receive a bonus this year.*
- *This new process will reduce time, improve quality, and costs.*
- *Our expenses are exceeding our costs, so each of us will need to submit a revised budget reflecting a 10 percent decrease in expenditures by next Friday.*
- *Our customer is concerned with health and well-being, and the best way we can accommodate these needs is to concentrate on making products that are fresh and flavorful and that contribute to a sense of well-being.*

Each of these messages is short and to the point. There is no ambiguity. The intent is clear. That is what you want to strive for when you create your message. You can also regard such a statement as the thesis, or the *why*, of the message. It contains why you are speaking and what you will say. The greater the clarity of your message, the greater the chance that it will be remembered. How can you create your message? The methods are as varied as the shades of color in a rainbow.

- *Think first.* You may wish to sit and think. Start with the obvious: What is it that I want to say, and what is it that I want the audience to remember when I leave the stage?
- *Ask somebody.* Talk to a trusted colleague. Tell that colleague what you want to accomplish and begin a dialogue to exchange ideas.

- *Brainstorm.* Gather a team together and start putting down ideas. What is it that we want to say, and how can we say it? Do not become overly complex or detailed. Remember, it's the message that you need first. Content comes later.
- *When it's over.* By starting with the endpoint, you focus on the outcome, your audience. By working backward, you can derive what you want to say and how you want to say it.

A word of warning: Do not feel that the audience must *like* your message. For example, if you are a union steward and you want to describe what the union will request from management, chances are that the membership will listen and will like what you have to say. You are their representative, after all. By contrast, if you are in management and your task is to present the company's side of the issues, you can be certain that much of what you are saying will be met with skepticism.

WHAT A LEADERSHIP MESSAGE DOES: THE FOUR I'S

Leadership messages must communicate information as well as open the door for participation by the listener. As such, the leadersh·· message must do these four things (see Figure 3-2):[2]

- *Inform* people of what the issues are and what they need to do. Leaders owe their people an explanation of the situation, whether the news is good or bad. Good examples of leaders who kept their people informed are Jack Welch of General Electric and Rich Teerlink of Harley-Davidson; both of these CEOs let people know what was going on in the business as well as attending and participating in events where stakeholders and other people voiced their ideas. Both men also spent time listening to customers, which meant that they were personally informed about issues, and that when it came time to communicate internally, they did so from a credible platform of knowledge. Also keep in mind that even when there is no news, leaders need to be seen and heard frequently. Absence in this case does not make the heart grow fonder, it gives rise to gossip.
- *Involve* others by soliciting their input. Herb Kelleher, founder of Southwest Airlines, was a master of getting other people involved. By traveling around on his airline, he met and mingled with employees at all levels of the organization, from executives to ticket agents and baggage handlers. His openness shattered the imaginary barrier between boss and employee, and in so doing invited people to raise issues and

FIGURE 3-2 Four I's Leadership Message Model

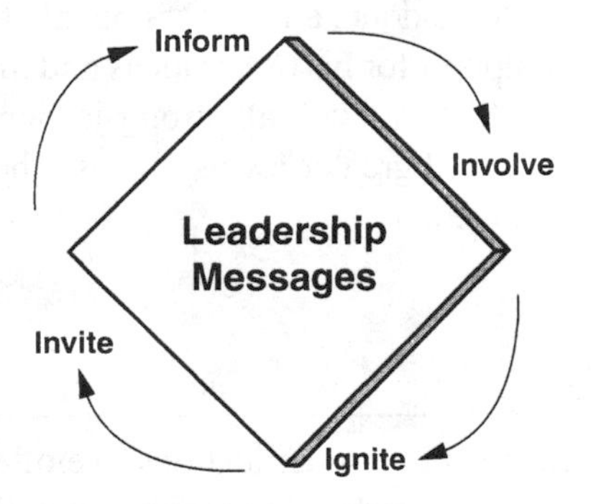

offer suggestions. Add to this the fact that Southwest Airlines is employee owned, and you have a successful model for involvement because employees have a stake in the enterprise.

- *Ignite* people's imaginations about what they can do to make things better for themselves and their organizations. Imagination is a powerful mental tool. Consider the example of Mohandas Gandhi in the independence movement in India. Gandhi's words and example, coupled with the charisma that sprang from his commitment and simplicity, rallied a nation to think about the possibility of becoming independent from Britain. While many thousands of leaders in every region of the subcontinent made separation possible, it was Gandhi who lit the flame and stoked it by words and example.
- *Invite* people to participate in the enterprise, whether it be the fulfillment of a goal or the transformation of a culture. Leaders who talk about what people can do *for* themselves and *by* themselves are leaders who understand their role as inspiring action or change. Joe Torre never batted, fielded, or pitched for his Yankee championship teams, yet he was the one who invited superstars and other players to play together as a team in order to win. His invitation made players of all abilities feel that they could contribute, and as a result, they did. Other successful coaches do the same thing, and in the process create win-win situations: a win on the scoreboard and a win for the collective psyche of the team.

All four elements need not be apparent in every message. Sometimes the leader's message is simply an update. Other times it's a call to action or an invitation to do something. But over the course of a leader's tenure, the success of leadership communications depends upon including these four elements over and over again.

When a leader informs his or her people, involves others in the effort, ignites ideas about what is to be done, and invites people to participate in the process, that leader gains support for his or her ideas and makes the process of achieving results possible. Also, as with all strong leadership messages, the leader makes it possible to build greater levels of trust, the bond upon which all leadership must be grounded.

COMMUNICATING UP

When we think about leadership communications, we often assume a downward flow of messages from the leader along with a bubbling up of messages from an engaged audience or individual. This communications loop from leader to followers and back again is not the whole story. Leaders also need to communicate upward. The recipient of such messages may be the leader's boss, a company director, or sometimes an advisory committee. These messages, like other forms of leadership communications, are grounded in the culture of the organization and are about significant issues related to vision, mission, and transformation. Likewise the purpose of upward leadership communications is the same: to build trust and drive results.

In his book *Leading Up*, Michael Useem describes examples in which leaders in subordinate positions strive to do the right thing. General Roméo Dallaire, commander of the U.N. troops in Rwanda, tried unsuccessfully to persuade his superiors, both military and civilian, to allow him to take aggressive military action to head off the threat of genocide. It was to no avail, as the majority Hutus and the minority Tutsi began a genocidal attack on each other; more than 800,000 people died during the bloodbath.[3] Charlene Barshefsky, as principal U.S. trade deputy, negotiated a trade deal between the United States and China that both permitted the latter's entry into the World Trade Organization and integrated the myriad special interests on the U.S. side, including those of business and labor. In other words, it was a job that balanced both negotiation skill and salesmanship.[4] Both Dallaire and Barshefsky employed effective communications; sadly, only one of the two succeeded. And there is a lesson in this. Leaders will not always succeed, but they must always communicate. And through the continual practice of communications, they will improve their likelihood of success down the line. When communicating up, it is wise to keep these points in mind:

- *Keep everyone on the same page.* People deserve to know what is going on. Leaders at the top often feel isolated from what is happening at the grassroots level, either with customers or with front-line employees, because they are shielded from it, either by layers of bureaucracy or by sheer negligence. The leader who keeps the boss informed is keeping the boss in the loop.

- *Separate facts from passion.* Facts are neutral; they tell what happened. Opinions color. When giving information, leaders owe it to themselves and to their listeners to keep their convictions separate from the facts. Let the facts speak for themselves. Good leaders know when to express a point of view and when to let the facts stand.
- *Sell when necessary.* Leaders have a point of view; it is part of their position of authority. When they believe something strongly, they will try to persuade others. It is perfectly acceptable, on most occasions, to share a point of view. But when expressing this point of view, frame it as such. In this way, the boss receiving the message will know what's fact and what's opinion.
- *Read the signs.* Keep the antennae up. Listen to what senior leadership is saying, or not saying. Often what is not said or expressed is as important as the words. Leaders who are communicating upward need to know how both the leader at the top and the leaders in the middle feel about the issues. Such knowledge allows the leader who is communicating upward to know how she or he must shape the message.

Upward leadership communications serve another purpose: They create a culture of dialogue and discussion. When employees see their bosses communicating regularly with their own managers, they soon learn that communications is integral to the leadership process. And while individual requests may not be granted or goals be met, the process of communications never ceases.

RESTORING CREDIBILITY

Credibility is the bond between leader and follower; it is almost sacred because it forms the bedrock of why people want to do what leaders ask them to do. Sometimes a loss of credibility occurs because the leader makes a mistake. Think of leaders who fail to fulfill their promises. Other times circumstances conspire against the leader and, through no fault of his or her own, problems arise. Think of economic slumps. None of us is perfect, even leaders. If a leader's credibility becomes damaged, what can the leader do (see Figure3-3)?[5]

- *Acknowledge the mistakes.*[6] When decisions do not turn out the way they were intended to, the leader owes his or her followers an explanation.

FIGURE 3-3 Restoring Credibility

3 As
Acknowledge
Apologize
Amend

Bill Clinton lied to the American people in the Lewinsky affair and turned an indiscretion into a political quagmire that harmed his presidency. When he finally did acknowledge his misdeeds, it was too late. His credibility was destroyed, and while he had nearly two more years in office, his presidency will always remain one of potential rather than achievement. By contrast, Jack Welch acknowledged that news of his lucrative postretirement perquisites was hurting G.E., so he stepped to the fore and voluntarily surrendered those perquisites rather than risk besmirching his former employer.

- *Apologize.* Admit that what you did was wrong and say you are sorry. It may be painful for the moment, but it can shorten the agony and enable the leader to put the incident behind her or him.[7] During the war in Afghanistan, our military was involved in several incidents that harmed civilians and friendly forces. Our military commanders acknowledged the mistakes and apologized immediately. Credibility between the wronged parties and the U.S. government was maintained.
- *Make amends.* Find ways to make it up to the people you have wronged. Make restitution to those you have harmed.[8] For example, if a company is found to have cooked the books, the perpetrators need to be punished. If those actions resulted in a loss of pension funds for employees, the company should find ways to make restitution. This is not simply courtesy, it is a way of repaying loyalty and ensuring its continuance.

The point must be made that the leader may not be the person who was directly responsible for misdeeds. As the leader of an organization, however, he or she owes it to the stakeholders to take responsibility and be accountable when things go wrong. Leaders who step forward and accept blame will often rise in stature, not decline. Why? Because they are seen as people who are trustworthy. Credibility, remember, is like currency; followers decide how much of it they want to buy, sell, or hold. The greater the holdings, the greater the levels of trust.

Communications Planner: Developing the Leadership Message

The leadership message is the most important part of the presentation. It is the core upon which the entire presentation depends. Think of the message as the 30-second takeaway that you want the audience to remember.

Here are some questions that you can use to spark your thinking process. The answers to these questions will help you formulate your message.

1. Why am I speaking, and what do I want to say?
2. How can I establish credibility?
3. What do I want people to remember?
4. How can I sum up my message in less than 30 seconds?
5. How will the audience react to my message?
6. How can I color my message to improve its clarity?
7. If I make a mistake, what steps can I take to restore my credibility as leader?

KATHERINE GRAHAM—LEADING FROM WITHIN

When you read Katherine Graham's autobiography, you get the feeling that this is a woman who was not certain of her selfhood until very late in life. Make no mistake: Katherine Graham was a giant who took a not very good newspaper and built into one of the nation's most respected, and at the same time created a media empire.

Along the way, she helped bring a president to justice, stood down a tough union, and survived a husband who demeaned her as he sank deeper into a suicidal depression. Underneath her society-bred manners and sweet exterior, Katherine Graham was one tough broad. As publisher of the most influential paper in the world's most influential capital, she was a powerful communicator and a shining example of how to learn to lead. At every step in her public career, the stakes got higher. And each time she rose to the challenge.

PROFESSIONAL EDUCATION

When Graham took over the *Washington Post* in the wake of her husband's suicide in 1963, it was not the powerful institution it would become. It was dowdy, parochial, and, except for its being in the nation's capital, inconsequential. In a way it was a mirror of Graham's self-assessment of her abilities. Although she had been a reporter in her twenties, she certainly was no businessperson. She took the helm out of family duty; her father, Eugene Meyer, had owned the paper, and Graham wanted to keep it in the family.

Despite her role as publisher and owner of the Washington Post Company, Graham was very much a creature of her upbringing. She did as she was taught; she deferred to men: first her father, then her husband, and later the male executives in her own company. She illustrates her naiveté in quotes taken from a *Women's Wear Daily* profile of her written in 1969, in which she admits, "I guess it's a man's world. . . . [M]en are more able than women at executive work and in certain situations. I think a man would be better at this job I'm in than a woman."[9]

LEADERSHIP AS LEARNING

In her autobiography, Graham attributes her success as a publisher and as a businesswoman to men. She extols Ben Bradlee, the crusading editor who stood behind reporters Bob Woodward and Carl Bernstein during the Watergate investigation. She also credits his journalistic integrity for helping to make the *Post* a great newspaper. Graham is warmly laudatory of financier Warren Buffett, who after buying a stake in the Washington Post Company became a sort of financial mentor, helping her to learn the business side of publishing.[10]

Graham's learning process stemmed in part from her ability to listen. She was comfortable with asking questions and integrating lessons into her actions. Complementing her listening was her writing ability, often expressed in letters. For example, she speaks of the letters she and Bradlee exchanged annually; it was their own private feedback on each other's performance. Such letters are a good way to air issues, settle accounts, and give due acknowledgement for success.[11]

Graham's views are not that remarkable. As one of the few high-profile businesswomen of her era, she had no female role models or peers. She was literally a pioneer in her field. What she demonstrated was her willingness to learn from others. She was not threatened by the presence of brilliant people. In fact, she relished their company. And the lessons she learned helped to give her the confidence she needed to become the leader she was capable of becoming. The sum of her collected learnings can be found in her autobiography, *Personal History,* which subsequently won the Pulitzer Prize.

LEADERSHIP RESOLVE

Inside her company, she also could be tough. Right after Watergate she went toe-to-toe with the pressmen's union, which was resisting modernization efforts. To her the *Washington Post* was family, and the strike was very painful for her. When rogue elements in the union vandalized the presses, she took it as a personal affront, and it stiffened her resolve. After more than 4 months, during some of which time she was personally vilified by members of the union, the strike was settled. She learned also that "when management . . . forfeits its right to manage, only trouble can result." She resolved to improve "communications within the company."[12] With the labor issues settled, the company prospered. In 1991, when she handed the reins of the company to her son, Donald, the company's revenues had grown from $84 million to $1.4 billion.[13]

LEADERSHIP UNDER FIRE

She had the final say on editorial and publishing decisions. In 1971, when her paper, along with the *New York Times*, published the Pentagon Papers (government documents about the United States' involvement in Vietnam that were leaked to the public by Daniel Ellsberg), it was her name that was on the injunction brought by the Nixon administration. It was a risky decision, not just because she was going against the administration, but because it coincided with the Washington Post Company's going public. Publicity of this sort would not be helpful. Graham persevered.[14] She quotes Bradlee as saying that it marked a "graduation of the Post into the highest ranks" of news organizations.[15]

Graham's will would be tested a short time later during the Watergate investigation. From the moment of the burglary at the Watergate complex on June 17, 1972, to President Richard Nixon's resignation on August 9, 1973, it was the *Washington Post* that led on the story, keeping it alive after Nixon's landslide election in November 1972, when few other papers had any interest. Bradlee, as executive editor, was front and center on the coverage, but Graham supported him. It was important to her. Watergate "was a conspiracy not of greed but of arrogance and fear by men who came to equate their own political well-being with the nation's very survival and security."[16] This is an apt statement about Watergate, and also about any other political scandal in Washington or any other capital.

And it points up the reasons why our nation needs a vigorous and free press as well as strong independent leadership at the helm of such media. Ultimately, as Graham wrote in her autobiography,

> The credibility of the press stood the test of time against the credibility of those who spent so much time self-righteously denying their own wrongdoing and assaulting us by assailing our performance and our motives.[17]

Not a bad epitaph for a woman who grew in her role as a leader and used her communications to demonstrate leadership in good times and bad, and in the process served as a good example for others.

Leadership Communications Lessons

Learn from others. Never be afraid to learn from those you respect. Graham assumed the helm of the *Washington Post* knowing little of business but something about journalism. She surrounded herself with strong leaders and learned from their example.

Make a stand. Abide by your principles. During the painful strike at the *Washington Post*, Graham stood down the powerful printers' union and won. It was a painful victory, but it opened the door to a greater future.

Be honest. Let people know how you feel about the issues. Graham's autobiography is such a powerful story because she is candid about her shortcomings as she emerged into a leadership role.

Believe in your people. Support the people you work with. Graham stood by her editor, Ben Bradlee, and her team of reporters through thick and thin.

Live your message. After the death of her husband, Graham's life was the *Washington Post.* She lived, breathed, and fought for the paper and the journalistic ideals it stood for.

CHAPTER 4

> The truth is it is almost impossible to kill a great brand, and marketers and agencies have to remember that. . . . The compulsion to change is often the wrong route. What they should do is accept who they are, and then express that in a meaningful and relevant way.
>
> *Shelly Lazarus*

LEADERSHIP COMMUNICATIONS PLANNING

THE NEW PERFORMANCE EVALUATION SYSTEM was not going over well. In fact, the new appraisal process was met with outright hostility—if hallway conversations were any indication, most managers were refusing to use it at all. The director of human resources was beside herself. This new appraisal system, which was designed to be easier to use as well as more comprehensive and more equitable, seemed destined to be dead on arrival. Although the new system was designed to be used online and replace the old paper-and-pencil form, managers were very suspicious. Employees, who were *encouraged to write self-appraisals and set forth new performance objectives, were leery, too. Their fear seemed to be twofold: first, lack of privacy, and second, how they were supposed to evaluate themselves. They feared that if they graded themselves too high, they might seem shallow, whereas if they graded themselves too low, they might get stuck with a poor review that would affect their compensation and their eligibility for promotion. As a result, the entire system, which cost $2 million to implement, was in danger of being written off. Worse, employee morale was sinking. Refrains of "Big Brother is watching" echoed in the hallways.*

Unfortunately, this situation is all too common. Whether the subject is performance evaluations, new project guidelines, or new policies governing overtime, the underlying principle is the same: The new initiative represents change, and people do not like change unless it is explained properly and put into the context of the organization.

The reason for the failure of this new performance evaluation system was not the system itself. It was the way in which it was introduced—or, frankly, not introduced. While a huge investment was made in the development of the system, little or no attention was paid to communicating the system to managers and employees. Rather, it simply appeared, as if from on high. The HR director was so involved with developing the application and the benefits of using it that she and her leadership team simply forgot to introduce it properly.

With the benefit of hindsight, it is easy to throw stones and accuse the HR director of being myopic and not in touch with the reality of the situation, but the fact is that organizations often institute change initiatives, big and small, without so much as a second thought about communicating them. Leaders seem to assume that whatever they introduce will be accepted. Months later, when the initiative fails, they wonder why. They tend to blame the initiative itself, when all too often it was simply the failure to communicate it properly. As a result, a great deal of time, money, and good ideas is wasted. Worse, the whole cycle is repeated when organizations seek to refine or redesign an initiative that probably would be good, if only it were explained properly.

Leadership communications plays a vanguard role in communicating change as well as in reinforcing organizational culture. Planning communications in advance is essential to developing a leadership message that is consistent with the culture, finding ways to communicate change, and ensuring continued credibility. Noted commentator and consultant on change Rosabeth Moss Kanter places a heavy emphasis on the role that communications plays in keeping a culture unified as well as helping to keep it together during a transformational effort.

ACTIVE VERSUS PASSIVE COMMUNICATIONS

Communications does not occur in a vacuum; it is part of the culture of an organization. As such, communications absorbs the character of the organization's culture. It is essential that those who *actively* create leadership messages be cognizant of those who *passively* receive those messages. Communications professionals need to be aware of what people are saying about products, people, and performance, both inside and outside the organization.

Active communications *(what goes out)* must reflect the reality of the world in which passive communications *(what comes in)* exists. Discordance between active and passive communications leads to an undermining of credibility; accordance ensures organizational alignment. Sensitivity to what's on people's minds is always important, but never more so than when communicating an initiative involving transformation. For this reason, leaders may need to prepare employees or customers for coming changes rather than springing the entire change initiative on them overnight with a single message. Leaders can introduce change with teaser messages prior to a major announcement, which may be given at an employee gathering or rally. Likewise, leaders need to follow up the message with a series of follow-on messages noting progress and keeping people up to date on what is happening.[1]

ASSESSING THE ORGANIZATIONAL COMMUNICATIONS CLIMATE

How do you find out what's going on within an organization? You ask people what's on their minds. As a leadership communicator, you need to discover the climate for communications. *Climate* refers to how open people feel about voicing their opinions or making suggestions. In places where the culture is repressive, many people are afraid to voice concerns even to coworkers, let alone to their boss. They also become distrustful of management because they feel that whatever anyone in management tells them is either untrue or bad news. By contrast, in nurturing cultures, people not only are open to one another, but feel free to make suggestions to their boss. Messages from the leaders are received with much more credence because people have learned to trust management.

Borrowing an approach from the social sciences, the best way to find out about the culture is to conduct a three-pronged study that uses interviews, focus groups, and surveys. Before embarking on any such study, you need to ensure the confidentiality of participants. Here's a sample disclaimer:

> We are doing this interview (focus group, survey) to get your opinion about the climate of communications. We value your opinions and your ideas. We will also keep all comments confidential. Your comments and ideas will not be linked to your name.

INTERVIEWS

Interviews are best for getting to the heart of what people think about the organization. Individual interviews give you the opportunity to explore a question or issue with someone in more depth than is possible with any other method. A skilled interviewer can make the interviewee feel comfortable by assuring confidentiality, opening with small talk, and having an open and friendly demeanor. When people feel at ease, they will reveal a great deal about how they see themselves within the context of the team or the organization.

Sample questions might include:

- *Has your boss set clear expectations for your job? Why do you say that?*
- *Do you know the objectives of your team/department? How do you know or not know?*
- *Do you know where the organization is headed? How do you know this?*
- *What is the climate for communications within your organization?*

The other factor in this type of research is choosing whom to interview. Consider interviewing at least two people from every function or organizational level. In this way, you get a more balanced understanding of what individuals think and what they do within the organization.

FOCUS GROUPS

Focus groups are good for getting different viewpoints in a short period of time. You can use the interaction within the group to stimulate conversation as well as to bring differing points of view to the surface. Keep in mind that some people are shy in groups and are uncomfortable voicing their opinions, particularly when those opinions might be contrary to what the rest of the group thinks or what the organization fosters. Use an experienced facilitator to draw out the opinions of the group. Group dynamics will have a big impact on the quality of the responses and the nature of the discussion; you need someone who is experienced and skilled in managing these dynamics effectively. In a focus group, limit the time to no more than 2 hours.

Sample questions might include:

- *How do senior leaders communicate to you?*
- *What kind of feedback do you receive from your boss?*
- *Think of what people are saying about your organization. Do their views differ from those of senior leadership? In what way?*

- *What happens when someone expresses an opinion that differs from that of his or her boss?*

SURVEYS

When you want to take the pulse of an organization and find out the extent to which an attitude or belief is held across the organization, use a survey. The survey typically will ask between 10 and 20 questions. It can be done using a paper-and-pencil format, or it can be done using email or the Web. The format selected depends on the culture of your organization and how people use technology. Usually, the computer-based formats get a better return rate than hard copy.

It is best to send surveys to as many people as possible. If the company has more than 10,000 employees, however, sending the survey to everyone may be impractical or too costly. In this case, you may wish to limit the surveys to people within a particular function (e.g., marketing, sales, or purchasing) or at a particular management level (e.g., supervisors, middle managers, or senior managers). If you receive responses from more than 50 percent of those surveyed, and this number is at least 30 (and preferably 100 or more), you can consider your results valid. There will, of course, be some bias as a result of differences between those who do and do not respond, but the numbers of returned surveys should give you a good idea of the issues and concerns facing people in the department, function, or organization.

Furthermore, if you survey the entire organization, you can slice (organize) the data according to specific groups. Specific groups will often have more or less concern about particular issues; this is typically due to the nature of their jobs, but it is useful to know this when designing communications plans. For example, supervisors may need more communications on issues related to hiring, while middle managers may need greater levels of communications on development planning. The information gained from the surveys can help you plan accordingly.

Suggestion: Get some help from an expert in designing the survey. There is an art and a science to constructing the questions so that you get valid and reliable results that you can feel confident in using to make decisions. And there are techniques for distributing and collecting the survey that will increase the likelihood that you will get a sufficient number of surveys returned.

COMMUNICATIONS AUDITS

Another form of survey used specifically for evaluating communications is the communications audit. While the audit may assess organizational climate, it is often used to measure the response to specific forms of communication, e.g., a video, a brochure, or a meeting. The purpose of the communications audit is to evaluate how well people understood the message and what they will do with the information they have received. For example, if you send out a video on changes to a benefits plan and follow up with a survey, you can ask whether people have the information they need in order to decide whether to make changes in their plan or keep it as it is, and whether they know where to go to seek further information.

Do you have to use all three methods of analysis? No, but the more types of analysis you use, the greater the validity of your conclusions. Also keep in mind that any one of these analysis methods is a form of intervention. And when you intervene, you must provide a context for it. For example, you must always explain why you are gathering data and what you will do with it.[2]

LEADERSHIP COMMUNICATION STRATEGIES

Once you know the issues facing an organization, you can plan your communication strategies. Communication strategies should echo the vision, mission, and business strategies of the organization. They should be telling people where the organization is headed, how it will get there, and what people need to do to make certain they are in alignment with the organization. The communication strategies are designed to

- *Develop and reinforce the bond of trust that must exist between leader and follower.* Position the leader as one who can be trusted and is worthy of support. Winston Churchill and Rudy Giuliani were the right leaders at the right time when people in peril needed their guidance and leadership.
- *Affirm the organizational vision, mission, and values.* Reinforce what the organization stands for and what people in it believe. Robert Redford founded Sundance Institute to support independent filmmaking, and he continues to actively support its mission through his actions and communications.
- *Facilitate a two-way flow of information throughout all levels of the organization, including manager to employee, employee to manager, and peer to peer*. Enable communications to flow upward from follower to leader. Upward communications keeps the leader in touch with the people and enables people to have their voices heard, thereby promoting a shared stake in the enterprise. Rich Teerlink at Harley-Davidson emphasized open and honest communications as the means of effecting lasting, positive change.
- *Create the impetus for organizational effectiveness (e.g., making things happen).* Tell people what is happening now, what will happen next,

and what will happen as a result of their actions. Steve Jobs lets people at Apple know why they should care about their work and gets them excited about the difference they are making in the world of design and technology.

- *Drive results.* Achieve what the organization is supposed to do: Make great products, deliver terrific service, improve people's lives, and so on. Jack Welch was a master at pushing the organization to achieve its stated goals, and he used his communications to prioritize the importance of making the numbers.

The other part of the leadership communications equation is giving people reasons to want to embrace the strategy. You develop your messages as reasons for people to support the strategy. Keep in mind that there is a natural overlap between purpose (as described in Chapter 1) and strategy; in some cases they are one and the same. Strategies and supporting messages echo one another to support organizational goals.

FOUR LEADERSHIP COMMUNICATION CHANNELS

Just as individuals use different forms of communications—words, gestures, signals of attentiveness—organizations use various communication channels. Typically an organization utilizes four types of communications, or channels (see Figure 4-1). While it may be advantageous to use all four channels to communicate a single initiative, it is often feasible to select a single channel for a particular message.

- *Organizational communications* refers to the ways in which individuals, teams, and the entire organization communicate one to one, group to group, or organizationwide. There are no hard and fast rules about what is and what is not "organizational communications," but think of it this way: It is the way messages are disseminated throughout an organization.

  Organizational communications can be as simple as a single email, or as complex as a media campaign regarding transformation. No single entity has ownership of organizational communications; it belongs to everyone. Why? Because communicating with others is each person's responsibility.

- *Editorial communications* refers to messages designed to elicit endorsement from a third party, typically the media and by extension the public at large. Public relations departments send out media releases to describe what is going on inside an organization; these releases may cover new products and services or discuss internal

FIGURE 4-1 Leadership Communication Channels

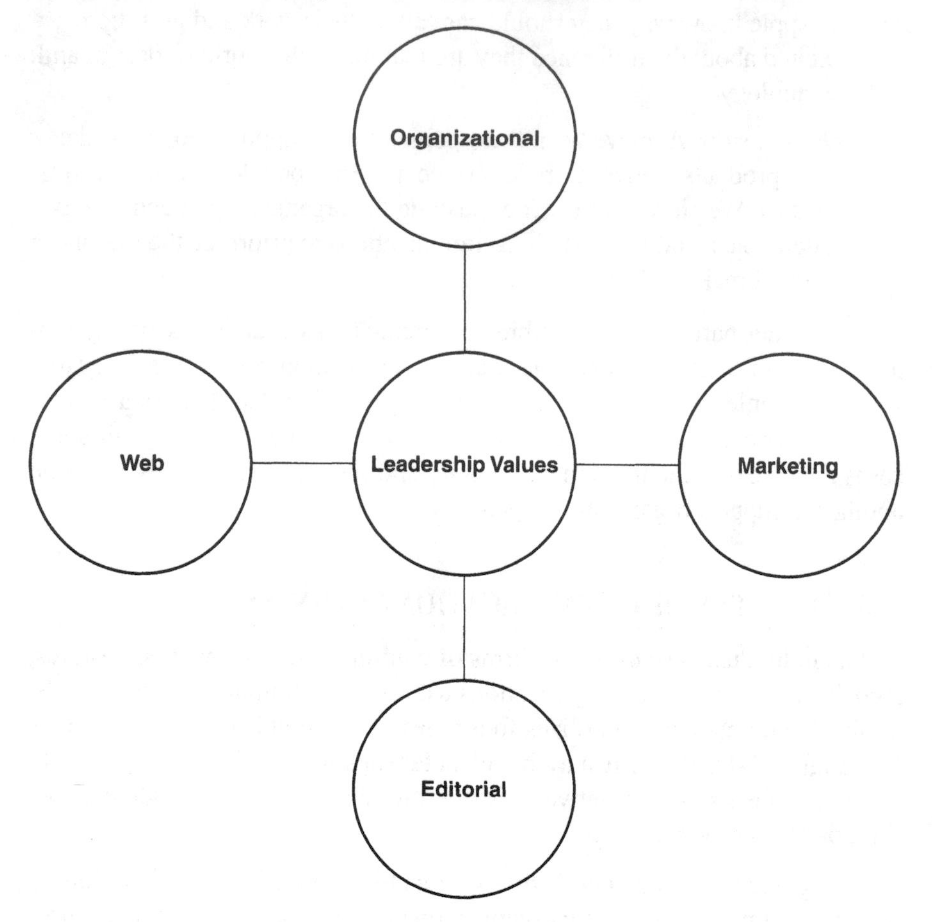

developments related to people and programs. By and large, these releases convey a single point of view that is favorable to the company. These forms of communications are designed to be used by external media (broadcasters, periodicals, newspapers, trade publications) to develop their stories, which the organization hopes will be both informative and positive.

Many large organizations also have in-house communication channels involving the development of articles for the organization's newsletter or web site. You can also consider a speech or a guest op-ed column by a company CEO as another form of editorial communications. In this instance, there is little filter between the leader and the public, since the leader's opinion is communicated directly, without benefit of interpretation by a reporter.

- *Marketing communications* refers to communications designed to present a point of view, e.g., to sell or promote. Think of advertising. What you see in a 30-second television spot or a four-color print ad communicates a message that is paid for by the organization. The same technique can be adopted by organizations that wish to sell the benefits of organizational transformation.

  Marketing communications is especially effective for communicating a sense of urgency. You can structure the message so that you concentrate on the WIFM (what's in it for me?) as a means of persuading people that the change, the program, or the initiative is good for them as individuals and for the entire company.

- *Web communications* are communications that reside on the web site. These messages may be developed solely as e-messages, or they may be retreads of articles, videos, and other media.

  The Web itself, however, can be a very powerful tool for enabling a leader to speak directly to his or her people. There are two popular methods. One is a webcast, which is a video telecast of a presentation or a conversation that is transmitted over the Web and restricted to subscribers, e.g., employees, dealers, media, or other groups. The other is a webchat, which enables a leader to respond to questions submitted via email. Sometimes the reply is sent out audio only or as a text message. Both methods are very direct means of getting to key issues. In addition, they can be replayed at the Web user's convenience or archived on the web site for later reference.

DETERMINING THE RIGHT MEDIA FOR THE RIGHT COMMUNICATION CHANNEL

Selecting the appropriate communication channel for a message is often as important as the message itself. The channel, which can be anything from an email to a speech to the masses, must be evaluated for its ability to convey the gravity of the message with the appropriate intimacy and leadership value. (*Note: Channel* refers to the method of communication (e.g., organizational, editorial, marketing, or Web); *media* refers to the vehicle (e.g., video, brochure, news article, or banner).

You can use just about any media in your communications channel—video, print, collateral, and so on. It is a common mistake to assume that video is only for marketing communications (e.g., a TV spot) and print is only for editorial. The truth is that you can use either or both—as well as other forms of media—for any channel that you like. The media you select are dependent upon the message. (Budget, too, plays a great role. Video can be expensive, as can four-color brochures.)

What kind of media you choose depends upon the importance of the message. All leadership messages have importance, of course, but some are more significant than others. Here are some suggestions you might consider:

- *Video* affords the leader the opportunity to speak directly to an audience and to augment the message with stories and visuals that underscore key points. For example, if the issue is the adoption of a new strategic plan, the leader may invite different people from throughout the organization to comment on their hopes and expectations, or to say what they will do to change the organization and carry out the plan. Additionally, the leader and his or her team can comment on what the new company will look like once the plan has been achieved.
- *An all-employee meeting* provides the opportunity to introduce the leadership message live in front of the entire organization. The leader needs to take a front and center role; she or he should explain the reason for the transformation, be it a new strategic plan or a new direction for the company. The leader may also wish to invite members of the leadership team to be on stage with her or him. It may even be appropriate for one or more of them to speak, to explicate the issue from their point of view. The meeting may conclude with a call to action, asking people to commit to the new idea. It should invite input and contributions from everyone.
- *Team meetings* can flesh out concepts introduced at the all-employee meeting. They can translate the broad vision into departmental and team objectives, i.e., what the team will do to carry out the mission, vision, and values. In other words, small meetings are where teams and individuals take ownership and make it happen. If they do not do so, the vision or the plan remains the property of the leader, and nothing gets done. Team meetings should allow for plenty of discussion. Ownership of an idea cannot be imposed; people have to warm up to the idea and talk about it first.
- *One-on-one meetings* are a team leader's opportunity to reiterate expectations and bring the leader's message to a personal level. The team leader should solicit the employee's opinion and conclude with a personal call to action, asking the employee to state what he or she will do to ensure the success of the initiative or plan. (Later in the chapter we will further explore ensuring feedback.)
- *Webcasts* are ideal for enabling the leader to speak live directly to the audience in a way that cuts through the clutter. The video image will be viewed on an employee's computer, so the setting will be intimate and

direct. Think of the message as the leader's opportunity to speak one-on-one with everyone in the organization. Keep it short; less than 10 minutes is ideal if a single person is speaking. (*Note:* Many organizations run their important videos as webcasts, but in doing so you lose some of the intimacy of a leader speaking live.)

- *Print media* formalize the message; they may include a brochure, a poster, or a wallet-size card. Many organizations print their vision, mission, and values on wallet-sized cards so that all employees have them. Other organizations take a more elaborate approach. Some companies have turned their vision and mission statements into drawings and printed them as posters. Many times the art is done by the employees themselves, adding an element of ownership to the process. There are other approaches. Kellogg's, for example, produced a four-color brochure delineating the company's vision, mission, and values for the sales team as well as expectations for sales performance.
- *Media releases* are designed to get the attention of the media: television, radio, newspapers, and the trade press. Use them to communicate important issues to the public or to the trade. Follow up with individual reporters to elaborate on these releases to ensure that your message is getting through. Keep in mind, however, that reporters are not publicity agents. They are seeking good stories that present all sides of an issue. If you maintain good relations with the media, you have a better chance of getting your story told. These relationships will play out especially well when the organization is going through a transformation, especially with senior leadership changes.
- *Banners* get attention and serve as reminders of the message. Post them in the cafeteria or in main traffic hallways. When you visit a military base, you will often see a banner with a slogan hanging from a key work area, such as an airplane hangar or tank garage. Peek inside a football team's locker room and you will find a banner with the team's slogan for the year hanging in a prominent place.
- *Email* works well for the reiteration of key leadership messages and announcements on progress toward milestones. Email may also be used for alerts, letting people know that an event (such as an employee meeting) is about to occur. Be selective. Most people receive far too much email already. Choose your moments wisely; otherwise the message will be ignored. (For more on email, see Chapter 5, "Leading with E-communications.")

- *Broadcast voicemail* is a method a leader can use to get the message out. You can use voicemail the same way as email, but it has one further advantage—the personal touch. Voicemail conveys the tone and personality of the speaker. And as with email, keep all voicemail messages succinct and to the point. Otherwise the message will be erased.

INTEGRATED COMMUNICATIONS PLANNING

Of course, for maximum impact, it may be appropriate to use two, three, or all of these media. If the gravity of the message is weighty, it deserves multiple channels and multiple forms of media. Leaders need to plan how their messages will be disseminated. We call this planning *integrated communications*—multiple channels and multiple media working together. The virtues of integrated communications are threefold: One, you can design a message to work in different ways for different media; two, you increase the chances of the message's being seen and heard; and three, you can use the media to keep the message fresh and alive—and therefore of greater interest.

A good example of integrated communications is the launching of a new vehicle. Commercials appear on television and radio. Ads show up in magazines, in newspapers, and on billboards. And the vehicles appear in dealer showrooms. Likewise, companies that want to communicate key issues may convene an all-employee meeting, send letters to employees' homes, and post banners in employee cafeterias. In both instances, the organizations are integrating channels and media to ensure exposure to the message.

FREQUENCY

Once is rarely enough; repeat, repeat, repeat is typically the rule. The gravity of the message dictates the amount of repetition. It is important to repeat the message frequently and in new and different ways. Varying the media used can assist in this effort. Use video for one announcement. Choose a meeting for a reiteration of the message. Post banners for thematic tie-ins. And use email to reinforce key points. In this way, the recipient receives the message in a variety of different ways over a period of time.

A word about budget: Video and print can be expensive, but in-house production facilities can reduce the cost. Furthermore, you can use other forms of media, like articles and webcasts, to carry the bulk of the message and be selective with more expensive media.

REACHING THE RIGHT AUDIENCE

The content and delivery of the leadership message are dependent upon the audience's needs and expectations. Just as advertisers target their messages to specific demographic groups, e.g., young males 18 to 24 or women 21 to 48, leaders can target theirs to specific interest groups, e.g., managers, employees, customers, or suppliers. The heart of the message will remain consistent, but the point of view may differ. For example, a message to employees about a new product launch will describe both the product and the support the employees must deliver to the customers. A product launch message to a customer will concentrate on features and benefits and describe the support the customer will receive.

In shaping the message, consider these points:

- *Select the key influencers.* Consider whom you want to reach first—those who can influence your message in a positive way. It may be appropriate to invite key members of the media for a preview of a new product or an inside look at an organizational initiative. This is a tried and true technique in public affairs circles as a means of creating buzz, i.e., excitement. At the same time, consider those who can adversely affect your message. It is appropriate to give them an inside briefing, too, so that you can address any potential negatives and defuse any negative reactions prior to general release of the message.
- *Target the message.* Adjust the content of the message to the audience you wish to reach. Sometimes the same message will be appropriate for all employees at all levels of the organization, and in this case everyone will receive the same content. It is often a good idea, however, to alert senior management to the message and even send them a prerelease message along with suggestions as to what kind of reaction they should expect from their people when the message is delivered. In this way, you gain buy-in of the leadership message and create a greater sense of shared destiny. All of us, no matter who we are, appreciate inside information because it makes us feel special and more in the know.
- *Reiteration is good.* People need to hear the message over and over again—once is not enough. Just as you repeat messages with different media, you repeat messages to the same audiences. You can tweak the content to keep it fresh, but it is essential for the leader to repeat the core themes over and over again. Repetition does two things: It increases the likelihood of retention, and it demonstrates importance. In particular, reiteration of a message underscores a leader's consistency, which leads directly to credibility.
- *Keep the big picture in mind.* Targeting and audience selection are important, but it is also important that you keep the whole story in front of you. It is essential that you make certain that everyone is getting the same big picture message. The leader must ask him- or herself

periodically whether key constituents have the information they need in order to do their jobs and have confidence in the leadership of the organization. People do not need—nor do they want—to know everything about everything. But they do need to feel that the communications they are receiving is accurate, honest, and truthful. If it is helping to strengthen the bond of trust between leader and follower as well as to drive results, then the communications is appropriate.

TIMING IS EVERYTHING

Once you have selected the right media, choose the right time to make an announcement. The most dramatic example of timing occurred in the immediate wake of September 11. Anything unrelated to the events of the day, including meetings, conferences, and advertising, was cancelled. While an event of this magnitude is thankfully a rarity, communicators need to be aware of events both inside and outside the organization. You want to strive for people's maximum attention. This is much easier said than done. During times of crisis, announcements of management changes or responses to the crisis are very appropriate. But when you are announcing a new initiative, don't do it during the holidays, when people are thinking of family and social obligations.

MAKING THE MESSAGE RESONATE

When it comes to ensuring that a message is seen and heard by the right people, leaders can learn from public relations professionals. In his book *Feeding the Media Beast*, Mark Mathis identifies a number of techniques that individuals or organizations that are seeking publicity employ to get noticed by the media. Three salient elements of raising awareness are relevant to leadership communications: difference, emotion, and simplicity.[3] Let's take them one by one.

- *Difference.* Leaders are about making a difference. We look to our leaders to give us the guidance to take us to places where we have not yet gone. Therefore, leaders need to link their communications to their difference. A leader's difference is both metaphorical and literal. The metaphorical difference relates to the difference the leader will bring to an organization: how he or she will make changes that will make things better for the stakeholders. Colin Powell is a master at delivering a message that explicates a policy and demonstrates the benefits. The second difference is literal. The leader must look to make her or his messages different (i.e., "fresh").[4] The freshness may emerge from the use of new and different words or stories to underscore key points or from the use of different forms of delivery. Speaker of the House Tip O'Neill was a master of the well-honed story; he had a treasure trove of tales that he was ready to tell at the right moment. Likewise, politicians on the campaign trail are good at finding new locales and venues for their messages; one day it might be a school, another day a factory, a third day a farm. By linking location to constituency need, they illustrate their vital difference as well as keeping the message fresh and alive.

- *Emotion*. All of us are bombarded by messages, both spontaneous and recorded, all day long. Most of the time the words and sounds run together. We stop in our tracks, however, when we sense emotion—or, better, passion. Governor Mark Schweitzer of Pennsylvania demonstrated passion as he addressed the media hour after hour during the Somerset mine disaster in the summer of 2002. When the miners were found alive and rescued, his passion turned to getting to the root cause of the disaster and determining how such disasters might be prevented in the future. Passion need not be oratory. Mother Teresa was a quiet, unassuming speaker, but her words echoed her passion for her mission of providing for the neglected poor.
- *Simplicity*. People have a lot on their plate. A leader needs to shape the message in a way that is straightforward and simple in order to make it accessible. Remember the KISS slogan (Keep It Simple, Stupid). Bill Clinton's first presidential election campaign adapted this phrase to "It's the Economy, Stupid" to remind everyone on the staff what the real issue was; it worked, and Clinton defeated an incumbent president. (Do not think that sloganeering is beneath you. It simply gives people a handle with which to grasp your message and begin to understand it.)

MARKETING THE MESSAGE

Advertisers also know how to make certain that a message resonates. Their job is to create awareness and provide a stimulus for action. Here are some things to consider (see Figure 4-2):

- *Generate buzz.* Get people talking about what you are saying. Take your cue from the *Star Wars* marketing team; they begin marketing the next sequel along with the current release, often years in advance of its premiere showing. Come opening day, you cannot pick up a newspaper or magazine without reading something about the phenomenon. Much of the promotion is free media. Leaders need to get people talking about

FIGURE 4-2 Marketing the Message

their messages, too. Select key influencers the way a marketer might select key media outlets or talk show hosts. Grant them access to what's going on and challenge them to spread the word.

- *Merchandise the message.* Give people something in return. Consider Bill Veeck, the legendary baseball promoter; his promotional concepts sprang from his love of the game as well as his respect for the paying customer.[5] Leaders need to do the same. Logos on hats, slogans on polo shirts, and banners in the hallways will get people exposed to the message. If you use the message as the theme of a sweepstakes and create some genuine excitement, people will get caught up not only in the fun, but in the meaning of the message.
- *Be novel.* Look for ways to make the message new and different. Advertisers do this by being creative. The U.S. Army introduced a high-end action adventure PC-based game entitled *Action Army* with two aims in mind: one, to attract potential recruits and get them to consider enlisting, and two, to demonstrate new forms of military tactics. Not only is this approach creative, it enables participants to experience the Army for themselves.[6]
- *Dependability.* Be seen as a relentless communicator. Get people used to seeing you articulate the message over and over again. Budweiser sponsors major sports because this gives it the optimum opportunity to reach its core market. Leaders must also find multiple ways to disseminate their messages—email, web site, video, telephone, and, yes, in person. When you become dependable, people will look to you for information as well as for inspiration.

- *Clarity.* Keep the message consistent with the culture of the organization. Volunteer-based organizations such as the Girl Scouts, the Salvation Army, and the U.S. Marine Corps excel at making their messages simple, direct, and in keeping with their cultural values. When you see an ad for one of these organizations, you know what the organization stands for; there is no ambiguity about its purpose or intention.
- *Repeatability.* It is overly optimistic (and maybe a little presumptuous) to think that people will remember a message the first time they hear it. Maybe the listener didn't hear it the first time, or perhaps it was not relevant to her or him the first time she or he heard it. It is the leader's responsibility to repeat the same message in different locations. The more times an audience sees and hears a message, the greater the chance that they will remember it. Think of advertising for your friendly local auto dealer. You see new ads for the business on television, over the airwaves, in the newspaper, and on billboards. Pretty soon you get the point of who the dealer is and what he sells. Leaders, too, need to be seen and heard frequently.[7]

ENSURING ORGANIZATIONAL FEEDBACK

Effective communications is a two-way street. All too often leaders spend the bulk of their time on crafting a message without stopping to listen to what people are saying about it. It is imperative that leaders provide avenues through which followers can voice their opinion of a leadership message as well as provide additional ideas that reinforce organizational values.

In this way, as mentioned previously, leaders enable the employees to take ownership of the idea. When you ask for feedback, you are saying, "We care about you, and we want your ideas." In return, the employee will feel a sense of obligation to contribute. In effect, asking for feedback is a kind of call to action.

The U.S. Army has a policy of expecting junior officers to challenge senior officers' opinions on matters related to the health and safety of the troops. During After Action Reports, the postmortem reviews of military exercises or actions, junior officers are encouraged to speak up and say how things might have gone differently. Why? Because the Army views AARs as learning tools. Continuous improvement will occur only when people can speak their minds. This does not mean that senior leaders need to agree; it simply means that they must listen. The same rule should apply in the civilian sector.

IMPLEMENTING A PLAN FOR SOLICITING FEEDBACK

Leaders need to understand that feedback will happen spontaneously. It is part of the *passive* communications environment discussed earlier in the

FIGURE 4-3 Ensuring Feedback

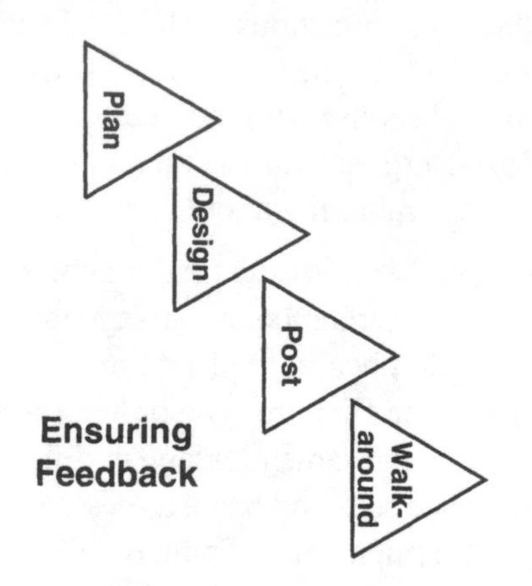

chapter. People will respond to the message in any number of ways: discussing it with colleagues, talking to their friends about it, or sometimes speaking to the media (off the record, of course). What the leader needs to do is to ensure an outlet for the feedback. You can do this in several different ways (see Figure 4-3).

- *Plan for feedback.* When you develop the communications plan, build a feedback loop into the process. As part of the planning process, let people in the organization know that you will be soliciting feedback and sharing the results of that feedback with them.
- *Design a meeting around feedback.* Encourage team leaders to hold feedback meetings. The only action item for such a meeting will be discussion of the issues. You can even provide a "meeting in a box" toolkit with questions to help managers who are unfamiliar with the feedback process to get employees to talk about the issues.
- *Post the feedback you get on your web site.* Select sample emails and post them on your web site. Omit the names of respondents; this protects the respondents' confidentiality as well as keeping people from focusing on the personality rather than the expression of the idea.
- *"Walk around" to get feedback.* Get out from behind the desk and walk the halls. Find out what people are thinking. A great way for leaders to do this is to make a habit of dining in the cafeteria at least once a week.

ENSURING THAT FEEDBACK IS HEARD

Many leaders say that they want feedback and even ask for it; the problem is that they never seem to find the time to respond to it. And let's be fair, leaders have many to-dos. The leader of an organization with hundreds or thousands of employees cannot be expected to respond to every email. What he or she can do is assign people to screen the mail and provide some response, and also respond personally to certain messages.

Another good tactic is to hold a webchat, which is an online question-and-answer session between leader and employees over a secure Internet connection. One way to begin the session is to have the leader sum up what he or she has heard so far and then open the session to questions from employees. (*Hint:* It never hurts to prepare a few questions in advance in case respondents are slow in submitting questions.)

YES, BAD NEWS HERE

Leadership brings with it isolation. As a leader moves higher up in an organization, he or she loses touch with the people at the grassroots level. Ensuring that feedback channels are kept open helps the boss stay in touch. But leaders need to do more. They need to establish ground rules that say that it's okay to deliver "bad news." Enron is a classic example of a company where the delivery of bad news was punished; people who asked probing questions, questioned decision making, or reported bad news were not promoted, and in some cases were asked to leave the company.[8] Enron is not an isolated example. Many companies do this, and in the process they isolate their leaders from the truth. Leaders themselves can make it clear that they want the unvarnished facts. Abraham Lincoln was constantly nagging his generals to give him the truth, especially when the Union was losing. Successful business leaders do the same.

Let's face it, isolation at the top is often the leader's own fault. He or she fails to meet and mingle with front-line supervisors or talk to customers. Worse, the leader promotes those who tell him or her what a good job he or she is doing and are always ready with the positive spin. Some leaders shun candid speakers because they fear that listening to them will reflect poorly on their leadership. In fact, the opposite is often the case. When small problems go unnoticed and untreated, they can mushroom into huge issues, even catastrophes. Colin Powell has said that if a leader is not hearing bad news, something is wrong. "The day soldiers stop bringing you their problems is the day you have stopped leading them. They have either lost confidence that you can help them or concluded that you do not care. Either case is a failure of leadership."[9]

The *Challenger* disaster is one such example. The engineers at Morton-Thiokol knew that the O-rings in the booster rockets were not certified to withstand freezing temperatures. Yet when NASA pushed for a launch in near-freezing weather, the engineers had no ready way to communicate their knowledge. The "no bad news" culture that permeated the space program at that time thwarted open dialogue between the suppliers' engineers and program leadership. All the engineers could do at launch time was watch in helpless agony as the *Challenger*'s booster exploded in midair. In contrast, years earlier, Gene Kranz, the legendary flight control director of the moon flights, was in the room when *Apollo 13* suffered an oxygen tank rupture en route to a lunar orbit. The astronauts in the spacecraft, together with the innovative flight team on the ground, devised a solution that brought the astronauts home safely. This culture of cooperation is an example of Kranz's leadership style; leaders and doers operated in an environment where information was shared openly.

GETTING FEEDBACK ONE-TO-ONE

Getting honest feedback from direct reports is no easy task. We humans have a strong instinct for self-preservation, so we don't bite the hand that feeds us. Therefore, when the boss asks us what we think of something coming from the top of the organization, our first reaction is to be positive. We don't want to say anything that will put our careers in jeopardy. Such a reaction may be human, but it is not healthy. We owe it to our leaders to give them honest feedback, but our leaders need to set the ground rules—i.e., they need to ensure that what is said to the leader will be kept in confidence and will not be used against the employee.

So how do leaders get feedback? First, they need to put people at ease. Make it clear that candor is the operative process. Demonstrate the benefits of honesty by accepting feedback in the spirit in which it was delivered. Next, leaders need to ask for feedback on a regular basis. You want to get people in the habit of expressing their ideas. No leader should expect to get instant candor, but when someone speaks out and does not suffer for it, others will begin to do likewise and may be more forthcoming. Still, the leader needs to work at getting feedback. Often what is not said may be the most revealing truth of all.

Of course, we need to separate the deliverer of bad news from the creator of the bad news. When people make a mistake, there will be consequences. Reporting the bad news, even when it involves your mistake, is a form of leadership; it's called taking responsibility for one's own actions. Merely reporting that news, however, should not reflect negatively on the messenger, if it's delivered in a way that is intended to keep the boss informed so that she or he has the information needed to take corrective actions. Leaders do not want to create a culture of tattletales; rather, they want to create a culture in which people can speak openly and share information in ways that reflect the credibility of the information and the organization.

THE BENEFITS OF LEADERSHIP COMMUNICATIONS PLANNING

Improved credibility results from strong and effective leadership communications planning. The benefits include increased levels of trust, improved alignment throughout all levels, better two-way communications, and the achievement of lasting results—all of which are a direct outcome of the strategies mentioned earlier in the chapter.

The planning process underscores the fact that everyone in the organization has a role to play in communications. The leader is the chief communicator, of course, but he or she should not be expected to shoulder the communications load alone. The leader should enlist the support of the leadership team as well as professional communicators. Furthermore, if the message is to be effective, everyone in the organization has to hear it. In addition, those at the top of the organization need to know what people are saying about the message. Communications is integral to an organization, and in the communications process you see just how important a role it plays in instilling the organization's vision, mission, and values. (For more on implementing a leadership communications plan, see Appendix A.)

Note: Surveys of organizational culture are another effective way to determine the communications climate. These surveys are designed to measure attitudes as well as business practices, customer service, operational focus, and mission, vision, and values. From these you can discern the communications climate. One of the best surveys of its kind is the Denison Organizational Culture Survey, which specializes in linking performance to bottom-line results. You can obtain more information by visiting Denison's web site at www.denisonculture.com.

Communications Planner—The Leadership Communications Plan

Much of this chapter provides direct information that you can put to use immediately. Use the following questions to help you determine the scope of your communications planning process.

1. Leaders need to be aware of what is being said about their organization by its key stakeholders. Make certain that you do the following:
   - Make a habit of asking at least three employees a week how they view the business.

- Eat lunch with employees at least once a week.
- Visit your employees' workplaces on a regular basis.

2. Conduct a communications survey/audit to assess the climate of the organization. Here are some suggested questions. Keep the number of questions to a minimum.

On a scale of 1 to 5, with 1 being poor and 5 being excellent, rate the following statements:

	1	2	3	4	5
Employees have the freedom to express their point of view.					
Leaders regularly communicate with their employees.					
Employees have a clear understanding of where the organization is headed.					
Employees are aware of what they need to do to meet future challenges.					
Leaders make themselves accessible to explain key issues.					

20–25 points: Excellent
15–20 points: Average
>15 points: Need more work

3. It is important to use all available channels of communications to communicate key messages.
   - Organizational
   - Editorial
   - Marketing
   - Web
4. Consider your target audiences.
   - Who are the key influencers?
   - What do the key influencers want?
   - How best can you communicate with them (e.g., email, one-to-one, video, meetings, or some other method)?
5. Leaders can learn from public relations professionals about shaping their leadership messages.

- What *difference* will your leadership message make in someone's life?
- How can you demonstrate *emotion* in your leadership messages?
- How do you keep the message *simple*?[10]

6. Advertisers are good at getting people to notice what they are promoting. Think of ways in which you might generate excitement about a leadership message.
7. Here are some steps you can take to ensure feedback:
   - Develop a "meeting in a box" for managers to help them communicate the leadership message.
   - Schedule a series of reminder emails encouraging managers to follow up on the leadership message.
   - Create a page on your web site for employee feedback.

SHELLY LAZARUS—A BRAND OF LEADERSHIP

She was young, pregnant, and working late. The man whose name was on the door of the firm for which she worked walked into her office. "He asked, 'Are you alright?'" then sat down and started to talk. . . . He did so every night [at six], on the dot, for the next month until I gave birth. We became great friends."[11] He was David Ogilvy, legendary ad man, and she was Shelly Lazarus, just beginning her career in advertising.

Years later, Lazarus became CEO of the agency. Now called Ogilvy & Mather Worldwide, the firm has offices in over 100 countries and billings in excess of $13 billion. It handles some of the bluest of the blue-chip brands, including American Express, AT&T Wireless, Coca-Cola, IBM, Ford, and Kodak. Lazarus also is a member of the board of General Electric. She has cultivated her own brand of leadership, one that is consistent with her own values as well as with the values she gained from her agency, including David Ogilvy. According to Lazarus, women have gone from "reaching for the engagement ring to reaching for the brass ring."[12] While she "crashed through the glass ceiling," her path was not without its obstacles; in particular, she recalls being told that jobs were not something to "waste . . . on a woman."[13] Still, Lazarus was prepared. She was a graduate of Smith College and held an M.B.A. from Columbia. When Lazarus tells her story today, she is reminding young women of their collective past as a means of educating them about their future opportunities, a classic model of leadership communications.

CHAMPION OF ADVERTISING

In an age when advertising agencies are bought and sold like commodities, O&M remains distinctive. As part of the huge WPP communications family, O&M has retained a unique identity as the agency of brands: identity, image, inspiration, and aspiration. At O&M they call it 360 Degree Brand Stewardship, touching all the points where the consumer meets the product or service—on the shelf, in a commercial, in a print ad, using the product, or dreaming of the product. "Once the enterprise understands what the brand is all about, it gives direction to the whole enterprise."[14] The responsibility for ensuring brand consistency falls on employees. "They are absolutely critical. If the people who work in a company don't understand what the brand is, if they can't articulate what the brand's all about, then who can?"[15]

At the same, Lazarus believes that you have to make the communications genuine. "People don't like being given messages," says Lazarus, "but they love listening to stories. I encounter fresh new examples every day of the principles I consider important. I find them at work, in my everyday life, in the media, and anecdotally. When I communicate principles using fresh, real life examples, stories that tell a tale, people always 'get it' that much better."

Her ability to be articulate has made Shelly Lazarus one of the most quoted advertising executives, not simply because of her gender but because of her insights. "Consider the value an ad agency brings. We help build brands, and a brand is the most critical asset a company has today. Sure, we're under more scrutiny from clients, but accountability means credibility."[16] Lazarus believes that an ad agency is really a "business partner" that is responsible for helping to grow the client's business. Toward that end, Lazarus would like to see the agency become a partner that can help to integrate advertising, marketing, and internal communications.[17]

The business of advertising is cyclical. Lazarus's belief in its power to influence is not. "The ad industry isn't struggling for a new set of principles or abandoning the ones that made it great from the start."[18] Despite downturns, Lazarus says, "I'm having more fun than at any other moment in my 30-year advertising career. The game is more interesting and more relevant than ever."[19] In 2001, O&M won more than $700 million in new billings. That same year, *Advertising Age*, the industry's top trade magazine, recognized O&M as "the outstanding American agency."[20]

INTEGRATION OF WORK AND LIFE

Lazarus has mingled her personal and professional lives in a way that makes her a role model. She and her husband, George, a pediatrician, both hold demanding jobs, but they make time for their three children, including finding time for skiing together. Her kids "insist that I ski alongside them without my cell phone."[21] When her children were younger, she took them to visit David Ogilvy in the south of France. "Seeing him play with my children made me realize how completely intertwined my career and family have become."[22]

Lazarus has come to an understanding of herself as a role model. *Fortune* magazine has included her in every issue of its annual "50 Most Powerful Women in American Business." Her example of making time for school functions "gives other women in the company, or clients, the confidence to be able to say, 'I'm going too.'"[23] Young women seek her out for advice. "There's one thing I say all the time: You have to love what you're doing in your professional life. If you ever want to find balance, you have to love your work, because you're going to love your children."[24] Most important, Lazarus believes in the direct approach to integrating work and life. "Encourage them, outright, to follow your example."

Her boss, Martin Sorrell, chairman of the WPP group (of which O&M is a member), says, "She has an incredible focus on people and understanding of this business and the way it is developing. But I wouldn't want [to say] she's just a great people person; she is a very good business manager who doesn't back away from tough decisions."[25]

SAYING IT ONCE IS NOT ENOUGH

Lazarus places great emphasis on reiteration. "I don't think you can ever communicate too much. Communicating to your organization is not something taken care of a couple of times a year in memos, or at the annual Christmas party speech. I know from my advertising background that the most effective communication is multilayered. One message builds on others."

As an advertiser, Lazarus understands the value of different forms of communications. "Emails are great for speed, but they never replace the face-to-face. Group meetings are fine for the camaraderie, but they never replace the intimacy of one-to-one. Formal communication—the written word—gives weight, but all the more so when it is supported by spontaneous and informal contact."

"Above all, you can never walk the halls too much," she says. "David Ogilvy once told me that as much time as he spent on people, it was never enough. Since people are the number one asset of any organization, I don't think you can ever spend too much time with them—in written communication, on the phone, in person."

SUSTAINING MERIT

Lazarus credits David Ogilvy with creating a sustainable foundation for the business. "[Ogilvy's] genius was in taking a very strong point of view about how to run an organization and from that point of view developing a set of principles . . . that have actually lived on in our people."[26] Lazarus believes that Ogilvy's befriending of her as a young pregnant woman stemmed not only from his sense of "democracy" but also from its being another way of "challenging the status quo."[27]

By telling and retelling her story and the story of her relationship with Ogilvy, Lazarus is building upon the virtues of the past as a means of creating the future—of growing the organizational brand, so to speak. Her stories remind others of the evolution of professional women as well as the opening of new doors of possibility for both men and women. As Ogilvy did, Lazarus, too, values a "meritocracy." People remain at O&M because they contribute. "[Ours] is a non-political culture. . . . It's an organization that holds its people accountable."[28]

Accountability is essential to leadership, and through her words and example, Shelly Lazarus, brand leader, demonstrates what it takes to lead by developing others and challenging them to find their own paths. Her stories provide illumination for others who are seeking to create their own way or to add luster to their own brands.

Leadership Communications Lessons

Understand the power of the media. Lazarus knows how to create excitement around a product or service offering. The same techniques that are used to sell products can be applied to selling leadership messages.

Take a stand. Lazarus has been an advocate for the integration of work and life and has made it a visible issue within her company.

Be visible. As an advertising professional, Lazarus understands the power of communications and uses it to disseminate messages. She is a frequent public speaker as well as a good person to interview on the role of women in business.

Strive for balance. A mother of three, Lazarus integrates her work and her life in ways that give meaning to herself and her family as well as set a good example for men and women in her firm.

Live your message. As one of the highest-ranking women professionals, Lazarus is both a role model for women and an example to men with working spouses.

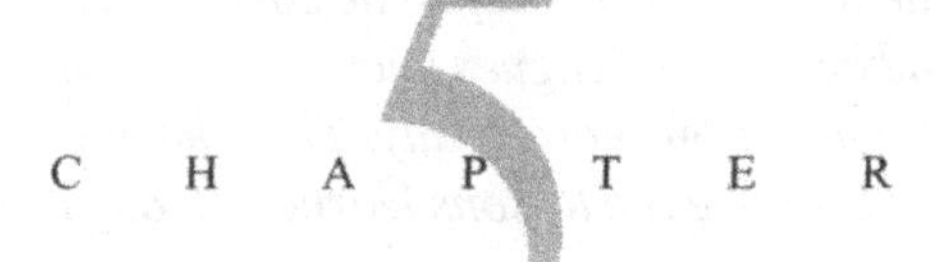

Communication . . . always makes demands. It always demands that the recipient become somebody, do something, believe something. It always appeals to motivation.

Peter Drucker

LEADING WITH E-COMMUNICATIONS

BILL IS A RELENTLESS COMMUNICATOR. As a marketing manager for a large packaged goods company, Bill understands the power of communicating with the consumer. He carries over this philosophy to his people. As one who operates in the realm where the application of knowledge about consumers and customers is power, Bill believes in liberating information so that his people can use it to do their jobs better.

Bill also is an early adopter of technology. He was among the first to embrace email as a means of sharing information as well as giving direction. Wireless communications is a boon to Bill; he prides himself on always being accessible and in touch. In addition, Bill set up a departmental intranet where employees could post updates on their work and also share documents. The team even works collaboratively online through the services of a departmen-

tal network. As a result, the department has a strong esprit de corps. This connectedness has spurred cooperation because colleagues know more about one another's projects and can share information more easily. This sharing has produced true organizational growth because the lessons learned on one project can often be carried to the next.

The e-communication revolution has certainly produced harmony in the ranks, but lately some employees are beginning to feel overwhelmed. While they appreciate Bill's keeping them abreast of developments, his emails, once a trickle, are now a veritable tsunami. And the emails don't stop when Bill is out of the office. Evenings, weekends, and out-of-town trips do not stem the flow. In fact, it seems that the more Bill is away, the more he sends messages. Accompanying his messages are the inevitable to-dos. His people cannot keep up. As a result, the happy workplace that Bill fostered so diligently is beginning to fray at the edges. People have become edgy, snapping at one another and going out of their way to avoid Bill. One or two refuse to check their email more than once per day for fear of getting another wave of things to do.

While the dot.com bubble may have burst, one of its legacies is thriving—e-communications (see Figure 5-1). From corporate intranets to e-newsletters as well as the all-pervasive email, we are all more connected, or e-connected, than ever before. Rosabeth Moss Kanter has written, "Communication is the core of e-culture."[1] Much of this connectedness is good. We can work from home, from the airport, from a remote office, or from a beach in the Bahamas—often more productively—thanks to the proliferation of e-communications. Being connected 24/7 is our mantra—always on, always available.

Hold on, though! Maybe all of this connectedness has a price, and a big one. A loss of privacy. A loss of free time. A loss of touch with the people who are nearest and dearest to us. A loss of everything except work time.

Leaders need to be aware of the power of e-communications. Leaders do a great deal of communicating electronically. In fact, most people will have more contact with the leader through email than face to face. The ability to express a leadership point of view in words only is essential. When used successfully, e-communications will help lay the foundation for a virtual community. The hub of the e-community is the web site. The lifeblood of the e-community is email.

Email also has its perils. Most of us are inundated with too much email. Leaders need to limit their use of it when sending leadership messages; otherwise it will not be read. Also, email cannot be a substitute for face-to-face encounters. There are times, such as in coaching, when only face-to-face

FIGURE 5-1 E-communications

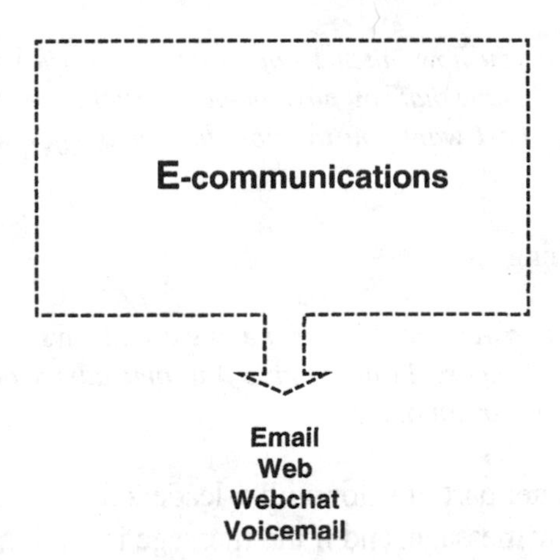

contact will do. You can follow up a coaching session or a team meeting with an email, but only after the personal connection has been made.

FORMING THE LEADERSHIP E-MESSAGE

Email facilitates the day-to-day commerce of an organization. It is used for this purpose in nearly every organization. Since people receive so much email (50 to 100 emails per day is common), you need to be selective. Choose your moments.

The leadership message, as always, must be rooted in the values of the organization and must be of significance to the recipient. It must be designed to further a sense of trust. Therefore, keep the messages consistent with your culture and your values. When Jack Welch used email to keep in touch with employees, it was an outgrowth of his habit of sending written personal notes.[2]

Here are some examples of effective leadership emails and their purposes:

Furthering the vision

- *Our vision challenges us to undertake some exciting new opportunities. We can be the organization we all want to be. Let me tell you how . . .*

Amplifying the mission

- *We are a people-centric organization. We attribute our success to your contributions. Let me take this opportunity to recognize some key contributors.*

Recognizing contributions

- *I want to tell you how much I appreciate the work you have been doing for us. I know that you have been sacrificing personal time for this project, and I want you to know that your effort has not gone unnoticed.*

Providing coaching

- *You are working very hard for us. People are always telling me what a hard worker you are. I want to give you some advice about how you can become better. First, . . .*

Brevity is the better part of valor with e-leadership messages. No one has time to read a lengthy message, and if the message is too long, people probably will not read it at all.

Note: Be careful when you send. Check that you have clicked the correct recipient. Do not copy people on e-coaching sessions. To do so may be a violation of trust between you and the employee.

FACILITATING TWO-WAY E-COMMUNICATIONS

Think of virtual communications as a great way for leader and employee to have a conversation. While nothing can, or should, replace the dynamism of the face-to-face conversation, virtual communications through email is an effective way for the leader to share his or her thoughts and to reiterate the leadership message, provide guidance and direction, and keep abreast of changing conditions by listening to feedback. Email invites response. With the exception of broadcast emails, which go to thousands, the email to a direct report typically carries with it the demand for a response. The leader needs to know, "Did you understand what I wrote?" and the leader needs to hear, "Yes, and let me offer my thoughts on this." When used in this way, email facilitates dialogue.

If both sides pay attention to what the other is saying (and keep in mind that the leader is communicating with more than one follower), you increase the capacity for trust to develop, which should always be the ultimate outcome of leadership communications.

BUILDING A WEB-BASED E-COMMUNITY

A web site devoted to leadership topics can be an invaluable resource for refreshing or extending the leadership message. The site can serve not only as

a communications center but also as a place for postin
related to development and evaluation.

The secret to building the successful e-commur
reason to visit. This means keeping the information
also means giving people a reason to return again
keeping the content fresh and up to date. The cent
the web site.

Leaders also need to keep in mind that in an e-community, transparency (openness) rules. As Rosabeth Moss Kanter puts it, the days of "mushroom management . . . keep[ing] employees in the dark, cover[ing] them with manure, and when they ripen, can[ning] them" are over.[3] In an e-community, information is everywhere and is freely shared. Such a community diminishes the opportunity for bosses to lord it over underlings because they have knowledge that no one else has. When people know the bigger picture, as happens in a transparent culture, they can make better-informed decisions for the organization and for themselves.

A note about access: You may decide to restrict access to members of the team or employees of the organization. You can also have levels of access, with everyone able to see the home page, but sections of the site being restricted. In this way, you can set up virtual workrooms where team members can collaborate. In this virtual space, members can share documents, edit them, and post new findings, with the information restricted to members only. Many corporate universities are doing this for their participants, enabling "students" to collaborate in virtual time and space.

TELEPHONE AND VOICEMAIL

In our age of e-communications, we sometimes forget to use the telephone. Often it is more appropriate to make an initial contact with an individual on the phone and follow up with email, or vice versa. Telephone and voicemail, as mentioned in Chapter 4, have the advantage of personal warmth and one-to-one connection. Also, a telephone conversation is a dialogue; the parties to the call can go back and forth quickly, amplifying and explicating in 30 seconds points that might take three or four rounds of email to sort out.

When leaving a voicemail, think about what you want to say first. Make your points quickly and in reasonable order. The person retrieving the message will thank you for your clarity and brevity. And, if you cannot think of exactly what you want to say, send an email. The time it takes you to compose the message will give you an opportunity to develop and organize your thoughts.

TAINING PERSONAL BOUNDARIES

our chapter vignette, Bill does a good job of building an e-community, but he ultimately goes too far. E-communications is a Janus-faced proposition. (Janus, you will recall from Roman mythology, was a god with two faces.) On the upside, email permits the boss and her or his team to exchange ideas at any time of the day or night. On the downside, all this emailing back and forth can erode personal time.

While it is true that for many the boundaries between work and home are blurred, the leader needs to respect the personal lives of her or his followers. A relentless flurry of email from the leader can set up the expectation that employees must do the same. The leader not only has to set limits on his or her own messaging habits, but also must make it clear that followers do not need to emulate them. In other words, just because a leader does email at two in the morning does not mean followers need to do so. Unless the leader is explicit in setting limits, employees will naturally assume that he or she expects people to be monitoring their email in the wee hours. For example, the leader can say, "I do my email in off-hours because it is my choice to do so, but I do not expect you to be waiting around for my messages. Nor do I expect you to work at those hours unless you want to." In this way, the leader sets limits and maintains a differentiation between work time and personal time.

Note: According to a survey by Pew Internet and American Life Project, 98 percent of people who have access to the Internet at work use it. They find email essential to their jobs, enabling them to accomplish their work. Most of them find email effective for conducting fact-based business, but less effective for "heart-to-heart" discussions. Many see email as "encouraging communications." Surprisingly, while anecdotal evidence shows that people feel overwhelmed by the amount of email they get, most users find it "manageable." Some 20 percent of emailers, however, fall into the "power email category," half of whom receive more than 20 emails daily, and a quarter of whom receive upwards of 50 per day. All in all, this study confirms what many employees already know: Email has become an integral part of the workplace.[4]

Communications Planner: Creating and Maintaining the E-community

Leaders can enable the building of a virtual community where key stakeholders can congregate to share information and learn from others.

1. Email is a terrific way to stay abreast of events and to provide ongoing coaching. Think of someone in your organization

whom you regularly coach. Face-to-face communications is paramount, but you can use email to:

- Clarify points raised in a coaching session.
- Provide feedback on specific points.
- Deliver ongoing e-coaching that is specific, able to be acted upon, and timely. (Remember, always open on a positive note.)

2. Establish a web site that can serve as a leadership resource. Consider providing the following materials:
   - Leadership programs: Descriptions of programs available within your organization.
   - Leadership evaluation tools: Career development tools and self-assessments.
   - Best practices: Descriptions of effective leadership within your organization. (Be certain to include examples of personal leadership from people who are not yet in leadership positions.)
   - Heroes of the workplace: Stories of men and women who have made a positive difference in the organization. Write them up as short features.
   - Leaders' exchange: A virtual gathering place where people can share ideas about leadership.
3. Create a work/life discussion about how virtual technology should be used. Operate from the principle that e-technology should be an enabler, not a disabler, i.e., focus on how technology can work for you, not against you. Begin with a team meeting where people discuss how to use technology to their advantage. Outline some parameters for email and virtual collaboration. Continue the discussion on your web site.

PETER DRUCKER—MANAGEMENT UNBOUND

He is known as the Sage of Claremont, referring to the school in southern California where he lives, teaches, and writes. He is still vigorous in his early nineties, and people come from around the world to hear him. And he comes to the world via satellite lectures. "I like bigness," he says. Today he splits his consulting time between fee-paying and *pro bono* clients. And in the process he is continuing to do what he has done for seven decades: persuade, nudge, and cajole organizations to regard workers as resources and management as the enabler of organizational effectiveness. He is Peter Drucker.

PIONEERING MANAGEMENT WRITER

Born in Vienna in 1909, Drucker recalls his earliest memory at age 5 as someone in his family referring to the "end . . . of civilization."[5] It was the beginning of World War I, which ended the spirit of the nineteenth century and ushered in the modern age, complete with its own horrors but also its possibilities. Somehow it seems fitting that Drucker, the creator of a new way of viewing management that would destroy an older form, would have this as his first memory.

First and foremost, Drucker considers himself a writer. In fact, he had been an accomplished financial writer prior to his emigrating to the United States from Germany as Hitler was coming to power. While his views have evolved over the decades, chiefly under the influence of behavioral scientists like Abraham Maslow, Drucker is noted for the significance of his work, the constancy of his message, and the frequency of his messages. He is a leadership communicator par excellence.

NEW IDEAS FOR A NEW AGE

His exploration of the management scene began with an assignment from a senior vice president at General Motors who wanted to find out what made his company tick. The result was *The Concept of the Corporation*. Alfred Sloan, the chairman of General Motors, hated the book, but he did not discourage Drucker from publishing it. Fortunately, Drucker did so. American management was never to be quite the same.[6]

The Concept of the Corporation made a strong case for a reexamination of the social contract between labor and management. Workers should be regarded as a "resource, not a cost," and they should have a role in the corporation's governance. Drucker also examined the dehumanization that occurs in large industrial corporations. At the same time, as his biographer, Jack Beatty, points out, Drucker was not a "Bolshie"; he argued that profit was "the pre-condition of industrial society." Furthermore, this was the book that introduced Sloan's concept of decentralization; over time, this concept was adopted by more than three-quarters of American businesses.[7] And while Drucker may have been unwelcome at General Motors, he emerged as a leading consultant to American businesses. (It is worth noting that General Motors has repaired the breach and now maintains good relations with Drucker.)[8]

MANAGEMENT UNLEASHED

Drucker's seminal management work—in fact, the work that many credit with inventing the field of management—is *The Practice of Management*. Appearing in 1954, this book quantified the role of the manager as the person responsible for goals (management by objectives) and concerned with the accomplishment of results through others, as well as having a total perspective on the business and its place in the competitive landscape.[9]

What Drucker did in this book, and 20 years later in *Management: Tasks, Responsibilities, Practices,* was to quantify the manager's role, not in some learn-by-rote, restrictive way, but rather in a Churchillian neo-heroic way that would cause the manager to see himself (and later herself) as one who can accomplish things, and in so doing aspire to something greater. That theme of aspiration for something better—a new system, a new management discipline, a new social order—is inherent in all of Drucker's work.

LEADERSHIP COMMUNICATOR

From where do Drucker's ideas spring? He learns as he talks to people, and he also discovers his point of view as he teaches or writes about it.[10] Curiously, Drucker credits a course in admiralty law, which he took as part of a doctoral program in Germany in the twenties, with giving him his management insights. To Drucker, management is "an integrating discipline of human values and conduct, of social order and intellectual inquiry . . . feed[ing] off economics, psychology, mathematics, political theory, history, and philosophy. In short, management is a *liberal art.*"[11]

Drucker is as much a social philosopher as he is a management consultant. His canvas is not limited to the boardroom, or even to the spans of a global corporation. Drucker has a wondrous ability to link the issues and challenges of modern management with history, be it ancient Greece, Rome, or China. He drops in historical anecdotes the way other writers use punctuation. The effect is to place management squarely within the entire span of human history. And lest we forget it, Drucker is a teacher; his books are his lectures, his visions, and his arguments for adopting new ways of thinking and doing.

At the same time, Drucker knows how to keep it simple. He loves organizing concepts into easy-to-remember paradigms, e.g., "The Ten Rules of Effective Research . . . The Five Deadly Business Sins . . . Two Cores of Unity."[12] The contrast between the grand themes and the plain and simple gets to the core of Drucker's influence—he is relatively easy to understand. He is not simplistic; his words, images, stories, and paradigms are used to make the abstract seem vivid and accessible.

LISTENER OR READER?

One of his later essays, *Managing Oneself,* applies his management insights to the individual. In the article, Drucker makes a striking insight into leadership communication styles with another of his historical allusions. He relates how General Dwight Eisenhower was loved by the press for his crisp, succinct responses to their questions. A decade later, President Eisenhower was reviled for his mumbling responses and his butchery of the language. The reason, writes Drucker, is that Eisenhower was a reader, and he read specially prepared briefing papers prior to his wartime press conferences. As president,

Eisenhower tried to rely on give-and-take with the press and wing his answers; it didn't work. Franklin Roosevelt and Harry Truman were listeners and could roll with the reporters' questions. For Drucker, it is a matter of knowing how you process information, orally or printed. Knowing what you are will enable you to communicate your point of view more effectively.[13]

Drucker devotes a chapter to managerial communications in *Management: Tasks, Responsibilities, Practices*. He draws a distinction between information and communication. Information is data—"formal" and "logical." Communications is perception—how we interpret the data. Communications then becomes, as Drucker says, "the mode of an organization," meaning how the organization uses communications to function. Commands (e.g., information) flow downward, but genuine communications (perception) stands apart from hierarchy; it is peer to peer or person to person.[14]

In *The Concept of the Corporation,* Drucker writes that "Management is the organ of institutions, the organ that converts a mob into an organization, and human efforts into performance."[15] For Drucker, it is management that tames the wild beast of anarchy and enables people working together to achieve great results. And it is Drucker's words and teachings that have made the topic accessible to generations of managers.

Leadership Communications Lessons

Draw analogies. Make use of metaphors and parables. Drucker is forever sprinkling his texts with artful images and little stories.

Illustrate with historical references. Reading Drucker is reading history. Whether he is citing the ancients in Greece or China or making reference to modern Europe, Drucker uses historical references to place his lessons in the context of history.

Share the learning. Teach what you know. Drucker is a teacher; he wants people to share his ideas.

Admit mistakes. Unlike some academics, Drucker admits his mistakes. He underestimated the role of behavior in management until he read Maslow. As a result, he changed his point of view and in the process made his lessons more instructive.

Live your message. Looking at the whole of Drucker's writings, we can discern consistency and constancy in his messages. Again and again he pleads the case for the besieged manager, always trying to show him or her a better way.

CHAPTER 6

> We are a fractious nation, always searching, always dissatisfied, yet always hopeful. We have an infinite capacity to rejuvenate ourselves. . . . We will continue to flourish because our diverse American society has the strength, hardiness, and resilience of the hybrid plant we are.
>
> *Colin Powell*

STRUCTURING THE STAND-UP LEADERSHIP PRESENTATION

THE ROOM IS DARK save for the light of a small overhead lamp. A figure is intently pecking away at the keyboard, watching the screen fill with words. The figure alternately expresses joy, optimism, indecision, and despair. Dollars to doughnuts this poor soul is writing his presentation. Lord, protect him. He needs help fast.

If you have found yourself in this situation, you are not alone. Every leader who crafts his or her own words, or even polishes them, sweats the details. Sometimes the words come in a torrent. Other times they trickle like raindrops in a mist. Other times, there ain't no drops at all. It's dry, man, dry!

Welcome to the world of making leadership presentations. Putting meat on the bones—that's what content is. And if you follow a simple step-by-step process, you will be able to add more meat faster and better than a turkey farmer can the month before Thanksgiving.

The secret, if there is one, is organization. Organization is fundamental to an effective presentation. The presentation that rambles is the presentation that is forgotten not as soon as it is over, but while it is still going on. And cheer up. You have already surmounted one of the biggest hurdles: You have your message. Now your challenge is to craft the content around it (see Figure 6-1).

CREATING THE PRESENTATION

Research the Topic

Get your stuff together. There are two ways to research the topic. One way is to gather material on it from print and media sources. These sources can range from newspaper, trade magazine, and periodical articles to corporate reports. Go through these sources to find material that you deem relevant and mark that material with a highlighter.

The Internet can be a big help in this area. You can search periodicals through their actual web sites or in a database. Sources like ProQuest and Lexis/Nexis catalogue millions of articles culled from newspapers, periodicals, and business, trade, and academic journals. In addition, many leading business and news publications provide their articles for a nominal fee. Some publications offer their articles free through their web sites; these include *The Atlantic, Fast Company, Forbes, Fortune*, and *Strategy + Business*.

The second way to research the topic is to go talk to someone. Ask your colleagues to provide you with information on the topic. If you are a guest presenter, do not be afraid to contact the host and ask for ideas about what the audience might like to hear. This technique can also be useful if you are making a sales presentation. As the sales expert, you know the material. Your challenge is to adapt it to what the customer wants to know. By doing so, you position your message to land on receptive ears.

Gather Anecdotes

During the research phase, it is important that you keep an open mind. Allow yourself to be receptive to ideas that are tangential, that is, that are not directly

FIGURE 6-1 Creating the Presentation

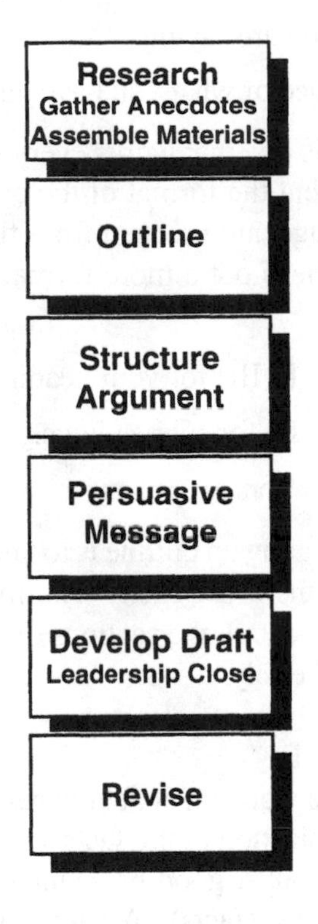

related to your topic but serve to add color. Look for stories that can embellish your presentation. To adapt the old Chinese proverb, one good story is worth 10 minutes of presentation.

These anecdotes can come from your own experience or can be gathered from other sources, such as speaker reference guides. Humor can be a good icebreaker, but always, always, always, keep it fresh, alive, and, above all, nonoffensive.

Assemble the Material

Arrange your research materials in a way that makes sense in terms of what you wish to say. You can organize it into subject files or keep everything together. The key is to put everything into an order that makes sense for you.

OUTLINE THE MATERIAL

Now you can begin to structure the material you have collected. Create an outline that makes sense for you. The important thing to remember is that organization is essential. Just like a paragraph, the outline for a presentation has three essential parts:

- *Beginning*: Tell the audience what you are going to say.
- *Middle*: Explain what you are saying.
- *End*: Remind the audience of what you have just said.

This is a formula, but it is one that works every time. The key to the outline process is organization, but the format of the outline is up to you. Some folks like to jot notes on a page and proceed from there. Others, particularly professional writers, like to flesh out a more formal outline. Here's a typical outline format:

- Use Roman numerals (I, II, III) for your headings.
- Use capital letters (A, B, C) for subheadings.
- Use numbers (1, 2, 3) for content points.

The operative point in creating an outline is to keep your ideas in sections. This way you can rearrange the order easily. The formal outline works well here because while it contains detail, the sections of the outline are freestanding and can be moved around easily.

STRUCTURE AN ARGUMENT

A leadership presentation or a well-run coaching session should be grounded in reason and logic. The organization of the facts should support the argument and flow to a logical conclusion. A good presentation will have good *claims* (results) and effective *reasons* (facts). Aristotle identified the grouping together of claims and reasons as an *enthymeme,* or logical proposition.[1]

- "Our prices are too high, so we had better lower them to attract new customers."
- "Our vision is to be the leader in our industry, and our leadership will enable us to set the standards for others to follow."
- "The competition in our segment is very strong, so we will need to develop new and better products that better meet the needs of our customers."

Enthymemes are not difficult to formulate. British philosopher Stephen Toulmin took Aristotle one step further by adding a third element to claims and reasons, which he called *warrants*. A warrant is "the connection . . . between your claim and your supporting reasons."[2] Think of the warrant as the product of the claim and the reason.

- *Claim:* We value diversity in our organization.
- *Reason:* Our diversity is an important strength when it comes to understanding our customers.

- *Warrant:* Our diversity will enable us to continue to develop products that customers want to buy.

Warrants are the "general principle that enables you to move from reason to specific claim."[3] They are the syntheses of your arguments, the statements that will enable people to latch onto your leadership ideas.

The leader needs to imbue his or her arguments with a mixture of fact and personality. A dry recitation of arguments will not sway anyone. When the arguments are invested with the leader's character, along with well-turned phrases, analogies, and stories, the presentation will take flight.[4] Winston Churchill and Martin Luther King were masters of the craft of augmenting their arguments with rhetorical flourishes that carried the listener on a kind of symphony of sound and reason.

THE PERSUASIVE MESSAGE

One of the chief responsibilities of a leader-communicator is to persuade followers to adopt her or his point of view. In fact, Drucker argues that persuasion lies at the core of all communications.[5] Except in times of extreme crisis, such as a battlefield or a pilot taking command during a thunderstorm, where time is of the essence, leaders must do more than say, "Follow me." They need to give reasons why people should follow them. And, during those crisis moments when the leader does not have the luxury of time, he or she must call upon the reservoir of credibility that he or she has established through consistent and repeated leadership messages. Robert Cialdini, a noted authority on the topic of persuasion, lists six key characteristics that persuaders use. Each is rooted in fundamental human behavior.[6]

- *Reciprocation* refers to the sense of obligation to "repay in kind" that we feel when we receive something that we perceive to be of value.[7] None of us likes feeling that we owe something to someone else, so we are inclined to pay it back as a matter of course in order to free ourselves from the obligation. When the leader describes what the organization has done for the individual or the team and then asks for something in return, she or he is using a form of reciprocation. For example, if a leader talks about how the organization has given individuals opportunities for growth and success, and how those opportunities have been fulfilled, employees will typically fall in line and do whatever the leader asks them to do. We are likely to reciprocate because we feel a sense of obligation.
- *Commitment and consistency* involves sticking with an individual or a principle because it is in line with what we have done previously.[8] A call to action is an example of commitment and consistency because it asks followers to do something as a consequence of the commitment they

have made to the organization. We see calls to action when organizations need to transform themselves in the face of crises and when they are trying to capitalize on new opportunities. The fact that people belong to the organization will make them inclined to respond to the call to action if they deem it consistent with organizational goals and values.

- *Social proof* involves people's going with the flow because others are doing it. Cialdini cites the example of canned laughter as a tried-and-true method of inducing people to laugh.[9] The leader who asks others to follow her or his example is employing the concept of social proof. The challenge for the leader is to follow through, to do what she or he promised to do. Social proof can be a validator of work/life integration; the leader who takes time off to participate in a child's school activity is leading by example if the same opportunity is afforded to others in the organization.
- *Liking* simply reflects the fact that people will associate with those whom "they know and like."[10] The leader who is often seen and heard, and who is perceived as someone that people want to be around, is an example of liking. However, while it is true that the leader whom everyone likes will have a better chance of getting others to follow, likability is not a leadership prerequisite. It may even be a detriment to leadership, because the desire to be liked may cause a leader to put off the tough decisions. When it comes to leadership, it is more helpful to think of liking as a form of respect. Respect can emerge from knowing the leader and liking what he or she stands for.
- *Authority* refers to an individual or a group's willingness to obey those who they assume are in positions of control over them.[11] Cialdini describes the Milgram experiment, in which "students were willing to deliver dangerous and severe levels of pain to another person because they were directed to do so by an authority figure." People will defer to power and will do what they are told. It is up to the leader, however, to use this power judiciously. The recent corporate finance scandals are examples of situations in which underlings went along with their bosses because they were told to do so. To speak up or point out the errors would have been to risk career suicide. Authority in the wrong hands can be a tool of the devil. Authority in the right hands is an instrument of judicious leadership.

  While authority and leadership are intertwined, position and leadership are not. People can be appointed to positions of authority, but they must earn their right to lead. People will defer to those in authority, but if that authority is abused, people will either tune out or comply out of fear.

In both cases, the leader has failed to win their respect. And when people have no respect for their leader, this often compromises their performance, i.e., they may not do as well as they would if they were more motivated.

- *Scarcity* is defined as "opportunities [that] seem more valuable to us when they are less available."[12] Leaders who talk about the "select few" who will have the opportunity to achieve if they are willing to put in the time, effort, and personal discipline are employing scarcity. Leadership development programs, both in the military and in the private sector, employ variations on the scarcity principle when either nominating or recruiting people for leadership positions.

In and of themselves, these methods of persuasion are amoral; they are characteristics of human behavior. They can be used for good or evil purposes. For example, marketers use these methods singly or in combination to provoke a desired response to a product or service they want us to buy. Someone with an evil intent, such as a Charles Manson or a Saddam Hussein, uses these methods to gain influence over others for some twisted purpose that is rooted in denigration and subjugation. When these methods are used correctly and with the right motives in mind, such as by someone like Mother Teresa who is acting for the good of the organization and the benefit of others, they can be valuable enhancers of the leadership message. The use of one or more of these methods will make for a more compelling, and ultimately more persuasive, leadership message.

A Stake in the Outcome

There is another caveat regarding persuasion: The leader must care about the message and should have a stake in the outcome. The leader must demonstrate that her or his vision or point of view is right for the organization. For example, a leader who insists on transformational change must demonstrate its benefits and be clear in his or her expectations for him- or herself and for the team. We see this when a new coach takes over a team or a new manager is hired to run a department. The fate of the coach or manager is tied to the fate of the team or the department. If the team wins, the coach and the players share in the victories. If the department achieves its objectives, the manager and the employees share in the rewards. In each case, the leader has a vested interest in the performance of the players or employees, and vice versa. The sense of shared destiny adds to the credibility of the message, and ultimately of the leader.

Persuasion gets to the core of leadership. When it is used with discretion and with the right intentions, it can be extremely powerful in accomplishing the leader's goals.

DEVELOP THE FIRST DRAFT

Okay, cue the lights. Spotlight on the writer. Bring up the music. Now comes the hard part: getting it down on paper. If you have followed the guidelines given earlier, your task will be easier. Your challenge is to put thoughts and words to your outline points. As you craft your words, you will have to keep some key points in mind.

- *What is your message?*

  Remember your message. It will serve as your compass. If what you are adding does not complement the message, it is better left unsaid.
- *What is your thesis statement?*

  The thesis and the message may be one and the same, but sometimes the wording of the two is slightly different. Regard the thesis as the reason why you are speaking and what you will say—e.g., "Tonight I will tell you why we need to cut costs and provide ways we can do it."
- *What are you using to amplify your message?*

  Amplification comes from the content that you add. You shape your message using your own knowledge and the information you have gained from the research materials and anecdotes.
- *What visuals do you have to illustrate your message?*

  Visuals can be anything from flipcharts and posters to electronic graphics. The rule of thumb is to use the graphics to support the message, not to present the message. You can, of course, use a photograph or a chart to tell part of the story, but you should not rely solely on graphics to tell the story.

When crafting your presentation, you have the option of writing it out word for word or preparing notes from which you will speak. Some people feel that word-for-word scripting enables them to think through precisely what they want to say. This approach is the soundest one, and it allows for the greatest amount of advance creativity. The downside is that it is time-consuming.

Other presenters prefer to work from notes. Not only is creating a presentation using this approach less time-consuming, but the approach also allows the presenter to be more flexible and responsive to audience needs. The presenter who is stuck to a speech may overlook the audience, while the presenter who is standing and delivering from notes can shift gears more readily according to audience needs.

Some speakers script everything in advance, then cull the words to note cards. By doing this, they determine their flow, precision, and word choice in advance, then deliver the presentation in a manner that appears to be spontaneous.

How Long Should It Be?

The subject of length is important. The presenter should ask in advance how long she or he is to present. For a set speech, a rule of thumb is that 15 to 20 minutes is good, but that unless the speaker is really first rate, the audience will go to sleep with anything longer. In contrast, sales or technical presentations may run for an hour or for an afternoon. In this case, the presentation should be more relaxed and informal. The speaker needs to engage the audience by asking questions frequently to ensure that everyone understands the material.

There is no right or wrong way to craft a presentation. What matters is the speaker's commitment to the material and the desired impact upon the audience.

The Leadership Close

Every leadership presentation needs to have a strong conclusion. The presenter has to give the audience both something to remember and something to do. Effective closes have two important elements: a recapitulation of the message and a call to action.

The recapitulation, or summary, is a simple restatement of the key points in the presentation and the leadership message. It is always important to remind the audience of what you have said; in so doing, you reinforce your message and its importance. A call to action is the action step of the presentation. It is asking the audience to do something in return. By asking for something, the leader is demonstrating a need for support as well as a confidence that that support will be received.

- Be specific. Give the audience a challenge and ask it to do something:
  - Implement a strategy or tactic, e.g., improve quality or develop a new product.
  - Perform an action, e.g., reduce absenteeism or have more fun in the workplace.
  - Demonstrate leadership, e.g., ask the audience members to be personal leaders to themselves and their people.

It is also appropriate to weave a story into the call to action. Storytelling is an ancient art, and stories are often used to develop an analogy between the present and a recent or past event. All of the world's major religions blend stories with calls to action. Why? Because the story makes the message memorable as well as relevant to the listener. The story itself may be personal—something the leader experienced—or refer to something contemporary or historical. At the conclusion of the story, be certain to include the action step; otherwise the story will lose its impact and the presentation will lack a leadership close. (For more on storytelling, see Chapter 12.]

REVISE YOUR DRAFT

No one said that this would be fun. Authors have their own adage: "Writing is rewriting."

Once you have crafted the presentation in a format that is comfortable for you, put it aside for a day or so. Then reread it and see how it sounds. Practice reading it out loud. When you do, you will find words and phrases that look good on paper but ring hollow when spoken. Adjust the phrasing. Remember, you are crafting a presentation that will be seen and heard, not read. Sound and images come first.

Review the Drafts with Colleagues

Share what you have crafted, either notes or speech, with your trusted colleagues.

Be prepared. Everyone has an opinion—once the words are on the page. For more than 40 years, the famous theatrical caricaturist Al Hirschfeld drew stylized drawings of leading actors and actresses that accompanied reviews of plays or musicals in the *New York Times*. In an interview, Hirschfeld said that not once during his lengthy career did an editor ever alter, or even suggest altering, a line. Yet, he said, he regularly witnessed the butchering of copy by everyone in the newsroom. Even the great Winston Churchill was not immune to the markings and slashings of the junior copy boys. So get used to it. People will make comments.[13]

Take all comments into consideration. But incorporate only those that have merit in light of your message, your audience, your intention, and your content. Throw everything else out. If you do not pay close heed to this rule, the finely sculptured horse that you have artfully created will slowly, but unmistakably, "morph" into an ugly, hump-backed camel. Ugh!

A word of caution: Disregard the previous paragraph if it's your boss who is making the suggestions. In that case, argue your point of view, but do not argue it to the point of no return. Unless you are writing the *Declaration of Independence* or the *Nuclear Test Ban Treaty*, do not jeopardize your promising career. Take what your boss says under advisement and try to find a way to make what he or she is suggesting work.

PLANNING AND PREPARING TO DELIVER THE MESSAGE

When you are developing the message, keep in mind *how* you will deliver it and *where* you will deliver it. The delivery of a formal presentation differs from that of an informal presentation. Location also has an influence on delivery.

- *Formal presentation.* You get on the stage in front of a podium. The audience sits in chairs and listens. You speak; they clap. You walk off the stage. Session over. That is a formal presentation. The location of a formal presentation can range from an auditorium that seats 2000 to a boardroom that seats 5. If you are standing and delivering a prepared message, the presentation is formal. When you present formally, you connote authority: "Listen to me. I know what I am talking about." Formal presentations are effective for presenting concepts, opinions, and information.
- *Informal presentation.* There is no podium. The audience may be standing or seated on whatever is available. You wander around the room as you speak. There is no single point of reference for the speaker. Sometimes you are in front of the audience members; other times you are behind them. What do you communicate when you shift your physical presence? That you are one of them. Yeah, you're just like the folks to whom you are presenting. Informal presentations may be as well rehearsed and well prepared as formal presentations, but the intent is different. You assume a consultative role. When you present informally, you connote collegiality: "Hey, I'm just like you." Informal presentations are effective for presenting a point of view or for enlisting support for an idea. They are ineffective for presenting abstract concepts.
- *Formal/informal presentation.* A leader who is in touch with how the audience is receiving the message will often alter the presentation format, sometimes on the fly. For example, you may start on the stage and end up in a chair. Or you may start on the floor and end up on a chair. Alternating between formal and informal messaging works best when you are trying to persuade, to win the group over to your point of view. You begin with an overview of the offering or idea, and then you home in on the benefits. As CEO of General Electric, Jack Welch varied his presentation style according to the situation. Like many corporate leaders, he would make prepared remarks and then open it up for a question-and-answer session where all pretense of formality was dropped. Welch was a big believer in humor and in what he calls "screwing around" at meetings, discussing things like the previous Saturday's golf tournament.[14]
- *Choice of venue.* Location is essential to the choice of presentation style. Will you be in an auditorium or in a cafeteria? Will you be speaking in a ballroom or on a factory floor? The location can make a difference. Auditoriums and ballrooms are typically used for formal

presentations; cafeterias and factory floors connote informality. Good presenters make the location work for them. Throughout his mayoral career, Rudy Giuliani made a point of showing up at scenes where he felt the community needed to see a leader. Of course, after September 11 we saw him every day at Ground Zero, as well as at funerals, memorials, and other public venues.

How and where you deliver your presentation may depend on your preference, or it may be set by the group to whom you are presenting. Knowing in advance how and where you will present is critical to ensuring that your message is understood and creates the right impetus for action.

Note: Part II contains much more material on delivering the message to audiences. For information on delivering the message to an individual, see Chapter 10, "Leadership Communications Coaching."

Communications Planner: Structuring the Stand-up Presentation

Organization is fundamental to an effective presentation. The presentation that rambles is the presentation that is forgotten not as soon as it is over, but while it is still going on. Try these techniques to get started:

1. Read. Read. Read. That's where you find ideas for your content.
2. Ask. Ask. Ask. Talk to people who represent your customers. What do they want to hear?
3. Find. Find. Find. Look for research material wherever you can find it. Trade magazines. The Internet. Corporate reports.
4. Brainstorm. Yes, you did this when you were coming up with the message. But guess what? It works for fleshing out content, too.
5. Write the draft by adding points to your outline. After a while, you will have the beginnings of a draft, but you will have created it by using an outline method.
6. Construct your arguments.
   - Claim: what you state
   - Reason: what you believe
   - Warrant: synthesis of statement and belief
7. As you write your draft, think in terms of analogies. Use the words in those analogies to color your content words. Here are some examples:

Topic	Analogy	Word Pictures
Growth	Gardening	Fertile, bloom, etc.
Change	Biology	Cell, embryo, organism, etc.
Conflict	Civil War	Division, skirmish, battle, war, etc.
Competition	Sports	Ball
Merger	Wedding	Bride, groom, ceremony, family, etc.
Celebration	Party	Milestones, champagne, cake, etc.

8. Review the methods of persuasion suggested by Robert Cialdini. Which of the six factors (reciprocation, commitment, social proof, liking, authority, or scarcity) is most applicable to your presentation? Develop a paragraph around one or more of the most relevant factors. Use it as part of your leadership message.
9. Develop your call to action in conjunction with organizational needs. Consider the following questions to help you craft your call to action:
   - What issues are facing the organization?
   - What problems are tearing at the organization?
   - What are the strengths of the organization?
   - What would the organization like to do to overcome its challenges?
10. Create links between sections. Examine the headings of your outline and think about how you can link one section to another. We call these points *transitions*. Transitions are essential to organizational unity and help to retain the attention of the audience. A transition can be as simple as Point 1, Point 2, . . . or Next, or it can be as creative as a story or anecdote.
11. When you ask colleagues to review your drafts, pass out candy or movie coupons. Folks will appreciate your gesture and are likely to go easy on your work.
12. Keep in mind that presentations are never finished, they are delivered. You may tweak your presentation until the moment you stand up and deliver it. If you keep an open mind, your presentation will remain fresh and alive every time you give it.

COLIN POWELL—THE CENTERED VISION

In the Washington stature game, few stand taller than Colin Powell. Washington respects power, and Powell has plenty of it. One reason is that his appeal is across party lines; as a black man in the party associated with the wealthy and powerful, Powell has few enemies on the left and even fewer on the right. Senator John McCain refers to Powell as "the most popular person in America."[15]

Powell parlays his power strategically. He is not afraid to speak his mind. As a military man who spent much of his career either as a political aide or as the highest-ranking general, he knows the value of deference, i.e., when to speak and when not to.

POWELL'S PERSUASIVENESS

As secretary of state in the George W. Bush administration, Powell shoulders America's foreign policy in time of war. Early in Bush's tenure, it seemed as though Powell was being shoved aside in favor of old hands like Vice President Dick Cheney and Secretary of Defense Donald Rumsfeld and newcomer Condoleezza Rice, the national security adviser. September 11 changed that power paradigm; suddenly Powell seemed to be in the right place at the right time for the right reasons. It fell to him to negotiate with President Pervez Musharraf of Pakistan for the right to use Pakistani air space. Only a statesman of Powell's stature, it seemed, could negotiate with this one-time ally, who was threatened by India on his border and squeezed by Islamic fundamentalists in his own military, and whose government recognized the Taliban government as legitimate. Powell prevailed, no doubt demonstrating the virtues of having the United States as a friend rather than an opponent. According to Richard C. Holbrooke, a U.N. envoy during the Clinton administration, "Powell and Musharraf have developed a relationship soldier to soldier, statesman to statesman, which is really important and has paid off by bringing Pakistan into the alliance against terrorism and preventing conflict with India."[16] Furthermore, Powell earned praise from President Bush: "He single-handedly got Musharraf on board. He was very good about that. He saw the notion of the need to put a coalition together."[17]

GLOBAL VIEW

As a soldier and a statesman, Powell strives to take the long view. He understands the ugliness of war, but at the same time he sees the need for taking a stand. Powell also looks at the post-September 11 world as a chance to redefine America's relationship with two former adversaries, arguing that terrorism was a common enemy. "Here was something that had nothing to do with any of the cold war models. . . . And it was something that everybody could join in against."[18] Powell is equally articulate in putting America's post-terror attack role into historical perspective. "Our record and our history is not of going out and looking for conflict, it is not one of undertaking pre-emptive acts for the purpose of seizing ... another people's territory, or to impose our will on someone else. Our history and our tradition is always one of defending our interests."[19]

As a result, after much soul-searching, Powell supported the administration's argument on pre-emption in the Iraq war as a means of national self-defense. Powell showed his mettle in pressing America's case before the U.N. in early 2003. All of Powell's skills as a communicator, anchored in his experience as an officer and statesman, came to the fore. Armed with a presentation packed with visual support, Powell was like a prosecutor as he tore apart Iraq's claims that it did not harbor weapons of mass destruction, like a statesman as he rose above the fray to present the international case, and like a soldier as he stated that the United States was ready to fight. For a man once derided by hardliners as the "Administration's dove," it was a presentation that came down forcefully against an outlaw government and on the side of international security. A tough act, but vintage Powell.

Powell's strength radiates from within. He not only speaks in complete sentences but expresses well-founded and well-grounded thoughts. Unlike some speakers, his speaking ability does not come merely from the use of rhetoric or clever language; it comes from deep within him. It is almost as if his words come from his soul. And his articulateness enables him to project the inner strength that emanates from deeply held convictions and his bedrock faith in his own abilities.

HIS ROOTS

The son of immigrants from Jamaica, Powell grew up in the Bronx, where he mixed freely with different races. He acknowledges in his autobiography that he was an indifferent student and that it was not until he joined the Army Reserve Officers Training Corps (ROTC) that he gained his focus—and his bearings.[20] He became a commissioned officer in 1958 and served two tours in Vietnam, being wounded twice and earning a Bronze Star. He experienced racism firsthand while serving in posts in the South. "I've been thrown out of places because I was just black enough not to be served. . . . I consider myself an African-American and proud to stand on the shoulders of those who went before me."[21]

Powell understands the symbolism of race in his role as secretary of state: "And it's always a source of inspiration and joy to see [foreign leaders] look at me and through me see my country, and see what promise my country offers to all people who come to these shores looking for a better life."[22]

MAXIMIZING EFFICIENCY

There is an efficiency to Powell's communications that stems from his military background. For example, he has a formula for making decisions; after gathering as much information as possible, much of it by making calls and asking questions himself, he assigns a numeric value to the intelligence he has gathered. Rarely do commanders have the luxury of 100 percent conviction; but when Powell gets to somewhere between P = 40 and P = 70, he applies his gut instinct.[23]

He also has developed what he calls "Powell's Rules for Picking People." Among the characteristics he values are loyalty, integrity, passion, energy, and—perhaps most of all—"the drive to get things done."[24] Those characteristics all apply to Powell himself, especially the ability to make things happen. And that is precisely what he brings to his position as secretary of state.

"TOWER OF STRENGTH"

When President-elect Bush introduced Powell as his secretary of state, he made reference to another former Army man: "I would say of General Powell what Harry Truman said of General Marshall: 'He is a tower of strength and common sense.'"[25] Marshall was chief of staff of the army during the Second World War and later served as Truman's secretary of state, where he was the architect of the European Recovery Act (later called the Marshall Plan), which helped rebuild Europe's social and industrial infrastructure. And there is something of Marshall in Powell, apart from their military pedigree. Both generals made the transition to statecraft by understanding both the advantages of power and its limitations.

And it is with regard to its limitations that Powell is sometimes criticized. "Caution is not a vice. I think it's a virtue. I know when to act. And if caution is such a terrible vice, then I'm sure various people I have worked for over the years probably would not have hired me."[26] One subject about which Powell is cautious is the use of troops. When he was chairman of the Joint Chiefs of Staff, he irked the Clinton administration with his sense of hesitancy about committing troops. That reluctance is born of his experience in Vietnam. Like many of his generation who served there, he knows war firsthand and he knows what happens when soldiers are thrown into battle without clearly defined goals.

As a lifelong army man, Powell knows from whence his soldiers come. He speaks of "Kmart parents"—those people of modest means who are the mothers and fathers of men and women in the armed forces. He insists that parents need to know why their sons and daughters are going to war, and that the reasons must be compelling.[27] In contrast to the situation in Vietnam, the goals of Operation Desert Storm were well defined, and the military, led by

Powell and a very capable cadre of senior officers, excelled, expelling Iraqi forces from Kuwait swiftly, efficiently, and with a minimum of casualties.

DISCIPLINE FIRST

Powell found himself an outsider after President Bush called for a regime change in Iraq through military means because of the suspicion that Saddam Hussein possessed weapons of mass destruction. Powell found himself at odds with Vice President Cheney and to a very large degree with Secretary of Defense Rumsfeld. Their differences arose from their approach toward Iraq; all parties agreed that Saddam was a tyrant who deserved to be deposed. Powell favored international action leading to his removal, a policy that involved allies as the Gulf War of 1990–1991 had. Cheney was a unilateralist, favoring the United States going it alone. Powell felt that an armed move would be preemptive and would risk disrupting America's fragile alliances in the Middle East, not to mention further upsetting the radical fundamentalist Muslims who dominated public opinion in the streets. As a result, Powell was the odd man out. Condoleezza Rice served as the liaison between him and the president. Nonetheless, Powell's decision to refrain from public comment on Iraq made his opposition to unilateral war obvious. To his credit, Powell worked behind the scenes to get President Bush to bring the Iraqi weapons issue to the United Nations. He was successful, and Bush eventually went to the U.N. and made a stirring address, one that by the way went through more than 20 drafts, the final ones bearing the ideas of Powell himself.[28]

In addition to the disagreement over the Iraq question, Powell has had his share of run-ins with the Bush administration; his decisions have been questioned, and he is not a favorite of the Republican conservatives, a bedrock support group for President Bush. Powell is not bothered: "Fights come and fights go."[29] And he is not above levity in such matters. In a lighthearted exchange with office secretaries over an empty jar of pretzels, Powell said, "Okay, that's enough. I've got to get back to work now—and by the way, I'm not resigning." His staff cracked up.[30]

NO TO HIGHER OFFICE

His son, Michael Powell, chairman of the Federal Communications Commission, appreciates his father's even-handedness. "[W]hen there was contemplation he'd run for President, the biggest speculation was, As what? I mean, what greater accolade to a soldier than you don't even know his politics."[31]

Powell acknowledged that his wife, Alma, was "unalterably opposed" to his running for the presidency, but he was comfortable with his own decision not to run.[32] Richard Armitage, a political insider and Powell intimate, quotes him as saying, "'On the mornings when I woke up and thought I'm going to run, I felt terrible, it was a terrible day. On mornings I got up and said, I'm not going to, I had a wonderful day.'" Powell, according to Armitage, believed that those who wanted him to run were looking for a "shortcut" to get "someone on a white horse." To his credit, Powell said, "That's not the way our system works."[33]

At his press conference in November 1995 announcing that he would not be a candidate, Powell summed up his place in history as well as his strong sense of self; he included the remarks in the afterword to his autobiography, *My American Journey*.

> Finally, let me say how honored I am that so many of you thought me worthy of your support. It says more about America than it says about me. In one generation, we have moved from denying a black man service at a lunch counter to elevating one to the highest military office in the nation and to being a serious contender for the presidency. This is a magnificent country, and I am proud to be one of its sons.[34]

Leadership Communications Lessons

Be firm in your conviction. Know yourself and what you really want to do. Powell demonstrates this in his willingness to forgo the presidency.

Demonstrate serenity. Powell exerts a sense of temperance, but when necessary he will elevate the emotion of the moment.

Be decisive. When the decision is made, act forthrightly. Powell's actions in Desert Storm demonstrate his ability to get results.

Be seen as the leader. Powell is a frequent speaker and mixes well with people from all ranks and stations in life. He stands out for his eloquence as well as his convictions.

Live your message. Powell's ability to inspire comes not simply from his words but from his lifelong example: soldier, author, and statesman.

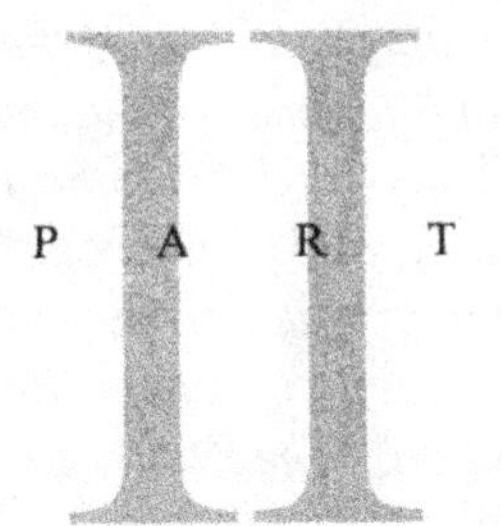

PART II

Delivering the Leadership Message

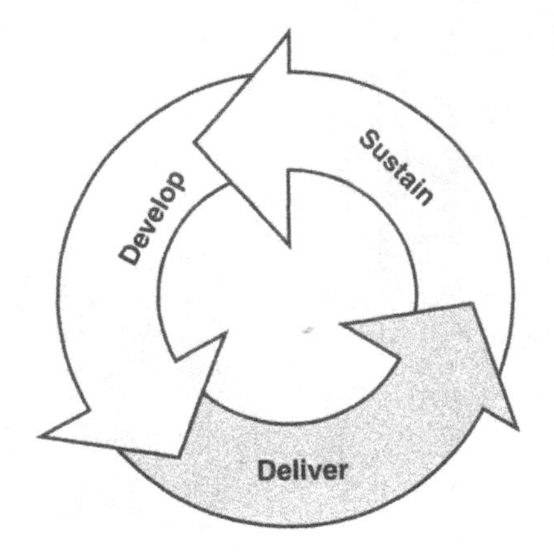

Once the message has been developed, it is up to the leader to disseminate it through words and actions. The ultimate test of the leadership points is the ability to deliver the leadership message with frequency, constancy, and conviction.

The chapters in Part II will help you amplify your message from concept to delivery and follow-through, chiefly by connecting with an individual or group through oral communications. The ability to stand and deliver either one-on-one or one-to-one thousand is the ultimate test of a leadership communicator. When communications is done correctly, people will be inspired to follow, and in the process will achieve inspired results for themselves, for the leader, and for the organization.

CHAPTER 7

To me, a ballpark filled with people is a beautiful thing. It's an epitome, a work of art. I guess I have seen everything in the country: Yosemite, Old Faithful, the Grand Canyon, and the most beautiful thing is a ballpark filled with people. Ballparks should be happy places.

Bill Veeck

ASSESSING YOUR AUDIENCE

THE EXECUTIVE HAD WORKED VERY HARD ON HIS PRESENTATION. He had been invited to be a guest speaker and receive an award for his services to the industry. It was a prestigious event.

So, as befit the occasion, the executive had collected his information; he had even hired a speechwriter to script the speech and a graphic services company to produce the visuals. He arrived early in the day to assess the room and even rehearsed on site. At the appointed hour, the executive was introduced, and he proudly took the podium. Looking out over the audience, he took a deep breath, smiled, and began his presentation. He was careful to note how proud he was to receive the award.

Everything proceeded well—for about 30 seconds. Then the audience began to grow restless, and after another minute or so it began a series of catcalls: "Come on. Hurry up. We're getting thirr—sty!" After another minute, individuals in the audience began to throw things. Bound and determined to be heard, the executive, like a St. Bernard in a snowstorm, plowed ahead. As the crowd grew more restless, he began to speak louder. When things hit the stage, he grew louder still, until after 3 minutes or so, he was shouting into the microphone.

Chaos ruled.

What went wrong? How could something that started so wonderfully and was prepared and rehearsed so carefully go so terribly wrong?

Simple. The executive had failed to assess his audience.

Not until later, when the speech was over and he had retreated to the safety of an anteroom, did the executive learn that he had been the only thing standing between the audience and the bar. It was the end of a long day, and the crowd of salespeople and industry representatives was in no mood for more talk. They wanted to "drown the day" with libations.

DEALING WITH HOSTILITY

What can you do when you face a hostile audience? One answer is to retreat and live to speak another day. But there is another approach.

After the American Revolution, George Washington returned to his beloved Mount Vernon to farm. Despite the Americans' victory over the British, nationhood was still a thing of the future. The Thirteen Colonies had devolved into thirteen independent states, all bickering with one another. As a result of this disunity, the soldiers of the Continental Army had not received money for their years of service. At one point, a group of disgruntled officers gathered in Newburgh, New York, to plot a coup against the government in an attempt to seek restitution. Washington learned of the meeting and asked to speak to the officers.

When he entered the meeting room, he strode to the podium and looked out over the group. He knew most if not all of them, and he reminded them of the hardships they had shared during the long years of the Revolutionary War. He then drew out a letter from a member of the Continental Congress. He attempted to read it, then stopped and apologized. He said that not only had he turned gray while fighting for his country, he had gone nearly blind as well. He then reached to put on his spectacles.[1]

That gesture broke the ice. Washington again won the hearts and minds of his former soldiers. The coup was forgotten. Washington had defused a volatile situation by reminding the audience of their shared past and their shared values.[2] No speaker can do more. It was an act of courage; moreover, it was an act of leadership.

Washington had assessed his audience accurately, unlike our poor executive. To be fair, Washington had a previous relationship with his audience to draw upon, whereas our executive was a stranger to his. Washington had something upon which to build; our executive had nothing. Washington was right to persevere, whereas our executive should have departed quickly rather than try to talk over the disruption.

TV talk show host Oprah Winfrey is a modern master at assessing audience wants and needs. As an experienced presenter, she has a sixth sense for what the audience wants to hear. Her entire show is based upon meeting audience expectations for information, emotion, entertainment, and sometimes insight.

Just as presenters have expectations for their presentations, audiences have expectations of presenters. And there are things you can do to determine those expectations and prepare for them.

FIND OUT WHAT THE AUDIENCE WANTS

The simplest way to find out what the audience wants is to ask in advance. If you are invited to present, take time to find out what the audience is expecting from you. Ask the individual who invited you. For example, if you are making a sales presentation, ask what kinds of features and benefits are most likely to be appealing to your audience. Does it want quality, efficiency, cost, or all of these?

If you are speaking to an internal group, find out what its issues are and find a way to weave those issues into your presentation. When you touch the concerns of the audience, you demonstrate that you understand its needs. Another means of determining audience expectations is to talk to people who will be in the audience. Find out what is on their mind. Think of ways to relate to their concerns without compromising your message.

MEET AUDIENCE EXPECTATIONS

Every presenter has an obligation to meet the audience's expectations. In this regard, you are like a singer or a musician who is hired to perform. The audience may not be paying you in currency, but it is paying you with something more valuable—its time.

On the simplest level, audiences expect a presenter to show up on time and finish on time. Most speakers have no problem with the first part; it is the second part that can be troublesome. If you are asked to speak for 15 or 20 minutes, aim for 18 minutes. The audience will love you for it. I have yet to hear an audience complain that a speech was too short, but I have heard plenty of complaints about presentations that seemed to go on forever.

Keep in mind that you are speaking at the pleasure of the audience, not your pleasure. People can get up and leave at any time. Most of them will not do so, but they always have that option. Bill Veeck used public speaking as a tool to drum up interest in his ballclubs; he would speak anywhere anytime if he thought it would help sell tickets. But Veeck didn't just show up; as a natural raconteur, he provided entertainment in the form of great stories, often at his own expense.

Audiences expect presenters to be prepared. If you are a salesperson, know your product or service better than you know the floor plan of your house. Likewise, if you are a guest speaker, be current on your topic. Know of what you speak. Keep in mind how prepared Colin Powell is when he gives a briefing; he knows the facts cold. The same is true of Rudy Giuliani. They are leaders who know the issues and can speak to them.

Audiences expect presenters to talk to them, not at them. If you are delivering a call to action, invite the audience members in. Don't order them to act. If you are preaching a message, speak as a member of the congregation, a sinner like all the rest of us, not as some anointed prophet. To paraphrase an old saying, "You will attract more followers with an acknowledgement of personal weakness than with an attitude of self-righteousness." One of the most saintly humans of modern times, Mother Teresa, never spoke of what she was doing for others; instead, she always invited people to share in the work that needed to be done for others.

And finally, audiences expect messages that are in tune with their wants and needs. Salespeople need to meet this expectation exactly. Others, however, can deviate somewhat. Often the presenter must deliver a tough message about hard issues, e.g., a corrective measure, a quest for improvement, or the big one—the need for change. Messages like this make us feel uncomfortable, so it is up to the presenter to find a way to make the message amenable without changing its content. A sure way to do this is to appeal, as Washington did, to a shared past and an attitude that "we are all in this together."

It is necessary to point out the difference between relating to the issues and pandering to the issues. Relating implies empathy; pandering implies playing to. For example, when Lyndon Johnson spoke about his plans for the Great Society, he touched upon his experiences as a poor boy growing up in Texas. He said he understood what it meant to have very little and how important government assistance was to those who had nothing. His themes related to the themes of those he was trying to persuade. By contrast, Joseph McCarthy stirred Americans' fears of communism by playing to their baser instincts of hatred and exclusionism. He lowered the level of debate rather than elevating it.

When you relate to an audience, you do not need to tell it what it wants to hear. You strive for the truth, but you present it in a way that is credible and understandable. At the same time, you need to avoid preaching or talking down to the audience. Both can be equally irritating to an audience.

OVERCOME OBJECTIONS WITHIN THE PRESENTATION

Facing a tough audience is not easy. But let's face it, sometimes it must be done. Management must talk to unions. Politicians must face voters. School boards must face parents. And so on. Not everyone wants to hear everything that you as a presenter have to say. Anticipating objections is part of the presentation process. If you follow the Toulmin argument process, you can formulate your rebuttals using the claim-reason-warrant methodology (see Chapter 6). With that in mind, here are some tips you can use to prepare yourself for those tough situations (see Figure 7-1).

- *Determine the objection*. Isolate the "hot potatoes." Before you stand in front of the audience, find out possible issues or concerns the audience may have with you or the organization you represent. Vince Lombardi was a hard-nosed coach. He knew that players would initially resist the kind of discipline and hard work he would impose, but this did not stop him from getting his message across. He would deflect objections through implication: If the individual players did not adhere to the regimen, they would be gone. If you are a salesperson, you need to know the account history before you try to sell. For example, if the salesperson before you was a jerk, your audience may harbor negative views about you. You need to know this before you walk into the room. Likewise, if you are an executive addressing a group of frontline employees, you need to know their concerns about their work, the management team, and possibly yourself.
- *Acknowledge the issue*. Say the issue out loud. If it is poor product quality or a tough question regarding management, spell it out—e.g., "I know you have an issue about this." As a former prosecutor, Giuliani was accustomed to dealing with objections. As mayor, he would freely give voice to the opposition as a means of acknowledging dissent. In doing so, Giuliani demonstrated that he was informed on and involved with the issues, even if he did not change his mind.

- *Empathize.* When issues on are the table, communicate your concern. This does not mean that you say whatever the audience may want to hear, it means that you demonstrate concern—e.g., "I understand the issues you are facing." With guests on her show, Oprah oozes sympathy in a way that gets the guest to open up and share a personal moment that will enable the audience to understand an issue more vividly and sometimes viscerally.
- *Remind the audience of shared experiences.* If you or your organization has a prior relationship with the audience, mention it. If it is a good relationship, say so. If it is one that soured, say so. The audience expects you to be honest. At Newburgh, Washington established the shared experiences at the outset. Katherine Graham made the *Washington Post* her life; her communications emerged from that commitment. Everyone who was part of the company understood that she stood for journalistic excellence and that by embracing that premise they could share in the enterprise.
- *Deliver the message.* Once you have laid the groundwork for your presentation through acknowledgement and empathy, you are ready to move into your message and deliver your content. You are free, however, to emphasize or deemphasize according to audience expectations; in this way, you remain responsive to audience needs. Actor-director Robert Redford is accustomed to fighting battles over causes he believes in. His public speeches, together with his professional commitments, give him a platform upon which to stand tall on an issue, even when he knows that people can and will disagree with him.
- *Open the door for compromise.* If the issue you must defuse is potentially divisive, you may wish to create a forum for compromise. Your presentation then becomes the first step in the healing process. You are entitled to present your views, but if you expect to create an action step—e.g., a sale or a dialogue—you need to open the door for action, that is, what's next? As a manager of 25 highly talented baseball players, Joe Torre lives by the art of compromise. He uses his communications to smooth over disagreements and open the door for cooperation. If you get beyond the objection, you can talk about how you would like to be part of the solution. You would like to help bury the hatchet and work out the issues together.

The good news is that when you can overcome objections within your presentation, very often you will win the audience over to your side and it will be receptive to your message now and in the future.

FIGURE 7-1 Overcoming Objections within the Presentation

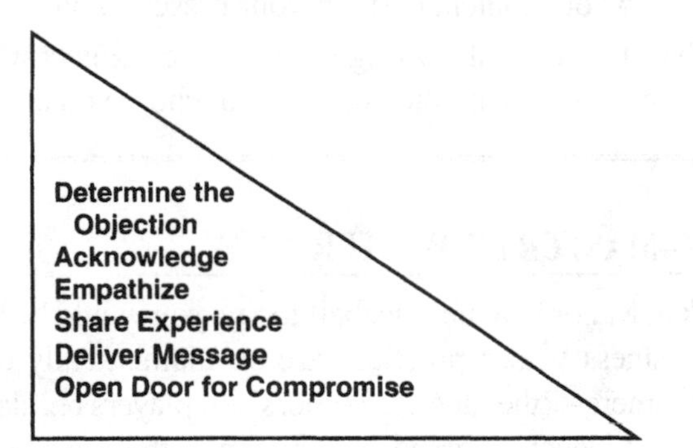

CREATE A RELATIONSHIP

If you get beyond the objection, you generate an opportunity for a relationship. The relationship may last only as long as the presentation, or it may last far longer. Relationships emerge from a community of understanding and a sense of trust. To use a gardening analogy, relationships do not bloom overnight, but they can emerge over time if the ground is made fertile and adequately watered. Oprah has taken the relationship with an audience to an all-time level; over the decades she has been on the air, she has forged a bond with her audience, which has come to understand her as someone who reflects its issues and seeks to make the world better for it.

Both the success of your leadership presentation and your personal credibility depend upon assessing audience expectations. You can establish a relationship only if you demonstrate that you understand and acknowledge audience issues.

Communications Planner: Structuring the Presentation

Audiences have expectations. It is up to the presenter to determine those expectations prior to the presentation or upon its delivery. Understanding audience expectations can make the difference between a forgettable nonevent and a memorable event.

1. Identify a key information resource.
2. Create a five-question survey. Mail it to key informants. Collate the data.
3. Ask what is on people's minds— e.g., "What issues related to what I will say should I be aware of?"

4. Make a list of relevant issues. Find ways to link those concerns to your content early in your presentation.
5. What story or analogy might you use to connect what you do and the issue facing the audience to whom you are speaking?

BILL VEECK—MASTER PROMOTER

When you look at Major League Baseball today, you would be hard pressed to find another business whose practices are so diametrically opposed to the needs of its customers—the fans. As owners and players regularly accuse one another of escalating levels of greed, it is the fan—the one who pays the escalating ticket prices—who gets left out in the rain like the family dog as the two sides bicker among themselves. In moments of despair for the National Pastime, it is useful, and hopeful, to recall that while owners and players have always been adversaries, there was one man in the game who marched to a different drummer—his own! He was Bill Veeck, and the cadence he marched to, wooden leg and all, was the same as the fans'. He loved the game as much as they did because first and foremost he was a fan himself. He was also passionate, opinionated, fun-loving, and dedicated to the value proposition "If you don't think a promotion is fun, don't do it!"[3]

And for an owner and baseball executive who had teams that finished first as well as last, no one ever had more fun than Bill Veeck. He was one part P. T. Barnum and one part Sam Walton— a combination of showmanship and customer value. Along the way, he irritated the plutocrats running the game and delighted the crowds who filled the stadiums. In his own unique way, Veeck was a leadership communicator who lived and breathed a message of honesty, integrity, and entertainment.

BORN INTO THE GAME

In a game going back nearly a century and a half as a professional enterprise and noted for its characters, Bill Veeck was unique. When he was 3 years old, his father became general manager of the Chicago Cubs. Veeck grew up in the game; in fact, he planted the ivy that adorns the brick walls of Wrigley Field. Later, as a junior executive in the organization, he ordered a new scoreboard, and when it wasn't finished on time, he hired a crew—and rolled up his sleeves—and assembled it in time for opening day. True to his character, Veeck paid the inventor in full even though he had not completed the scoreboard on time. But Veeck also was a businessman. When the inventor wanted to bid on the exploding scoreboard for the Chicago White Sox many years later, Veeck said no.[4]

THE STUNT

The stunt that transcended baseball and won Veeck a place in American mythology is the one involving Eddie Gaedel. As Veeck tells us in his autobiography, in 1951 he was the owner of the St. Louis Browns, "a collection of old rags and tags . . . rank[ing] in the annals of baseball a step or two ahead of Cro-Magnon Man." Looking for ways to get fans to the park, Veeck hit on the idea of hiring a midget to pinch-hit. He signed Gaedel to a contract and assigned him the number 1/8. Eddie walked on four pitches and into the history books, taking Veeck along with him. "I have always found humor in the incongruous, I have always tried to entertain. And I have always found a stuffed shirt the most irresistible of all targets."[5]

Veeck was not one to exploit the misfortunes of others. As one writer put it in the introduction to the re-release of Veeck's autobiography, *Veeck—As in Wreck*, now back in print 40 years after its first printing in 1962, "Physically, of course, Bill was not all there. His body was a mosaic of broken parts on borrowed time."[6] He wore a prosthetic leg, the legacy of a war wound suffered as a Marine in the South Pacific in World War II. The leg, along with his "impish smile," became his trademark.

EXCELLENT COMMUNICATOR

Veeck knew his fans not simply because he was one, but because he spent time with them. Stories of him sitting in the stands with the paying public at Wrigley Field or Comiskey Park are legion. He was accessible. Another way he stayed in touch was by speaking frequently to groups in his market area.

Bill Veeck would never win an award for his presentation skills; however, his speech teacher in college said that despite breaking all the rules for giving a good speech, Veeck was effective.[7] Pat Williams, a sports executive and speaker in his own right for whom Veeck was something of a mentor, attributes Veeck's speaking success to his storytelling and his humor. His standard opening line was, "I used to own the St. Louis Browns, and I'm not used to seeing so many people gathered together like this."[8] Famous for not wearing a tie, he once addressed a formal dinner where the men were dressed in tuxedoes: "First time I ever saw 1500 waiters for one customer."[9]

Veeck was also a "really good writer," says his coauthor, Ed Linn, who edited Veeck's copy. Aside from Veeck's autobiography, the two of them wrote *Hustler's Handbook,* which is considered the "virtual bible on sports promotion."[10] A compendium of tricks and insights for bringing fans to the ballpark, it is also a good read, chock full of good stories. Later Veeck became a columnist for the *Chicago Tribune* and *USA Today*. As Pat Williams says, "The reason [Veeck] wrote so prolifically and so well was because he had so much to say. Just to listen to the words pour forth from the page was an engrossing journey into the complexities of his mind."[11] An indifferent student, Veeck was an autodidact who loved to read; in the process, his span of knowledge became encyclopedic and he was able to converse learnedly on literature, history, tax law, and even gardening.[12]

PROMOTION AS A CORE VALUE

Promoting the product was what Bill Veeck was noted for, and his ideas for promotions were as broad and diverse as his reading habits. Veeck was the first to give away free bats, and his reach in promotion knew few limits: free balls, free pickles, free hot dogs, free lobsters, free ice cream, and then . . . free tuxedo rentals, along with pigs, chickens, mice, eels, pigeons, ducks, and, yes, 50,000 nuts and bolts.[13]

And this is only the free stuff. Veeck did more than freebies; he was the impresario of event packaging— Squirrel Night; a bicentennial-themed opening day in 1976; Music Night with free kazoos; special games for A students, teachers, bartenders, cabbies, and transit workers; and even Disco Demolition Night. (Well, even Veeck might go too far once in a while.)[14]

Veeck's promotions revolved around a desire to tickle the imagination. "You give away a radio or a TV— so what? What does that do for the imagination? Nothing. . . . If I give him 50,000 nuts or bolts, that gives everybody something to talk about."[15] And Veeck knew that when people are talking about your product, they will be more inclined to pay money to come out and see it. Veeck's promotions sprang from his values; he was a "giver."[16] He wanted to entertain his customers, and he wanted them to have something extra in return for their patronage. Veeck's final bit of advice on promotion was, "No one has a monopoly on ideas. You can always think of something."[17]

GRAND STAGE

Upon the death of Bill Veeck in 1986, Tom Boswell, baseball writer and thinker for the *Washington Post*, wrote: "Cause of death: Life."[18] Not a bad epitaph for a man who loved and lived life to the fullest and brought us along for the ride.

Leadership Communications Lessons

Listen to the fans. Ask your stakeholders what they need, want, and aspire to. Bill Veeck did this and made a business out of it.

Know the score. Veeck realized that the media could make or break his business; he played the game with them and made certain that they had good stories to write and good times to write about.

Be seen and be accessible. Spend time with your people. Veeck watched games from the bleachers with the fans, the people who paid his bills and those of his enterprise.

Give back something. Leaders need to show their appreciation for their stakeholders. Veeck gave the fans something of himself—a sense of surprise, showmanship, and fun.

Have fun. Life can be deadly serious, but that doesn't mean we should be. Veeck knew how to have a good time and invited everyone along for the ride.

Live your message. Bill Veeck lived life to the fullest. His business philosophy flowed from his core values; he adhered to them faithfully and in the process delighted, excited, and entertained generations of loyal baseball fans.

CHAPTER 8

> Real communication is an attitude, an environment. It's the most interactive of all processes. It requires countless hours of eyeball-to-eyeball back and forth. It involves more listening than talking. It is a constant, interactive process aimed at [creating] consensus.
>
> *Jack Welch*

DELIVERING THE MESSAGE

SHE WAS NOT BEAUTIFUL. She was overweight. She was confined to a wheelchair. And she was one of the most dynamic speakers of her age.

Despite her cosmetic challenges, Barbara Jordan had the voice. You only had to hear it once to never forget its powerful resonance. Her diction was always precise, clear, instructional, and at times reverential. She spoke with the conviction of a preacher, but the insight of a scholar. Born to a poor black sharecropper, she earned a law degree from the University of Texas and became a law professor there. She represented her Texas district in Congress in the 1970s and served for a number of terms until her health forced her to retire.

The important thing to remember about Barbara Jordan is that she was a speaker's speaker. Where others are professional, she was artful. Where others are sincere, she was passionate. Where others are intellectual, she was a scholar. Where others are sensitive, she was human. And it is important to remember that while at first glance she might appear to be something other than what she was, the moment she spoke was the moment the audience listened.

Her eloquence was particularly piercing during Watergate. She sat on the Impeachment Committee that weighed the evidence against President Nixon. In those dark days of government, her words and her voice served as reminders that one of the strengths of our country is its adherence to law and the pursuit of justice.

When Congresswoman Jordan spoke, she created moments of truth. These result when a speaker's message and content meet the expectations of the audience live and on stage for all to see. How can you prepare for such moments of truth? Well, as the old man said when asked the way to Carnegie Hall, "Practice, practice, practice!"

THE AUTHENTIC PRESENTER

Establishing credibility is fundamental to leadership. As we have discussed, leaders affirm their believability through the content of their leadership messages. Vocalization of the message also plays a role; in other words, the way you look and sound as you present is critical to your credibility (see Figure 8-1). Emerging leaders often ask their speech coaches or trusted advisers how they should present. The answer most often given is, "Be yourself!" This is the correct answer, but it doesn't tell the whole story. The leader must be him- or herself on stage or in a coaching session, but he or she may also need to do more. Here are some suggestions:

- *Reflect the mood of the moment.* Know the situation. Is the organization upbeat and optimistic, or is it fearful and dreading tomorrow? Take your cue from the mood and adjust your presentation style accordingly. For upbeat audiences, a lighter approach is acceptable; for uptight audiences, being direct and to the point may be more appropriate. Humor, however, can be a terrific way to lighten the mood and break the ice.

FIGURE 8-1 The Power of Authenticity

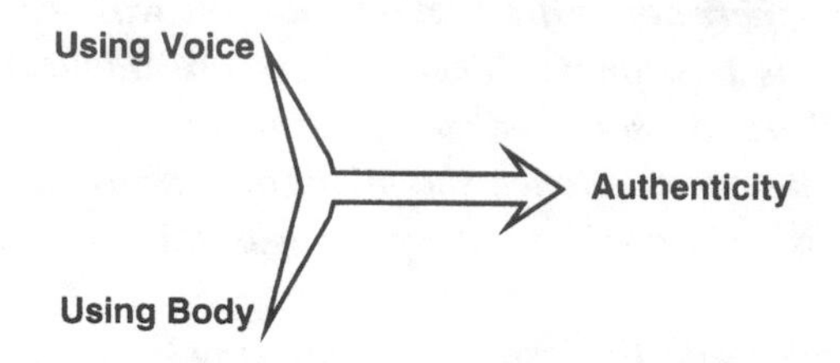

- *Emulate, don't copy.* Be the speaker you are. Do not try to replicate some orator from the past. Use your own words. It is okay to quote, but do not try to copy the manner and gestures of someone else. You will only do yourself a disservice and raise questions about your believability.
- *Act the part.* Speaking out loud, as discussed earlier, is acting. It is the art and practice of giving voice to your thoughts and words as a reflection of your leadership style. Sometimes women feel that they must raise their voices if they are to be heard, but instead of just being louder, they may come across as shouting. This situation plays into the stereotype of male speakers being more authoritative than female speakers. The truth is that men and women are equally believable or equally disingenuous as speakers, depending upon their ability to communicate the authenticity of their messages. Using a microphone will enable the speaker, male or female, to speak in a voice that captures his or her natural cadences and voice colorations. And don't hide behind the podium; use a wireless microphone so that you can stride across the stage or walk among the audience as you speak.
- *Take the message, not yourself, seriously.* Audiences love it when the speaker shares something of her- or himself. Self-deprecation, or making a joke at your own expense, is a great way to connect. You can be serious about the message without being strident and overly intense in your presentation style.

Effective leadership communicators need not be polished orators. Winston Churchill was an accomplished master of the art form, but Katherine Graham had to force herself to become a public speaker. Both, however, radiated conviction in their communications.

THE AUTHENTIC COACH

Not only is authenticity essential in the public forum, but it is equally important in private. Being themselves in a one-on-one coaching situation may be easier for some leaders than presenting to an audience because the intimacy of the moment is closer to the way we communicate in our daily lives. Some of us are more comfortable than others in interpersonal discussions. If the leader is naturally shy in such situations, he or she must find ways to overcome this. Leaders owe it to their people to be honest and direct, especially when delivering constructive criticism. (For more on coaching, see Chapter 10.)

USING YOUR VOICE

Your most valuable asset as a speaker is your voice. Effective speakers vary the pitch and inflection of their voice for emphasis. Think about all the monotone lectures you had in college. Remember how boring they were? One reason was that the professor never varied his or her tone of voice. Big points melded with small points into some kind of tasteless stew of ideas that never boiled, never simmered, just remained lukewarm. And was forgettable.

But with practice, you can move to the head of your class by putting some zip and zest into your voice. Here's how.

- *Give voice to your voice.* Practice using rising and falling inflections for meaning as well as for questions. Inflection is a form of audio punctuation. Use it!
- *Hear your message.* Record yourself speaking. After you get over the hurdle of what your voice actually sounds like (trust me, everyone hates the sound of his or her own voice), listen to what you are saying. Ask yourself:
  - How am I using inflection?
  - Do I sound credible?
  - Would I buy from this guy?

This final question applies to everyone, not just salespeople. As presenters, all of us are pitching something, so we need to ask whether the audience is buying it, i.e., is receptive to the message. When speaking about Sundance or his commitment to the environment, Robert Redford employs his actor's ability to reflect his conviction through his voice. You recognize his sincerity in an instant.

USING YOUR BODY

Much discussion has been devoted to shaping your content and delivery. Most of what we have explored thus far involves the mental processes of thinking and writing. However, the physical process is also important. Unless you plan to deliver the presentation as a disembodied voice from behind a curtain à la *The Wizard of Oz*, you need to put some physicality into your speaking. Steve Jobs is an accomplished public speaker. Strolling or even prowling the stage, alone or with a strategic prop (a new Apple product), he projects a sense of confidence and knowledge. His physicality underscores the power of his message because it says subconsciously, "I know what I am talking about and I am in control."

- *Visualize a speaking style.* How do you see yourself delivering the presentation? From behind the podium, walking the stage, or moving into the audience? Ideally, polished presenters do some roaming. But until you are totally comfortable, it is better to use a podium where you can mount your speech or notes. Teleprompters, where words are projected on television monitors out of the audience's sight line, free the speaker to wander the stage without having to refer to notes.
- *Get involved physically.* At a minimum, you must do a few simple physical things:
  - Make eye contact with the audience.
  - Periodically shift your gaze from one side of the room to the other and from back to front. Actually, the process is remarkably similar to the one you use when you drive as you shift your gaze from the road in front of you to the rearview mirror and sideview mirrors.
  - Look up from the podium. Keep your nose out of your notes.
  - Do not read the words in your visuals (if you have them). Instead, interpret what it is you have to say. (An exception is cartoons. They are little stories, so it is acceptable to read them.)
- *Use gestures for emphasis.* Use a hand motion or wave an arm. When you are more accomplished as a presenter, get out from behind the podium. Move about the stage or speaking area.
  - Get your shoulders in motion.
  - Stand still momentarily, then stride to one side of the room.
  - Make grand gestures occasionally.
  - Engage the audience with an occasional question, e.g., "Wouldn't you agree?" or "Am I clear?"

If all of this sounds theatrical, that's because it is. If you do not feel comfortable doing it, then do not force it. Too much animation is wearing not only on you, but also on an audience. But gradually, over time, you can get physical to a degree that is comfortable for both you and your audience.

- *See your message.* Videotape yourself. Again, you won't like yourself on the screen at first. But when you get over that, ask yourself the following questions:
    - Am I gesturing appropriately?
    - Do I look credible?
    - Would I buy something (a message or a product) from this guy?

The success of a presentation depends upon its delivery. Talk show host Oprah Winfrey radiates empathy and understanding. Rosabeth Moss Kanter, a professor, radiates energy and the enthusiasm of having something important to say. When the words match the voice and body, magic can occur. It is a matter of practice and commitment to giving the audience something it can remember.

REHEARSAL: PUTTING CONTENT TOGETHER WITH VOICE AND BODY

No one likes to rehearse. Frankly, it is a pain. And with all the work you have put into the presentation, you know the material, so there's no need to worry. Right?

Wrong!

Rehearsal is important to the success of the presentation. Delivery is where the content meets the audience. Essentially, you are taking a two-dimensional presentation of words and pictures and moving it into three dimensions by the addition of yourself. You are adding life to the presentation. In this instance, you are the actor. And, to be blunt about it, actors rehearse.

Before you rehearse, take a good look at the room, starting from the rear. If you stand at the back, you can judge for yourself how large or small you will appear. Keep that in mind. If you plan to reveal something small, make certain that everyone can see it, or else don't show it.

Then go to the stage and take a moment to get familiar with it. Where will you enter? Where will you exit? If you have visuals, where will they be? Then go to the podium; how does it feel? Adjust the microphone to your height. That way you can walk right up and speak. (If you have to adjust it in real time, do it. Don't try to talk without one.)

If time permits, run through your entire presentation, complete with visuals. Practice as much as you can. After your rehearsal, thank the stage crew, if there is one. Your friendly demeanor can do a lot to improve the mood of the crew. Treat the crew members respectfully and they will do wonders for you. Then walk away. If you are happy, get a good night's sleep. Read over your speech in the morning and maybe practice in the mirror. Focus on the outcome and relax. You are ready to stand and deliver.

A note about using a teleprompter. A teleprompter (a term that has come to mean any form of prompting device that projects words in front of the speaker) is an aid that many speakers use. Used well, a teleprompter is a godsend. It helps the speaker look at the audience and still keep his or her place in the text. Used poorly, it can be as restrictive as a straitjacket on a mental patient. There is an art to using a teleprompter, so if you have never used one, practice with it first. If you are unsure about it, decline it unless you have a couple of hours to practice. (If you use a teleprompter, you will need to get your text or notes to the teleprompter operator in advance, preferably in computer form, so that the operator can enter and format it for you.)

SELL THE MESSAGE

Part of delivering the message involves selling it—putting something of yourself into the message. In Chapter 4 we discussed marketing the message, finding interesting and sometimes novel ways to distribute it through different channels. Selling the message is about persuasion and conviction, putting the leadership commitment into it. Failure to do so can be hazardous, as Senator Trent Lott discovered on the eve of becoming Senate majority leader. In the wake of publicity about his offhand remarks in praise of fellow Senator Strom Thurmond's failed 1948 presidential bid on a segregationist ticket, Lott repeatedly tried to apologize. To many, his remarks seemed to lack sincerity and even credibility, given that he had made similar statements in the past. Lott was criticized by politicians on both sides of the aisle and rebuked by President George W. Bush. (As a result, Lott resigned his leadership post prior to assuming it.)

In contrast, watch a successful salesperson make a sale. She is fully engaged; she knows her offering and can make it come alive for the prospect. More important, she is attuned to the prospect's slightest nuance—a raised eyebrow, a glance at a watch, a look of consternation, a breaking of eye contact. These are telltale signs that the prospect is otherwise engaged and that unless the salesperson acts quickly, she will lose the sale. So what does she do? She shifts gears and tries another approach: asking a question, mentioning another feature, demonstrating a key benefit. She works the prospect, looking for signs that the message is reaching home.

Effective leadership communicators do the same. Whether it is Rudy Giuliani or Jack Welch, Mother Teresa or Shelly Lazarus, the communicator reads his or her followers, looking for signs that the message is being received loud and clear. When delivering a message, either one-on-one or to an entire group, the leader can judge for him- or herself whether the message is hitting home. Are people looking at the clock, looking concerned, or just not looking at all? Good communicators, like good salespeople, can shift gears and, like actors, find new ways to connect. How? Here are some suggestions:

- *Ask questions*. If you want to know what is on people's minds, ask them. Good leaders are always asking questions as a means of gauging interest as well as finding ways to connect the offering to the individual. Engage the people in your audience in conversation. Find out what they are thinking. And don't be afraid to ask for feedback; it's important to know how you are coming across.
- *Make the benefits real.* People need to see, hear, and experience the leadership message. The leader needs to connect the message to the individual. Show each person how what you are asking her or him to do will benefit her or him personally. Rich Teerlink made the benefits of a transformed Harley-Davidson real to employees, dealers, and customers through constant repetition. Give people a reason to believe, and they will. Human nature predisposes us to belong to something larger than ourselves.
- *Echo the values.* All communications from the leader need to echo the values of the organization. The leader's interpretation of those values transforms them from platitudes to behaviors. For example, if a company prides itself on being people-focused, the people in the company need to see that behavior echoed by the leadership. When employees see a leader spending time with a customer or lending a hand with an employee, the rhetoric of "we're a caring company" becomes real.
- *Ask for the sale.* Never leave 'em hanging. Ask for support. The call to action close to a presentation is a perfect example. As we said in Chapter 6, be specific about what you want your people to do. You can employ the same method when speaking one-on-one. Ask people to get behind what you want them to do. Statesmen such as Colin Powell ask for support for government initiatives. Business leaders like Jack Welch ask for an employee's commitment to a business objective. The very asking makes the person feel important, as if he or she has been singled out to do something special.

Leadership communications—in contrast to the sales cycle, which has a definite beginning, middle, and end—never really ceases. Messages may have cycles, but the communications process continues.

PLAY FOR PASSION

When you were a youngster learning to write, no doubt you were instructed to write first about what you know. Leaders elevate the stakes. They are required to communicate what they know through their words and actions. But they need to do something else as well: They need to demonstrate *passion*—the conviction that they care. As recipients of messages throughout the day, at work, in the media, and in our daily lives, we have become very adept at discerning whether truth is coming from the speaker's platform. It has become almost reflexive for us to assume that all politicians are lying or that all businessmen are being evasive. Of course these are gross exaggerations, and unfair ones, too, but the perception remains real. So what's a leader to do?

Speak with conviction. The passion that a leader brings to the message is essential. Recall the passion that our civil rights leaders brought to their messages in the fifties and sixties. Their conviction was born of the injustice they had personally experienced. Today we see some of the same conviction in human rights workers who work on behalf of victims of hunger, war, and land mines. Their passion is genuine. As a leader, you probably feel a similar passion for what you do. Your challenge is to transfer what is inside of you to what is coming out of your mouth. If you speak simply, honestly, and straightforwardly, your conviction will ring true.

Keep in mind that you will not be feeling your best every time you speak. You may be feeling overworked, tired, or even bored. The last thing you may want to do is get up and speak about some new initiative, but remember, that's your job. You owe it to your followers, those who place their trust in you, to speak with clarity and conviction. You need to deliver the passion, even when you are feeling about as passionate as a wrung-out dishcloth. At times like this, you have to trust your instincts and use your acting abilities. Acting is not about faking conviction; it is a set of tools that you use to articulate your message in a believable manner.

COMMUNICATIONS THEATER

Communications, as has been discussed, involves far more than verbal exchanges between speaker and listener. It is also a form of theater, a pageantry of drama, history, and symbolism. It is important for leaders to keep a dramatic image in mind. We find such moments everywhere.

When the last pile of rubble was hauled from the site of Ground Zero at the World Trade Center, there was a marking of the moment. Again and again we heard that there would be no music, no speeches—just silence. It was a fitting moment of reflection to remember those who had died in the horrible and unprovoked attack.

Conventions are another form of communications theater. Whenever people united in a single purpose are gathered together, whether it is an annual convention of union members or a quadrennial presidential political convention, there are set activities that occur. Some groups open with the Pledge of Allegiance and close with a song. Political conventions are designed to peak at the selection of the presidential candidate and the candidate's address to the group and the nation. These are moments with a time-honored tradition. Consider them as part of the liturgy of the organization. They are rooted in the culture of the event. Therefore, leaders must know their meaning and abide by their significance. Here are some considerations to keep in mind.

- *Use symbols*. Symbols are metaphors for organizational values. In our legal system, the judge wields a gavel to begin and adjourn sessions and to call for order. The gavel is a symbol of power, of coming together for a joint purpose. The range of symbols is endless. In sports, the Stanley Cup, which is given to the winner of the National Hockey League playoff series, is a potent symbol. One at a time, players and coaches skate around the rink hoisting the cup over their heads in victory, sharing the moment with the fans. The name of each player and coach is engraved on the base of the trophy. And in a spirit of genuine celebration, each member of the team gets to keep the cup for 48 hours. Traditionally players take it to their hometown and have a party so that all the player's friends and relatives can share in the moment. In recent years, the cup has traveled to Europe to the hometowns of players from Sweden, the Czech Republic, and Russia. This gesture brings the tradition of the NHL to other hockey-playing nations and demonstrates the international spirit of the game.
- *Dress the hall.* Gatherings of people mean more when the room is "dressed" for the occasion. Create an environment that will remind people of the strengths of the organization and why they should care about it. The room may contain nothing more than a banner with a logo, or it may be dressed to the nines with pennants, banners, video walls, and product displays.
- *Choose your clothes carefully.* Wear something that is appropriate to the expectations of the audience. Mother Teresa adapted her nun's habit to local custom. The white garment trimmed with blue served a dual purpose: It symbolized both her commitment to her religious faith and her order, the Missionaries of Charity, and her solidarity with her adopted land, India. Hamid Karzai, the leader of the post-Taliban Afghan state, uses his manner of dress to make a similar statement. He combines a Western suit with the colors, capes, and headwear of his native land.

  Closer to home, a union boss addressing a group of hardhats is best off not wearing a tie, the symbol of management. Likewise, a politician who wants to curry union votes will don a jacket emblazoned with a union logo. This is not a jacket that he would wear in a corporate setting.

Likewise, the CEO who dispenses with a tie in a factory or wears cowboy boots is one who is demonstrating outwardly that he is one of the people.

- *Wear the hat.* Hats are another form of dress. We live in the age of the baseball cap. Every leader wears one bearing the logo of the group that he or she is visiting. Hats have significance. Calvin Coolidge was photographed wearing an American Indian chief's headdress of eagle feathers. Jack Kennedy dispensed with a hat during his Inaugural Address and thereby established a trend. (*Caution:* Choose your hat carefully. Candidate Michael Dukakis agreed to wear an army helmet during his run for the presidency. Rather than appearing presidential, he looked ridiculous.)
- *Think music.* Every baseball game, and for that matter every major sports event, in America begins with the National Anthem. Every Rotary Club meeting begins with a song. Music can serve two purposes: It can remind the audience of who they are as a people (the National Anthem), and it can get people up out of their seats and make them feel more energized (the Rotary Club anthem).
- *Consider the backdrop.* Politicians are adept at creating the picture-perfect moment where the setting makes more of a statement than the words of the speaker do. For example, when Bill Clinton spoke up for the environment, he did so in a national park in the West. George W. Bush has made a strong case for schools. When he delivers a speech, he does it in a school gymnasium, drawing parallels between the immediate location and the universal values he espouses.
- *Respect silence.* A moment of silence to reflect on the events of the day or in memory of others is a time-honored tradition. While this technique may be common among both politicians and preachers, a selective use of silence can be powerful. Leaders may use the dramatic pause to underscore their points as well as to enable people to reflect on the meaning of the words.

Communications theater is a time-honored tradition. The selection of the right background or the proper use of symbols can make the leadership message resonate more deeply than words alone can and allow it to be understood on an emotional level that rings true and helps bond the leader to her or his followers.

THEATER OF ONE

The concept of communications theater also has applicability to one-on-one communications. The leader needs to demonstrate respect for the listener in ways that go beyond words. During a formal coaching session, the leader may assume the role of host. Invite the employee into the office, offer refreshments, make certain that the person is sitting in a comfortable chair, and, if appropriate, close the door to the office. These are little things, to be sure, but they reflect courtesy for the other person, not as a performer, but as a fellow human being.

Leaders can extend these same courtesies at meetings in a variety of ways. Offer to get coffee for the group. If the meeting will run more than 60 minutes, consider treats or snack foods. Rotate the assignment of running the meeting. Do not be the first one to speak; allow others to voice their opinions first. Again, these are small measures, but when taken together they demonstrate a leader's concern for others.

Communications Planner: Delivering the Message

Content + Preparation + Audience = Moment of Truth. Use these tips to help you prepare for your moment of truth.

1. Consider your leadership message. Imagine yourself preparing to go on stage.
   - What does the audience want to hear?
   - How can you bring your personality to bear on the message?
   - What story can you tell on yourself that might break the ice and put the audience at ease?
2. Listen to your voice on tape. Make notes about your tone and inflection.
3. Imagine a presentation style. When I speak, I like to keep the mental image of Rob Petrie from the *Dick Van Dyke Show* in mind. If you recall the show, Rob (played by Van Dyke) was thin and lithe, and exuded a great deal of physical comedy with seemingly little physical movement. His movements, including the pratfalls, were polished and practiced.
4. Practice speaking in front of a mirror. It's probably the oldest technique in the world, but there's a reason for this: It works!
5. Watch yourself on videotape. Make notes about your movements and your voice. Do they work in concert?
6. Plan your rehearsal time. Plan what you will do in advance; that way, you can maximize your time on stage.
7. Watch the professionals. Attend lectures or speeches whenever possible. Watch what the pros do, and as you do so, make

notes on the following points:

- How do they walk on stage?
- How do they welcome the audience?
- What gestures do they employ?
- How do they make the audience feel? Why do they do this?

8. Consider a situation in which a facilitated dialogue might be appropriate. [A facilitated dialogue is similar to a focus group where a facilitator (or even the speaker) asks questions designed to elicit opinions and ideas of the audience. See Chapter 9 for more on a facilitated dialogue.]

- What is the issue that you would explore? Why is dialogue more appropriate for it than a straight presentation?
- What questions would you pose to yourself and the audience?
- What would you want as the desired outcome?

9. Think about your next meeting or coaching session. How will you employ some elements of communications theater to underscore your leadership message?

JACK WELCH—THE STRATEGIC COMMUNICATOR

He has been called the greatest CEO in America. On one side, you have an unparalleled record of earnings growth, sustained profitability, and growth in market capitalization that stretches for more than two decades. On the other side, you have a man who can be tough as nails, brusque, and at times impatient, yet who speaks reverentially of his late mother, to whom he attributes much of his success. He is Jack Welch, chairman and CEO of General Electric from 1981 to 2001.

So much has been said and written about Welch that you would think that he invented the role of the modern CEO. He, of course, would be the first to disagree. For one thing, he would laud his predecessor, Reginald Jones, for preparing him to lead the company. More important, he would attribute his success to a couple of seemingly simple themes: focus, execution, and people. Inherent in all three is communications. And it is his relentless commitment to disseminating the message that accounts for much of his success.

KEEPING IT SIMPLE

The facts of Welch's professional life are pretty straightforward. He got a

Ph.D. in chemical engineering, then went to work for GE Plastics. He rose through the ranks, becoming a general manager at 33, then rising to a vice presidency and later to vice chairman of GE Credit. At age 45, he was named CEO.[1] According to Welch, his tenure at GE was focused on "three fundamental things": hardware, behavior, and work processes. By hardware, Welch means business priorities, i.e., being first or second in every market segment. Behavior refers to "boundarylessness, open idea sharing" among business units. Work processes concerns finding ways to improve the way the work gets done.[2]

These fundamentals coincide with the three phases of Welch's career in the top slot. During phase 1, he was called "Neutron Jack," getting into and out of businesses and engaging in heavy layoffs. Phase 2 was called "Work-Out"; managers worked with their people to determine strategies and tactics. Senior leaders sketched the issues and left teams to "work out" solutions; the boss could reject or accept these solutions on the spot or ask for more information—but always with a timetable. Phase 3 was Six Sigma, a quality-centric approach to business and people, or, as Welch put it, "transforming everything we do."[3]

USING COMMUNICATIONS TO LEAD

Each of these phases required a "sell-in" period, and that's where Welch earned his stripes as a communicator, getting the word to GE's vast multidisciplinary business operations throughout the world. His secret? Simplicity. Welch intuitively understands how to break things down into simple parts to make them understandable by all.

Welch repeats himself purposely. "In leadership you have to exaggerate every statement you make. You've got to repeat it a thousand times. . . . Overstatements are needed to move a large organization."[4] Welch is careful to point out that you need to back up the overstatements with action. For example, when he spoke of getting rid of people who achieved but in the process trampled on other people, he meant it, and those people were systematically rooted out of the organization.[5]

An additional method for getting buy-in is to give the audience a reason to believe. Welch tells the story of the time he asked people to cut travel expenses by 30 percent. To forestall a backlash, Welch wrapped the message in the context of integrating work and life. "Look, you've [managers] been telling me your biggest problem is that you don't see your families enough. Now you're going to be seeing your families 30% more."[6] Linking the leadership message to a strategy, or, better yet, an individual benefit, helps overcome resistance. Such linkage may require some clever thinking, but as Welch showed time and again, it is essential to ensuring buy-in and uniting people for a common cause.

Welch has said that a CEO's greatest failing is "being the last to know."[7] A leader who never hears bad news is hopelessly out of touch. Welch made a point of surrounding himself with people whom he referred to as "business soul mates." These were individuals who could be counted on to give him the straight scoop on the issues. Another way Welch stayed tuned to the organization was by asking questions, sometimes for hours on end, until he learned what he needed to know.[8]

POWER IN PEOPLE

Development of others is essential to Welch's success as CEO. Welch was an active and vigorous participant in what GE calls its Corporate Executive Council, which meets quarterly. Strategy and succession are principal themes of these meetings. At the 2½-day sessions, senior leaders meet to "share best practices, assess the external business environment, and identify the company's most promising opportunities and most pressing problems."

Apart from getting perspective on the business, Welch used these sessions to coach and observe managers interacting with one another.[9]

During another set of meetings, known as Session C, Welch worked with senior line managers and human resource leaders to assess managerial talent. "Candor" and "execution" were the buzzwords. When Session C concluded, Welch followed up with his handwritten assessment. In keeping with Welch's claim of backing words with action, it is GE's policy to link all management development to strategic business goals. Meritocracy is what GE strives to create, and this is the thing of which Welch claims to be most proud.[10] It is no surprise, then, that many people refer to GE as the boot camp for managers, or "CEO University."[11] The ranks of American corporations are filled with GE grads, including Larry Bossidy (Allied-Signal and later Honeywell), Robert Nardelli (Home Depot), David Cote (TRW), and Jim McNerney (3M).

Some of the luster of Welch's legacy was tarnished when the perquisites that he continued to receive from GE after his retirement were revealed during divorce proceedings from his second wife. The amenities included a rent-free apartment in Manhattan, use of the corporate jet, and private security for overseas travel. The cost of these perquisites, according to Welch, amounted to less than the lump sum that GE's board had originally offered as part of his 1996 contract extension negotiations.[12]

Welch, never one to flinch from a challenge, responded with an op-ed piece in the *Wall Street Journal* in which he defended his compensation as well as his legacy. But not wishing to reflect negatively on the company for which he had worked so long and so hard, Welch agreed to give up his perks package and reimburse GE for expenses that had been previously covered, including the New York apartment and corporate jet service. This bill, according to Welch may be $2.5 million annually, but as he says,

> [Perception] matters. And in these times when public confidence and trust have been shaken, I've learned the hard way that perception matters more than ever. . . . I don't want a great company with the highest integrity dragged into a public fight. . . . I care too much for GE and its people.[13]

CORPORATE STATESMAN

In the wake of the corporate governance scandals, Jack Welch emerged as a statesman on corporate and shareholder interests, confessing that he was as shocked as anyone by the financial foul play perpetrated by companies like Enron and Global Crossing. He traces the rise in CEOs' pay to the alignment of management compensation with shareholder value. When companies' stock soared, as happened in the nineties, senior management compensation grew at the same rate. "If you focus on pay for performance, and if you focus on results, and you focus on delivery to shareholders, you will get a system that works."[14] He admits that his total compensation for building GE's equity was generous, but he argues that it was determined fairly and honestly and for the benefit of shareholders and employees alike. He draws a distinction between the fraud perpetrated by a few and the honest earnings of the vast majority of senior leaders. Welch remains a true believer in the long-term future of his company, refusing to sell when the stock spiked, a move that "more than halved" his net worth: "I've gone up with it and I've gone down with it."[15] In his speeches, Welch reflects the same spirit of optimism about corporate America that he injected into GE "We need to have an atmosphere where CEOs are out taking risks, are out doing things positively, are out creating an atmosphere that we can win again."[16] To Welch, born into a union family and educated at a state school, it's all part of the American free enterprise system, of which he is a loyal and proud proponent.

FINAL THOUGHTS

Welch has a capacity for self-criticism. He says that his biggest mistake was not going fast enough. "I went too slow in everything I did. Yes, I was called every name in the book when I started, but if I had done in two years what took five, we would have been ahead of the curve even more."[17]

In a reflective interview with the *Harvard Business Review* after he had left office, Welch was even more philosophical. "My success rate was 50-50 at best. . . . That improved later because I turned out to be pretty good at it." As for strengths, Welch considers himself only "marginally" creative, but "very intuitive. I don't get fooled very often."[18]

In this same interview, Welch said that he wanted to be remembered as a people person, in contrast to earlier names like "Neutron Jack" or even "Neanderthal Jack." Why? "I like people. . . . People I work with like me."[19] Welch's affinity for others gets to the heart of his strength as a communicator. Leaders who care and respect the employees in the organization will make the time to ensure that those employees understand the message, both for the good of the enterprise and for the good of the individual, enabling him or her to give the best and get the best in return.

Leadership Communications Lessons

Embrace change. Welch does not accept the status quo. He believes that complacency is the enemy of progress, and he pushes his people to look to the future and consider alternative options as a means of growing the business.

Focus on developing people. Welch restlessly seeks to promote other people to positions where they can contribute and succeed. One measure of his success is the number of GE alumni who have served or are serving as CEOs of other companies.

Communicate relentlessly. Clarity of message coupled with frequency is a Welch hallmark. His expectations for people and the organization were always high. And he communicated those expectations clearly and frequently throughout all levels of the organization.

Be decisive. Once the decision is made, act forthwith. Welch backed his words and those of his team with actions. The Work-Out sessions are a classic example of decisiveness.

Be seen as the leader. Welch was the personification of GE during his tenure. He communicated what he wanted people to do, and he expected them to do it. His standards for execution were the envy of the business world.

Live your message. Welch's ability to lead stems from his ability to see the issues clearly and to persuade others to come along for the ride.

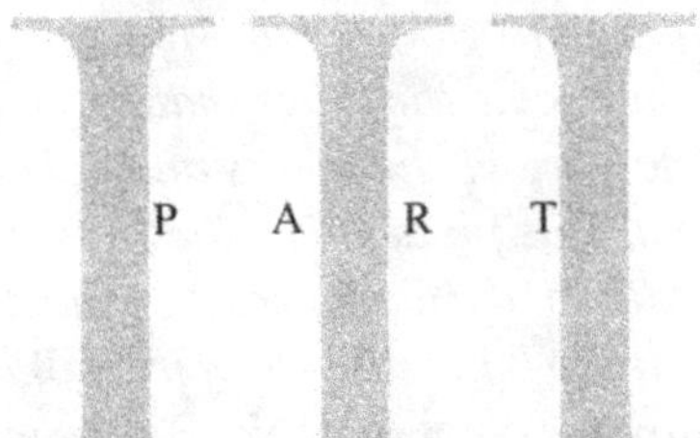

Sustaining the Leadership Message

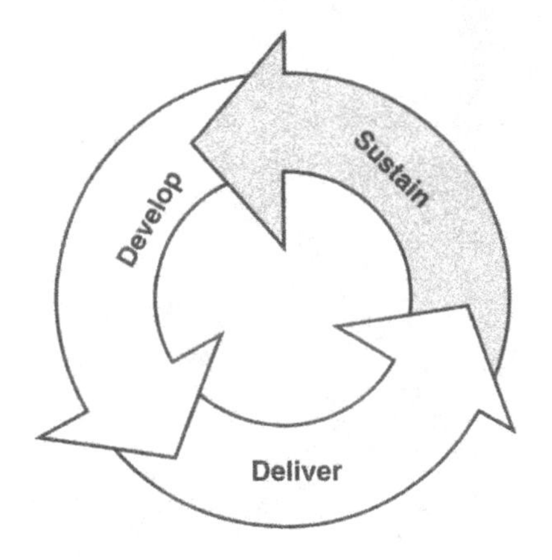

LEADERSHIP COMMUNICATIONS IS A CONTINUOUS JOB. Messages must be communicated and recommunicated in ways that make them understandable and credible to various audiences and able to be acted upon by those audiences. This process is called sustaining the leadership message. In addition, the leader must connect with his or her people on a personal level in order to build a sense of trust. When a bond of trust has been established, the future becomes possible. People will be inspired to follow, and in the process they will achieve inspired results for themselves, for the leader, and for the organization.

Part III focuses on sustaining the leadership message through a variety of communications methods, including coaching and storytelling. You will learn how to use communications as a core leadership behavior to achieve inspired results through the actions of the people you lead.

CHAPTER 9

Remember before you speak, it is necessary to listen, and only then, from the fullness of your heart you speak and God listens.

Mother Teresa

Morale is the state of mind. It is steadfastness and courage and hope. It is confidence and zeal and loyalty. . . . It is staying power, the spirit which endures to the end—the will to win. With it all things are possible, without it everything else . . . is for naught.

George C. Marshall

CONNECTING WITH PEOPLE BEYOND WORDS

WE LIVE IN AN AGE OF THEATRICALITY. You can see it everywhere. In shopping malls. In TV news programs. In music programs. Even in the supermarket. There is a reason for this: People who have a product to sell or a message to communicate feel the need to intensify the delivery of their message. Merchandisers use high-impact graphics and artful staging to display their products in the most appealing manner. Advertisers produce creative messages for TV, radio, and the Internet as a means of gaining attention. As a result, the rest of us feel that we need to put some pizzazz into our messages in order to be heard and, better yet, understood.

As a result of this pervasive theatricality, the straightforward stand-up presentation may appear tired and dated. At times, it may actually be so. When that occurs, you can extend yourself beyond words and pictures in order to connect with the audience (see Figure 9-1). There may be occasions when you want to think like a promoter and present like a professional actor.

In fact, actor-turned-President Ronald Reagan spent the bulk of his time doing what he did best—communicating. He worked hard at his speeches, and he delivered them with the practiced skill of an actor. In fact, Lou Cannon, his biographer, has written that Reagan was very proud of his acting ability; he took umbrage at political enemies who sought to dismiss him and his policies by calling him a lousy actor. Reagan wondered how anyone could function as president without acting experience.[1]

ENGAGE THE AUDIENCE

The key word to remember is *engagement*—getting the audience to look, listen, and respond. But how do you engage an audience? By appealing to its

FIGURE 9-1 Connecting with the Audience

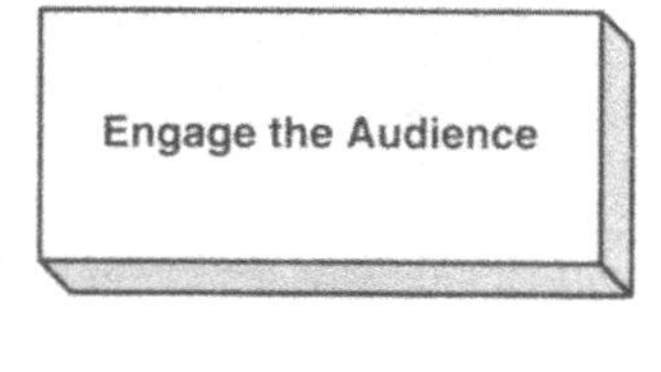

intelligences. All of us have more than one type of intelligence. According to psychologist and author Howard Gardner, we have at least seven, covering mind, body, and spirit. All too often, presentations appeal only to the intellect, ignoring our physical, emotional, and spiritual sides.[2]

Good leadership communicators strive to reach both the head and the heart. They want to pitch ideas to the mind, where we figure things out with logic and reason. But they also work to reach the heart, our emotional side, where decisions are made. Leaders need to make a strong emotional case for a vision statement; they need their followers to see, touch, and feel what the future will be like once the vision becomes reality.

Leaders can borrow lessons from salespeople. Salespeople are practiced masters at knowing how to close when the customer is excited and emotionally involved. Leaders can capture the same kind of engagement as they seek to sell their message. Effective presenters must connect with the audience in at least one and often more of the following ways.

- *Stimulating the intellect. Cogito, ergo sum* wrote Descartes four centuries ago. As a presenter, you want to engage the audience's attention through the reasoning of your presentation. This is why you want to give your presentation a strong structure, augmented with compelling facts. General George Marshall was not a scintillating orator, but when he briefed Congress on war issues, everyone listened because he knew his stuff.
- *Appealing to the emotions.* Touch the emotions. Make people feel the power of your presentation by awakening their emotions. You can do this with stories. You can do it with pictures. You can do it with games. CEO Steve Jobs captures attention with his body language and his skillful product demos for Apple Computers.
- *Engaging the body.* Create movement. Encourage the audience to get up and move with you. Revivalist preachers invite those who feel the spirit to come to the front. Why? Because they know that when a person is engaged physically, she or he is more likely to be engaged in mind and spirit. Colin Powell is a polished professional speech-giver; he gesticulates on cue, but with conviction. By contrast, Bill Veeck was a jumble of seemingly distracting activities—he would tousle his hair or scratch his wrist.[3] But each of these men used his physicality to make appropriate points.

How can you develop your presentation so that you do this? You are limited only by the range of your imagination. Here are some ways to get the audience to focus its attention on you and your leadership message.

FACILITATE RESPONSES

Audiences are accustomed to sitting and listening. If you can reach out and encourage them to speak up, you have broken the invisible barrier separating the presenter from the audience. Here are some simple things you may wish to try:

- *Invite the audience to stand and stretch.* If the audience has been sitting for a while, invite people to stand and stretch. They will appreciate your gesture.
- *Pose questions to the audience.* Possible questions include the following:
    - *How is everyone today?* If the response is tepid, pose the question again. You can go back and forth until you hit the right level of enthusiasm.
    - *Why are we here today?* This is a good one for getting people to speak up. You can have some fun with the audience.
    - *Where are you from?* Invite people to stand when you call the name of their city or state. (*Note:* Find out in advance where the majority of the people live so that you can mention those areas first.)
- *Create an ongoing dialogue with the audience.* Find points in your speech where you can ask rhetorical questions. You can even pause for a group response. Watch how Oprah shifts from asking a question of the interviewee to asking a question of the audience. This helps the audience connect with the guest as well as with Oprah.
- *Thank the audience.* Entertainers are perpetually thanking the audience for its patronage. Leaders can learn from this example. Recognize individuals in the audience for special achievement. Take a moment to thank the group for achieving a milestone or even for coming to this gathering. Do not overdo it, but acknowledge the audience for its participation. Mother Teresa thanked contributors to her mission through speeches and words, but she also thanked God for enabling her to carry out her mission. These types of communications reflected on how Mother Teresa saw herself—as an instrument in the service of a higher power for a greater good.

USE INTERACTIVE TOOLS

Interactive is the twenty-first-century word for getting people involved in what you are presenting. Here are some ideas you may wish to consider. Pick and choose those tools that complement your style and the expectations of your audience.

- *Interact with games.* Those who teach adults, either as instructors or as trainers, typically have a selection of books containing games. Ask to see these books or seek them out in bookstores. Icebreakers, those that encourage people to interact with one another, work best. Keep the exercise to less than 5 minutes.
- *Interact with music to set the mood.* Before you step on stage, play some "walk-on" music, i.e., a light, easy-listening melody that encourages the audience to settle down.
- *Interact with lighting.* Arrange to lower the light level before you go on stage, then bring it up gradually. Maybe lower it when you are making a dramatic point.
- *Interact with your product.* If you are presenting a product, let the audience experience that product for itself. You can explain the features and benefits, but let the product demonstrate itself. Invite the audience to touch and feel the product.
- *Interact with the Internet.* Many presenters augment their presentation with images from a web site. Some even hold teleconferences over the Internet. If you choose this e-avenue, make certain that you use a projection screen large enough for everyone to see.
- *Interact with props.* One effective technique is the lone chair. Place it on the stage. You may sit on it, place your foot on it, or even create an imaginary dialogue with it.
- *Interact with clothing.* Something you wear can be a prop. Often a presenter who is wearing a suit will stride to the podium and make a point of taking off his jacket and rolling up his sleeves. By doing so, the presenter sends a signal that the mood will be informal and down to earth.

Engaging the audience is a presenter's chief responsibility. As we have shown, there are many ways to stimulate an audience response. The challenge for the presenter is finding the right balance between message and staging. Sometimes words alone are enough. Other times, you may need both visuals and interactive games. Whatever the method, the outcome must be the same: engaging the audience's attention.

Theatricality may not be suitable for all occasions. It may be expected of professional presenters, but it may be frowned upon when you are presenting to the board of directors. Boredom is your enemy. Do what you can to banish it from your presentations forever.

ALTERNATIVE PRESENTATION FORMATS

Leaders continually need to ask themselves *why* they are communicating. On one level, it is to impart the leadership message as it relates to vision, mission, and values. On a deeper level, it is to strengthen the bonds of trust between leader and followers. Therefore, the manner in which a leader communicates is less important than the content of the message and its impact.

Much of Part II concentrated on developing a coherent presentation, using both words and visuals. All of the rules of message structure are valid, but the presentation methods may vary. For example, the presenter may choose to give the presentation as a dialogue, asking questions of the audience and proceeding into discussion, debate, and maybe resolution. Other times, the leader may just make an opening statement and invite questions from the audience. As a third option, the leader may come out, tell a story about the business, and invite comments from the audience. The methods of presentation are endless; what is important is the message and its content.

FACILITATED DIALOGUE

One method that is fast gaining in popularity is the facilitated dialogue—inviting a skilled facilitator to conduct a dialogue between the leader and the audience. Turning things over to a facilitator leaves the leader free to concentrate on the message—what does she or he want to say, and why? The facilitator will be briefed in advance and told what points need to be made; it will be up to him or her to bring out these points from the leader and from members of the audience. A facilitated dialogue will still require much preparation—drafting the messages, shaping the presentation ideas, even providing visual support, if desired.

The advantages of a facilitated dialogue are that it encourages the participation of both leader and audience. It enables people to contribute their own ideas, and it enables the group to build on the ideas of others. The leader becomes an active participant in shaping the process. Leader and followers collaborate in a shared process that can lead to greater understanding, and ultimately to greater levels of trust.

One thing to remember: The leader should have the last word in a facilitated dialogue. This enables the leader to sum up the meeting and take ownership of the process. The leader may invite others to offer their final words, but he or she should be the one to close. This act affirms her or his leadership and responsibility for leading the group.

Hints on Facilitated Dialogue

When staging a facilitated dialogue, consider the following:

- Brief the facilitator beforehand. Let the facilitator know the issues and the topics to be discussed.

- Ask the facilitator to develop a list of questions to ask the leader.
- Invite the facilitator to provide periodic summaries of the discussion so that everyone in the group stays together.
- Require the facilitator to keep the meeting on time and on task. The facilitator should focus discussion on the issues, not go into extraneous topics. (There may be times, however, when there will be a deliberate veer in the dialogue in order to cover hot issues or deal with unexpected surprises.)
- Ask the facilitator to summarize, but then invite the leader to close the dialogue.

The bottom line is that leadership communications is about content and meaning. A facilitated dialogue can be a wonderful way to explore new ideas as well as to affirm organizational values and create deeper levels of trust.

Communications Planner: Connecting with the Audience

Getting the audience's attention and maintaining it is the presenter's chief challenge. Beyond words and visuals, presenters can use their imagination to grab the audience's eyes and speak directly to their souls.

1. Develop a "get to know me" pitch for the start of every presentation. This should let the audience know who you are and what you will do in your presentation.
2. Consider learning a magic trick or a simple juggling maneuver. Practice it until you can do it in your sleep, or in front of your friends. Look for opportunities to introduce it into a presentation. It may be an opener; it may be a closer. Think about how and where you can use it.
3. Practice different ways to demonstrate your product. If it is something tangible, let the audience touch and feel it. If it is a service, invite the audience to experience it. Consider reversing the order of presentation. Maybe you will lead with the benefits and close with the features, or perhaps you will lead with the features and close with the benefits.
4. Talk to corporate trainers. Find out what games they use to engage the audience's attention. An easy way to find some titles is to do a search in a virtual bookstore. Choose the words *games for trainers*.

5. Window-shop. Look at how the merchandisers have dressed the store windows to attract your attention. See how the lighting and staging present the merchandise in the most appealing fashion. Ask yourself if there is a way you can present yourself more theatrically. Perhaps you could wear a new suit, a funny tie, or a clown nose.
6. Have a conversation with an elementary school teacher about how he or she maintains attention when presenting a lesson. You will be surprised at the variety of tools that teachers of the very young use: pictures, songs, musical instruments, and toys. One or two may be appropriate for your next presentation.
7. Visit the theater. Watch how actors add body movement to the words as a means of bringing their characters alive.

MOTHER TERESA—A LIFE OF HEALING

She radiated holiness pure and simple. She was drawn to the poorest of the poor, and as a result the world was drawn to her. She was Mother Teresa. Founder of a religious order and a Nobel laureate, she lived as she died, in Calcutta tending to those in need. One of the ways she was able to achieve what she did—always for others—was through her unique ability to communicate. Through prayer, through meditation, through interviews, and through her own writings, Mother Teresa demonstrated an ability to bring people to her cause.

MACEDONIA TO INDIA

The facts of her life are straightforward. Born in Skopje in what is now Macedonia, Agnes Gonxha Bojaxhiu was Albanian by heritage. She was inspired to go to India after learning about it from missionaries who spoke at her school. She joined an Irish order, the Sisters of Loreto, moved to India, and became a school principal. Wanting to do more, she founded her own order, the Missionaries of Charity, based on Franciscan principles of service to those most in need. She founded her order with some fellow nuns in 1948 with no funds to speak of. Upon her death nearly 40 years later, her order had grown to include 4000 nuns and 120,000 lay workers treating the disenfranchised who were suffering from leprosy or AIDS as well as hunger and malnutrition in some 450 missions around the world. She also became a citizen of India, demonstrating her solidarity with the people she served first.[4]

BURDEN OF SAINTHOOD

Mother Teresa was not comfortable with the label of "living saint." It is true that she had an aura, a kind of charisma, that drew people to her. But she was also very human. A documentary about her, done over a 5-year period, depicts in gritty detail the world that was her life. As one reviewer put it, "The frail figure huddled inside the Indian sari is clearly a force, a soft-spoken lode of iron reserve. The deeply committed no-frills humanity comes through."[5] When asked what it is like to be a living saint, Mother Teresa responds, "I have to be holy in my position. That's nothing extraordinary. It's my simple duty. We have been created for that."[6]

Also depicted in the film is her visit to Beirut in 1982 at the height of the fighting between Muslims and Christians. Mother Teresa wishes to retrieve a group of spastic children who were isolated in an abandoned hospital. A priest says it's a good idea, but it's impractical because the hospital is in a free-fire zone. To which Mother Teresa responds, "It's not an idea. It's our duty." At her insistence, a cease-fire was arranged and the children were rescued.[7]

WORDS TO LIVE BY

Like many leaders, Mother Teresa was a powerful storyteller. Many of her writings tell of the people she has encountered and what they have taught her. Rather than assuming some kind of superior role, she paints a portrait of herself as a seeker. She was famous for telling the story about the first person to whom she ministered. The woman's body was half-eaten by rats; instead of revulsion, Mother Teresa saw "Christ in his distressing disguise."[8] And in her Nobel Peace Prize lecture she tells the story of a bedridden man whose only joy was smoking. He abstained from tobacco for a week and sent Mother Teresa $15 for the mission. "It must have been a terrible sacrifice for him but see . . . how he shared. And with that money I brought bread and I gave to those who are hungry."[9]

Although Mother Teresa was strictly Catholic in faith, she was liberal in reaching out to others, seeking to help all regardless of their faith as well as receiving aid from anyone of any faith. She also saw her ministry as taking care of the poor and sick, not as proselytizing: "Love has no other message but its own. . . . If we do any preaching, it is done with deeds, not with words. That is our witness to the gospel."[10]

A considerable body of literature is growing up around Mother Teresa. Some of her writings have been collected as inspirational texts. Another book is a collection of reflections from the famous (e.g., Senator Ted Kennedy), from religious leaders, and from ordinary people who met her only once. All of these are testaments to the power of her example, and these communications serve to extend her message further.

TRUE TO HER BELIEFS

Those from the secular world found Mother Teresa a holy individual, but many of them did not agree with her doctrinaire support of the Church's position on contraception and abortion. Mother Teresa did not turn them away. Similarly, she accepted an award from dictator Baby Doc Duvalier of Haiti and laid a wreath at the tomb of Enver Hoxha, the communist tyrant of Albania. Critics assailed her. Mother Teresa was not bothered. She "saw Christ in them, and believed they could be redeemed."[11]

DEEPLY HUMAN

For all the talk of Mother Teresa's saintliness, she also was very human. In excerpts from her diaries published after her death, we see a woman who is more like us—plagued by doubts. "In my soul, I feel just the terrible pain of loss, of God not wanting me, of God not being God, of God not really existing." Those words were from a journal she kept between 1959 and 1960, when she was urged by her confessor to keep a record of her thoughts.[12] Thirty years later, she seems much more at ease. "I have begun to love my darkness, for I believe now that is a part, a very small part, of Jesus' darkness and pain on earth."[13]

Mother Teresa writes eloquently of love as a healing force and how it is necessary to love others in order to heal their physical afflictions. She also writes of the joy of giving, doing it for love, not for duty. "God loves a joyful giver. . . . A joyful heart is a normal result of a heart burning with love. Joy is strength."[14]

And as befits someone who is in tune with herself and with others, Mother Teresa had a good sense of humor. She writes: "Someone once asked me, 'Are you married?' And I said, 'Yes, and I find it sometimes very difficult to smile at Jesus because He can be very demanding.'"[15] Likewise she joked in her Nobel speech, "If I don't go to heaven for anything else I will be going for all the publicity [which has] made me really ready to go to heaven."[16]

WORK CONTINUES

The greatest legacy of a leader is the continuation of his or her work after he or she has passed from the scene. In the year following Mother Teresa's death, the Missionaries of Charity added some 20 new centers. Her successor, Sister Nirmala, accounted for the growth this way: "It's God's work. If it was Mother's work, maybe in the course of time it would [have ceased], but since it's God's work, it is the same."[17]

Whether God has anything to do with it is an eternal question. What there can be no question about is this: It is the example of Mother Teresa that continues to bring the poor to her missions and to draw people who are committed to serving them as she herself did.

Leadership Communications Lessons

Understand the power of words. Mother Teresa wrote a number of mediations and reflections. These help readers gain a perspective on life and the world.

Take a stand. Mother Teresa vowed to work among the "poorest of the poor" and did so, overcoming many obstacles in her journey.

Enlist the support of others. Mother Teresa was forever inviting people who came to visit to help her cause. Some stayed and worked as she did; others provided support in other ways.

Use the media. At first Mother Teresa sought no publicity, but soon she realized that if she were to achieve her aims, people throughout the world would have to hear her message.

Live your message. Mother Teresa is the embodiment of living the message. The sanctity of her life resulted from her commitment to others and her selfless desire to help the least fortunate.

GEORGE C. MARSHALL—THE GREAT MOBILIZER

"I feel I could not sleep at night with you out of the country," said Franklin Roosevelt. And with those words General George C. Marshall's lifelong ambition of commanding troops in battle was denied. Dwight Eisenhower, an officer he had developed and promoted, would get the supreme command in Europe. Roosevelt had given the choice to General Marshall himself, but, ever the soldier, Marshall had declined. The decision belonged to the commander in chief. This selfless gesture assured the president that the best man for overall command would remain in Washington.[18] As a result, Eisenhower would become the more famous of the two; after all, as Roosevelt himself once said, "Ike, you and I know who was the Chief of Staff during the last years of the Civil War but practically no one else knows. . . . I hate to think fifty years from now practically no one will know who George Marshall was."[19]

As Roosevelt conjectured, the contribution of General Marshall has faded from memory. True, World War II was won by the blood, sweat, and sacrifice of millions of citizen soldiers who were fighting for the freedom of others against the evils of totalitarianism. Yet although Marshall did not fight in the trenches, his story is equally heroic, for it was through his efforts and will that America and its soldiers received the men, material, and leadership they needed in order to wage war. While Marshall himself never took fire in this war, he sacrificed his lifelong ambition to lead troops so that he could better serve his nation and the army. In Marshall we have an example of a leader as manager for a heroic purpose; his skillful use of communications was essential to his aims and those of our nation.

THE RIGHT MAN FOR THE JOB

In 1939 General Marshall was appointed army chief of staff. It was the fulfillment of a dream for a lifelong soldier who had devoted himself to the service of his country. Marshall had had a slow rise through the ranks from second lieutenant in the Philippines in 1902 through outposts in the American West, service under General "Blackjack" Pershing in World War I in France, and then service in Asia, including China. Now, as chief commander of air and ground forces, it fell to Marshall to mobilize the American military for war should it come.

The challenges that Marshall faced were enormous. While President Franklin Roosevelt was a supporter of intervention, the American people for the most part were not. Fortunately, Marshall had the organizational skills necessary for the task. The army grew from a force of less than 500,000 at the outbreak of war to 12.9 million at the end. Marshall mobilized American men, women, and material. It was he who made certain that troops were equipped for battle and that generals had the troops, supplies, and armaments that they needed in order to wage war.[20]

LEADER-TEACHER

It is said that the modern army took shape under Marshall's guidance. He served as an instructor at the War College for several years, and he also served as chief instructional officer at Fort Benning, Georgia. Dispensing with textbook planning, Marshall pushed for more realistic exercises, in which commanders would need to make decisions with only partial information, just as on a real battlefield. In doing so, he reinvented the way the military educates its officers.[21]

One of Marshall's chief assets was his ability to pick the right person for the right job. At Fort Benning, Marshall identified future leaders and did what he could to promote them. He created the American general corps of the Second World War. His choice of military commanders was meticulous: Generals Dwight Eisenhower, Omar Bradley, Mark Clark, and George Patton were but four of many standouts—all of whom earned a place in his little black book.[22]

THE RIGHT WORDS OF DIPLOMACY

Time and again Marshall proved himself adept at communicating his point of view without creating rancor, and in the process he gained respect for his position as well as for himself. With Congress, Marshall could be charming as well as informative. He was the same with the Allies, especially Britain. Having seen the folly of disunity among the Allies during World War I, he argued forcefully for a unified command during World War II. He wanted an American commander, but he was willing to put British generals into leadership positions, or even to put an American officer in a subordinate position to a British officer as a means of demonstrating a willingness to cooperate.[23]

Marshall drew a distinct line between the military and politics. Throughout the war, by virtue of his position, he was required to testify before Congress. Even though the process was time-consuming and took him away from his military duties, he prepared himself and underwent the rigor of testifying. He also ordered full cooperation with the Truman committee's investigation of military purchasing, rather than stonewalling. The result was twofold: First, Truman's committee uncovered waste and sometimes fraud and in the process ended up saving the nation billions of dollars, and second, he and Truman had the opportunity to assess each other; this paved the way for greater understanding when Truman was thrust into the presidency after Roosevelt's death.[24]

MILITARY VERSUS POLITICAL

Marshall also recused himself from the summits among heads of state that took place periodically throughout the war. He did not think it was wise for a military man to influence political outcomes. At the same time, Marshall was not a political neophyte. Although there were suggestions that he run for office, even for the presidency, he always declined. He knew how Washington worked, and he prided himself on his reputation for being honest and without guile.[25] Periodically, he had to undergo what must have been humiliating examinations—for example, in late 1945 during the investigation of the lack of preparedness at Pearl Harbor, and in the early 1950s when he was wrongly accused by the red-baiting McCarthyites of undermining America's resistance to communist forces, particularly in Asia.[26] With this latter charge, scurrilous though it was, Marshall took the high road, refusing to dignify McCarthy's charges with a rebuttal. His reply: "If I have to explain at this point that I am not a traitor to the United States, I hardly think it's worth it."[27]

The decision to drop the atomic bomb on Japan was one that Marshall did not want to make. He fully endorsed the development of the bomb and in fact was the chief overseer of the project: General Lesley Groves reported to him. Marshall understood that the decision to drop it was one that would have profound moral consequences, and for that reason he deemed its use not a military decision, but one for the government to make. However, Marshall endorsed the use of the atomic bomb as a means of shortening the war and ultimately saving the lives of both the American soldiers and the Japanese civilians and soldiers who would be killed if Japan were invaded.[28]

THE STATESMAN

Truman so admired Marshall that he twice called him into his cabinet, first as secretary of state and later as secretary of defense. It was in the former role that Marshall gained recognition as a humanitarian. In a speech at Harvard when he was given an honorary degree, Marshall spoke of Europe's suffering and slow recovery and its need for assistance in the wake of the war.

> The remedy lies in breaking the vicious circle and restoring confidence of the European people in the economic future of their own countries and of Europe as a whole. . . . It is logical that the United States should do whatever it is able to do to assist in the return of normal economic health in the world, without which there can be no political stability and no assured peace. Our policy is not directed against any country or any doctrine but against hunger, poverty, desperation, and chaos. Its purpose should be the revival of a working economy in the world so as to permit the emergence of political and social conditions in which free institutions can exist.[29]

Direct and to the point, Marshall made the case for providing political stability by ensuring economic viability. This speech introduced the European Recovery Act, soon known as the Marshall Plan. This plan fostered cooperation among nations, staved off communist expansionism, and laid the foundation for a more united Europe. Years later, after he had retired, Marshall was awarded the Nobel Peace Prize, in part for his efforts at helping to rebuild Europe. Acknowledging the irony, even modest dissent, of giving a soldier an award for peace, Marshall said in his Nobel address:

> The cost of war is constantly spread before me, written neatly in many ledgers whose columns are gravestones. I am greatly moved to find some means or method of avoiding another calamity of war.[30]

COMPASSIONATE ALOOFNESS

Very few people called him George; he was always the General. He had an aloofness to him that terrified junior officers, but to Marshall it was a way of getting to the point: A commander's time is limited, and he must maximize his effectiveness.[31] Yet Marshall, like all good commanders, viewed his soldiers as people; the genesis of the USO show was Marshall's requesting entertainment for his troops stateside before the war. During the prewar mobilization, Marshall directed his staff to prepare a summary of messages that newly enlisted men were sending home; many of these messages were complaints.

Forrest Pogue, Marshall's biographer, estimates that Marshall spent "twenty minutes a day" reviewing these summaries and personally answering some of the complaints himself. Marshall also visited with the troops as well as keeping in frequent contact with those he had promoted and developed. He understood that he was mobilizing an army of civilians; the military would mold them into soldiers, but they were nonetheless civilians and wanted nothing more than to return home and resume their lives. Their sacrifice and their service were "the essence of democracy" and "what the fighting was all about." [32]

SAYING NO TO YES

Another of Marshall's traits was a willingness to listen. General Omar Bradley tells of being called into Marshall's office in 1939, a week after the outbreak of the war in Europe. Marshall expressed his disappointment in Bradley and his fellow officers: "You haven't disagreed with a single thing I have done all week." The next day the officers returned with a recommendation that in Bradley's recollection seemed "questionable." To which Marshall replied, "Now that is what I want. Unless I hear all of the arguments against something I am not sure whether I have made the right decision or not."[33]

After Pearl Harbor, Marshall called Ike to his office and told him to draft a plan to save the Philippines. Ike took a few hours, then reported that it was not possible but suggested alternatives. Marshall said, "Eisenhower, the department is filled with able men who analyze their problems well but feel compelled always to bring them to me for final solution. I must have assistants who will solve their own problems and tell me later what they have done."[34] To General Marshall, leadership was not about pleasing the boss or *saying* the right words; leadership was *doing* the right thing. This was the creed by which he lived.

"GREATEST LIVING AMERICAN"

Anyone who came into contact with George Marshall respected him. His sense of virtue was palpable. Throughout his long years in the military, often doing jobs he did not particularly want, he did his duty. His greatest disappointment was failing to obtain divisional command. He was a lifelong staff officer, who served the army and the nation well, and he was worthy of Harry Truman's appellation: "the greatest living American."

Leadership Communications Lessons

Communicate your conviction. People need to know where the leader stands. Marshall was clear and forthright on the need for the army to prepare for war, and he let Congress and the president know where he stood.

Overcome roadblocks. Leaders have to deal with opposition. During World War II, Senator Truman headed a commission to investigate fraud and waste in military spending. While Marshall would have preferred to concentrate on war issues, he understood the benefits of cooperation and won Truman to his side. The commission also saved the American taxpayers billions in unnecessary spending.

Be persistent. Achieving goals may take time. Marshall is the embodiment of persistence; it took him more than 30 years to become a general, and not until he was nearing retirement did he become chief of staff.

Be willing to make sacrifices. You may have to put aside your ambition in order to lead. Marshall wanted to lead troops, but his skills as a manager kept him in staff roles, and as a result he was the best officer for the job of mass mobilization prior to World War II.

Be sensitive to morale. Leaders need to create conditions in which people can do their jobs. Combat is not where soldiers want to be, but Marshall insisted that they be fed, equipped, and supported adequately. He also wanted them to have some touches of home; hence the establishment of the USO shows to entertain the troops at home and abroad.

Know your limits. A leader must know where he or she can do the most good. As a general, Marshall steered clear of political strategizing, believing that a soldier had no role in it. Later, as secretary of state, he proved to be an adroit statesman.

Be seen as the leader. Let people know that you are in command. Marshall not only led the army, he helped lead Congress as it wrestled with decisions on armament for a nation preparing for and waging war.

Live your message. For more than a half-century, Marshall put service to his nation first—as a soldier and a diplomat. His integrity and his honor were forthright and are stellar examples to us all.

CHAPTER 10

> [T]he new leadership is in sacrifice, it is in self-denial, it is in love and loyalty, it is in fearlessness, it is in humility, and it is in the perfectly disciplined will. This . . . is the distinction between great and little men.
>
> *Vince Lombardi*

> As a young teacher I learned never to promise anyone instant success. Instant success does come for some gifted pupils, but for the average pupils, success is a journey of testing their intention.
>
> *Harvey Penick*

COACHING—ONE-TO-ONE LEADERSHIP COMMUNICATION

THE YOUNG CADDIE WAS A CONSTANT COMPLAINER; nothing was ever as it should be. Everyone else had it better than he did. Things always seemed to go against him. The young man's complaints were so frequent that he was known among his fellow caddies as Willie the Weeper. Things came to a breaking point when, while he was out hitting golf balls, he roke the hickory shaft of his club. Willie began wailing. Tom Penick, head caddy and Harvey's older brother, charged up to him and let him have it, then gave him two rules. First, life isn't always "fair"; second, if you want "to change your life you have to change the way you think." The words quieted Willie for the moment, but they stuck with Harvey for a lifetime.[1]

As a golf coach and club pro, Harvey came to understand that some of his players had an inordinate amount of talent, others only a moderate amount. Talent, however, was only the starting point; what was more important was attitude—how you approach practice and how long you practice translate into how well you play the game. That insight is fundamental to coaching—getting the individual to understand that his or her ultimate success or failure will begin with an attitude of how. To put it another way, coaching begins with preparation, preparing to improve one step at a time.

It was always Harvey Penick's philosophy that if a player was prepared for the little things, that player would be prepared to handle the major challenges that he or she would encounter while playing in tight games, where one decision or one movement could determine a championship. More important, Penick, like all good coaches, was a teacher, and he was preparing his players for the larger arena: life after college, after sports—in the "real world."

Preparation is one of the greatest lessons any coach can teach his or her players. Preparation is really another word for investment, and that is essentially what coaching, or teaching, is all about: It is an investment of time and care in the life of another individual that prepares that individual for the challenges that lie ahead. The challenge may be a project that needs completing, a new job that needs tackling, or the selection of a new career path. Coaching is the investment in human capital that opens the door for individual and organizational performance improvement.

Leadership communication leads to a personal connection between leader and follower. This connection can form the foundation of a coaching relationship that enables the leader to challenge the individual to achieve while providing support built upon trust.

Coaching is also a key leadership behavior. Effective leadership, after all, is an investment in the good of others for the good of the whole group. Leaders who succeed are those who incorporate the agendas of others into their own agendas. Leaders who coach are essential to the health of every organization. Good leaders are natural coaches in their own right. Some business leaders serve as cheerleaders for the achievements of their teams; they want the teams to win and succeed. Other leaders work one-on-one, or behind the scenes, to develop their people so that their people are prepared to assume ever-greater leadership responsibilities.

Like communications, good coaching is a two-way street. To be successful, coaching requires the commitment of the individual player or employee. Coaching enables individuals to fulfill their potential, to be what they are capable of becoming for themselves, their team, and their company. Organizations succeed because of the people running them. The more exciting the enterprise—be it in business, government, or social service—the more commitment it requires.

One of the maxims of coaching is that its purpose is to move people from *compliance* (going along with the flow and not making waves) to *commitment* (making a difference and creating waves if necessary). Commitment can occur, however, only if the goals of the individual and the goals of the organization are in synch. If they are, then good things can happen; if they are not, then it is up to the coach to help get them into alignment. The coach can persuade the individual that the organization needs and wants her or him, and that therefore the individual should make a commitment. For example, if a computer engineer is not demonstrating the right degree of care and attention to detail in his or her work, it is up to the team leader to point out the engineer's deficiencies and suggest improvements. Furthermore, the team leader may draw a link between individual slackness and weakness in corporate return on investment. The leader then demonstrates that the engineer's deficiencies are hurting not just the engineer, but also the entire company. In this way, coaching plays a role in both individual and corporate development.

ALIGNMENT OF PERSONAL AND CORPORATE GOALS

Coaching can be an effective means of aligning individual aspirations with organizational goals. It is the coach's responsibility to bring out the talent within the individual and to ensure that there is a good match between that talent and the organization's needs. For example, an accountant wants to work in a place where she or he can use her or his analytical skills and make a contribution to corporate objectives. The company needs good accountants to manage its finances in order to achieve its fiscal goals. In this situation, the goals of the employee and the company are aligned. Sometimes such alignment of goals may not be possible. If, for example, an employee prefers working solo rather than as a part of a team, an organization where team culture rules may not be a good fit. The coach can advise the individual that he or she might be happier working somewhere else, in a more autonomous environment. And this can be good news. A number of successful entrepreneurs have left the shelter of large organizations because they craved the independence of running their own business. And some will admit that they based their decision to leave on the advice of well-intentioned coaches.

Note: When addressing the role that coaches play in organizational alignment, I prefer to focus on organizational goals rather than organizational values. *Goal* refers to objectives—what the organization wants to achieve. You can draw a direct parallel between organizational goals and individual performance objectives—what an individual needs to achieve. *Values* refers to what an organization stands for and believes in; the same applies to individuals. And while an employee should reflect the corporate values, such as integrity, honesty, and ethics, these are central to the individual's character and typically are not what coaches focus on. I do not think you can coach a person into a value system, e.g., a dishonest person cannot be coached into honesty. It is more authentic and powerful to have a coach's behavior reflect the corporate value system. However, an individual can be coached to achieve performance objectives that are in alignment with organizational goals.[2]

Here are eight ways to begin to develop a strong coaching technique (see Figure 10-1).

ESTABLISH TRUST

Trust is at the core of every coaching relationship. To build a sense of trust, a leader-coach must communicate that he or she has the individual's best interest at heart, and that whatever he or she says or does is done with the individual's best interest in mind. Once the coach and the recipient understand each other, they can create a relationship of mutual benefit. The

FIGURE 10-1 Coaching Model

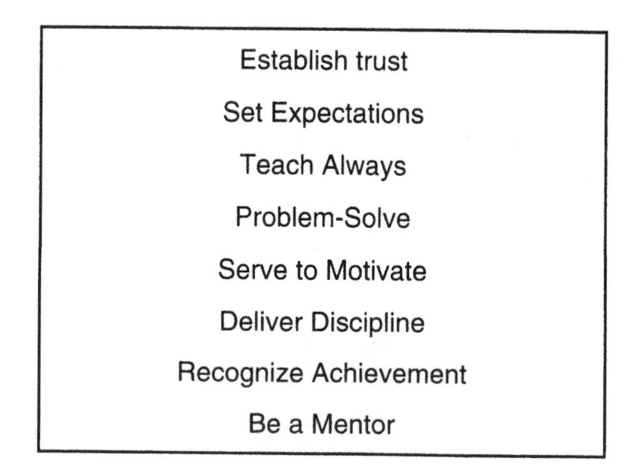

coach helps the individual achieve personal goals, and the individual helps the coach realize organizational goals. Harvey Penick, throughout his seven decades of coaching championship golfers, founded his relationships on trust; players understood that Penick wanted them to excel, and so they should listen to his counsel. At the same time, Penick did not mold players to a specific swing pattern; he worked within the physical capabilities of each player. This approach depends fundamentally upon respect for a player's talent and engenders trust.

Few things earn the respect of a team more than a coach's willingness to accept criticism in public. In sports, good coaches never publicly blame the players or their assistants for a defeat. They take the criticism. Behind closed doors, within the confines of "family," a coach will rip into players who need ripping into, just as he or she will praise those who are deserving of praise. Corporate leader-coaches can do the same. They should stand up for their people in front of senior management and do whatever is possible to provide their employees with the support and the resources they need if they are to perform. Advocating on behalf of employees is a sure way to gain employees' respect. But a coach must be skillful about this; he or she cannot alienate the management team. Coaches, too, need to maintain the trust of the bosses.

SET EXPECTATIONS

The individual needs to know what is expected of her or him, and it is up to the coach to be specific about what is needed. As an extension of the goals alignment, the leader-coach needs to make certain that the department is aligned with the organizational goals. Furthermore, the coach needs to ensure that the individuals on the team know what they are supposed to do. Many managers ask their direct reports to set their own performance objectives. This practice is a good one, but the manager owes it to both the team and the individuals to contribute to those objectives. A simple sign-off is not good enough; the manager owes the employee a conversation about it.

As part of the conversation on performance, the leader-coach must get the individual's buy-in. And it is here that the manager must be very clear and specific. Make certain that goals and objectives are in writing, and gain agreement on what the individual will do by when. Timeliness and deadlines are essential. If this is not made clear, the employee may legitimately state that he or she will do it when he or she gets around to it. The deadlines add a sense of urgency and lead naturally to the manager's following up and following through. In the wake of the Super Bowl, Tom Brady, as quarterback of his team, set expectations for himself that he wanted to repeat, and as team leader he thereby established expectations for everyone. Brady backed those expectations with a commitment to off-season training.

TEACH ALWAYS

Teaching is fundamental to coaching; providing information and ensuring that learning occurs is what coaches do. Vince Lombardi, who began his career in coaching as a high school teacher of math and sciences, was first and foremost a teacher. With a piece of chalk and a blackboard, he could talk for hours to players or to fellow coaches at clinics about the Xs and Os of football. Dressed in a sweatshirt and a baseball cap and with a whistle around his neck, Lombardi was the archetypal image of a football coach of his era. Coaching instruction can take many forms. It may be explicit: Pointers on how to operate a piece of machinery, or tips on how to structure a report. Or the instruction may be implicit, such as a parable or a story that the coach relates. What is important is that the coach relates the instruction in ways that the individual can accept and understand.

For this reason, coaches must be active listeners, attentive to communication clues. Blank stares or bored looks indicate that the lesson has no meaning. Conversely, head nods and questions mean that the lesson may be getting through. The coach must work to find methods to engage the employee's interest and hold it so that learning does occur.

It is no coincidence that many coaches are good storytellers. Stories offer the opportunity to impart important life lessons in a manner that is accessible and even enjoyable rather than condescending and preachy. For this reason, coaches keep a personal inventory of stories intended to evoke the appropriate emotion for the situation—admiration, inspiration, tears, or laughter. Importantly, all of these stories contain a pithy message wrapped neatly inside. (See Chapter 12, "Leader as Storyteller.")

PROBLEM-SOLVE

Coaches must possess a sixth sense about individual performance as well as team performance. In basketball, when one team begins a scoring run, the opposing coach will often call a time-out. He will pull the team together (*physically and mentally*) to focus its energies on the task at hand. He will point out both what the team is doing wrong and what it is capable of doing. Great coaches can turn around team performance in a matter of minutes. In business, good coaches have similar abilities. They can rally a team around a goal and provide direction. When the team encounters an obstacle, the coach finds ways to overcome or avoid the problem. Specifically, good coaches go around to each team member and ask what type of help that team member needs: time, resources, or staff. Coaches then affirm the individual's value to the project and provide ongoing encouragement. Jack Welch, a Ph.D. chemist turned manager, learned early that a successful career in management depended upon an ability to solve problems. He continued to preach that throughout his career.

Similarly, if there are personality conflicts, it is up to the coach to intervene. Often the coach cannot impose a solution, other than forced separation, but he or she can try to get to the root of the problem and discover ways for the individuals who are at loggerheads to work together. Ideally, a solution will come from the two parties themselves, but it will be the coach who brings them together and gets them talking.

And keep in mind that coaches do not wait for problems to occur. As leaders who exemplify the "management by walking around" philosophy, they have their antennae tuned to the rhythm of the team. They are responsible not simply for maintaining morale, but for invigorating it. When coaches sense that something is amiss, they seek out the cause immediately. Likewise, when a crisis occurs, they do not hesitate to intervene. Good coaches drop everything and move to solve the problem immediately. Quick action has three benefits: It can provide immediate relief and ameliorate the situation, it can prevent a small problem from growing larger, and it demonstrates to the organization that the coach has people's best interests at heart.

SERVE TO MOTIVATE

Good coaches are known as masters of motivation; they prod their teams to win. Motivation, of course, cannot be imposed upon an individual; it stems from the person's inner drive to achieve. What coaches can do is establish an environment in which individuals can thrive. They can, as mentioned earlier, provide alignment between the goals of the individual and the goals of the organization. At the same time, good motivators need to know when to push and when to hold back. Some individuals need someone prodding them all the time; others prefer a laid-back, hands-off approach. It is the coach who designs a system, or an approach, that is tailored to bring out the best in the individual for the good of everyone. Part of that system includes a healthy dose of recognition for a job well done. Joe Torre of the Yankees is a coach who knows how to do all three—prod the player who may be slacking, encourage the player who is struggling, and frequently recognize everyone who is doing a good job.

DELIVER DISCIPLINE

Not everyone responds to advice. Metaphorically speaking, sometimes the stick *can* be more effective than the carrot. Discipline connotes compliance with the rules, be they rules of quality control or rules of conduct. Delivering discipline, therefore, is another form of maintaining standards and ensuring that behavior has consequences. We see this often in the world of sports. A coach will bench a star player because the player is not practicing hard enough, or because the player is not demonstrating commitment to the team. In the workplace, a leader-coach can call aside an employee who is not pulling his or her weight, e.g., not sharing information with other employees, showing up late for meetings, or regularly leaving work early. The coach can warn the employee that if the deficient behavior does not improve, the employee will suffer the consequences: restriction of perks, forfeit of bonus pay, or the loss of a promotion.

Discipline will be effective, however, only when it is backed by trust. Every coach must focus on behavior (what the person does) rather than personality (what the person is) and must communicate that any punishment is due to deficient behavior. Vince Lombardi was famous for having a star player or two whom he could publicly excoriate. Sometimes this was deserved; other times it was an act to get the team's attention. Lombardi did not want to play favorites, and when he purposely went after a star player, everyone else would fall into line.

Discipline need not always connote punishment. Discipline can take the form of adhering to a value system, even in the face of adversity. Coaches teach discipline not so much by their words as by their example. When employees see a coach making a tough decision, particularly one that involves personal inconvenience, they learn to respect that coach. Effective discipline ultimately leads to self-discipline, with employees taking responsibility for themselves and their actions. When this occurs, the coach has done the job.

RECOGNIZE ACHIEVEMENT

The flip side of discipline is recognition. Individuals who do a good job need to be recognized. Recognition accomplishes several things: It lets the person know that she or he is doing a good job, it helps raise the person's confidence and encourages him or her to continue achieving, and it lets others know that the individual is doing a good job and is appreciated. Rudy Giuliani recognizes the contributions of his people by mentioning their names in his writings and his public statements. Shelly Lazarus at Ogilvy & Mather fosters a culture in which individual contributions matter; she calls her agency a "meritocracy."[3] Mother Teresa believed that recognition for service has its own rewards, the sense of serving God by serving the people who are most in need.

It is important to separate the concepts of recognition and reward. Recognition is the acknowledgement that someone has done a good job; reward is the benefit associated with the recognition. In other words, employees are recognized for a good job and rewarded with a gift or bonus. Many companies practice pay for performance, awarding bonuses for the achievement of goals. While people may debate the benefits of this system, in such a system it falls to the manager, who sometimes also functions as coach, to evaluate an individual's eligibility for bonus. This practice clouds the development role of coaching because it equates development with compensation. The two are independent of each other. Compensation is linked to job performance; development is linked to individual growth and improvement. Good coaches, therefore, must learn to separate their role as arbiters of compensation from their role as developer of talent—not an easy task.

BE A MENTOR

What is a mentor? A friend, colleague, and adviser, all rolled into one. A mentor is a friend in the sense that he or she has the person's best interests at heart. A mentor is a colleague who is not afraid or unwilling to dispense advice that the individual may not want to hear, but needs to hear. A mentor is an adviser who looks toward the future, who dispenses wisdom that is directed toward the current but mostly the future needs of the individual. Yiddish has a wonderful word for mentor, *mensch*, a person who can be counted on to be a good friend and to be of assistance in times of need. That's not a bad summary of mentorship.

People have a desire for guidance. Just as children are taught life values by their parents, employees are taught workplace values by their "superiors" (*managers, old-timers, retirees*). Counsel is a form of advice. The good coach aligns advice within a value system. For example, a coach may advise an employee to show up on time as a means of demonstrating a commitment to fellow employees. Timeliness is a lifestyle value that extends far beyond the work environment. Likewise, the coach may advise an employee to listen more attentively when a colleague speaks. Again, a good life lesson.

Very importantly, coaches give counsel through example. The old adage "Do as I say, not as I do" cannot apply to coaches. A coach who advises an employee to listen, but always talks over other people, undermines her or his own advice. Leader-coaches do not have the luxury of slacking off when it comes to advice giving.

Mentoring, by the way, can be a temporary or a long-term commitment. General George C. Marshall was a mentor to many up-and-coming officers. He kept their names in his famous "black book," and when the time came for a new generation of leaders to rise to the challenge, as happened at the outset of World War II, Marshall knew whom to promote. Many people come back to their mentors for ongoing advice at various stages of their lives. Others seek a mentor for a given assignment. Mentorships, by the way, are gaining in popularity within the corporate arena for two reasons: First, young employees need guidance, particularly when it comes to navigating the sometimes-treacherous waterways of corporate channels, and second, mentors need experience in giving advice as a form of teaching. By being mentors, they learn more about themselves and their potential for greater leadership positions. Mentorship does have mutual rewards.

ACTION COACHING MODEL

Coaching should be an integral part of a leader's job. It is not something that should be undertaken lightly. It requires preparation, critical thinking, and follow-through (see Figure 10-2). Leaders also need something more—a healthy dose of emotional intelligence, e.g., the ability to understand someone else and your relationship to that individual.

- *Plan ahead.* Identify the individual you wish to coach. Schedule a time to meet. Allow at least 30 minutes, and preferably 1 hour. Look at the work the individual has been doing. Ask coworkers about the individual. Look for problem areas. Keep in mind that you are looking for areas of weakness, not to punish the individual for them, but rather to strengthen her or him. That's what coaching is all about.
- *Uncover the motivational tick factor.* Think about what motivates this individual. Is it an opportunity to be promoted? Is it more money? Is it the quest for a better life for her- or himself and her or his family? Does this individual value time off in lieu of overtime pay? Discovering the motivational tick factor opens the door for understanding.
- *Give feedback.* Open with small talk. If you know the individual well, you will know his or her likes and dislikes. Some of us like to talk

FIGURE 10-2 Action Coaching Model

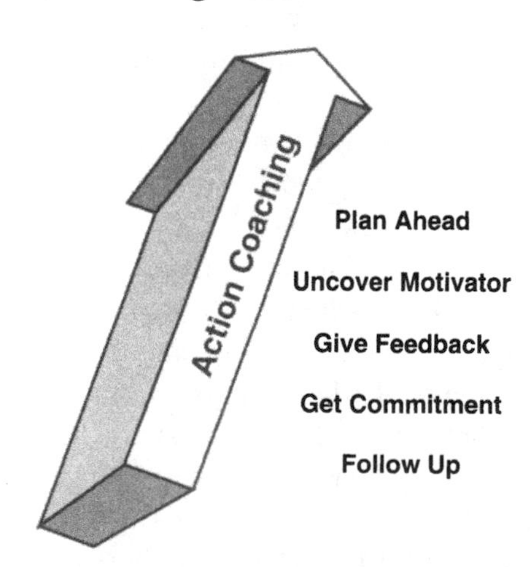

about our families; others prefer not to. Some of us like sports, cooking, camping, biking, you name it; others could care less about any or all of these.

As the coach, you need to identify an individual strength—something that the person is doing very well. Say something positive about the person's performance. Then move to the areas of weakness, things that the individual could be doing better. Call them "opportunities for improvement." First find out what the individual thinks about the situation.

Ask if there is anything holding the individual back or preventing her or him from doing the job. These obstacles could be a lack of resources, not enough time, or another individual—even the leader. Typically such problems not only are harmful to the individual but may be harming the entire team. Emphasize your willingness to help. Ask the individual if he or she has any suggestions for improvement.

- *Get commitment.* Identify solutions to the problems. Ask the individual to commit to improvement. Gain agreement. Establish a time frame for resolving the problem. Again, gain agreement. Close the session on a positive note. Thank the individual for his or her contributions. Ask for feedback on your coaching style. Was it helpful? How could you have made it better? (If you are open and forthcoming, you will get honest feedback. It may take a few sessions for the individual to open up, but in time she or he will—if you have established the proper boundaries of trust.)
- *Follow up.* Check on the individual periodically. Feedback during the workweek is perfectly acceptable. Do not ride the person. Just be available. When the agreed-upon deadline is reached, check on the status of the situation. If the problem has been resolved, recognize the individual for meeting the commitment that he or she made. If the problem has not been resolved, ask why. You may need to schedule another coaching session, or at least keep a close watch on the situation.

As the leader, you want to be able to resolve any issues, but you also want to enable individuals to solve as many of the difficulties as possible for themselves. Too much intervention indicates that you are doing too much, to the detriment of others on the team. This also thwarts the growth of the individual. Too little intervention leaves the individual to sink or swim. Sometimes that is appropriate; other times it is not. When you follow up, make certain that you ask for feedback on your coaching style. Again ask how you can improve.

CONTINUOUS COACHING

As mentioned, coaching is integral to leadership. While coaching sessions need to be planned in advance, informal coaching can occur at any time or at any place. Often this is nothing more than giving feedback, positive or negative. Keep to the rule of opening with a positive and ending with a commitment to improvement.

One more point: We have emphasized coaching as a leadership behavior, assuming a leader-to-subordinate direction. Peer coaching is equally valuable. And so is "upward coaching"—e.g., coaching your boss. Follow the same process outlined in the action coaching model. The outcome will be increased trust and improved performance. And whenever you can bring that out in another person, it's a leadership action.

COACH AS LEADER

Coaching and leadership go hand in hand. From creating trust through discipline, reward, and mentorship, coaching behaviors exemplify leadership behaviors; in fact, they *are* leadership behaviors. All coaching behaviors are centered around strong organizational goals and work together to reinforce the coach-individual relationship. In doing so, they create a situation in which the individual as well as the team can thrive.

Fundamentally, coaches, like leaders, are teachers. They teach by their words as well as lead by their actions. Harvey Penick and Vince Lombardi draw life lessons from the task at hand. Through coaching, the individual acquires job skills, but more important, she or he also gains knowledge about life itself. It is the life lesson that matters most in a person's development. It is an investment in the person's future to which leader-coaches must continually strive to contribute.

Communications Planner: Coaching One-to-One

Communications is essential to effective coaching. It is essential that all good leaders coach their people. The suggestions provided here will help you use your communications skills to improve coaching.

1. *Establish trust.* Before you begin coaching, ask the following questions:
   - What do you like about this job?
   - What do you dislike about this job?
   - What do you see yourself doing in 6 months?
   - Where would you like to be in 5 years?
   - How can I help you to achieve your goals?

2. *Set expectations.* Align the individual's performance with the team or department's performance.
    - Relate team or departmental goals and objectives.
    - Link the individual's performance to those goals.
    - Gain agreement on performance
    - Commit to deadlines.
3. *Teach always.* Find out the individual's professional interests.
    - What do you want to learn more about?
    - What can I teach you about our business?
4. *Problem-solve.* Uncover problems that may be hindering the person's performance.
    - Is there anyone (or anything) standing in the way of your achieving your objectives? Explain.
    - What do you need in the way of assistance from me to solve your problem?
5. *Serve to motivate.* Create condition in which the individual can motivate him- or herself.
    - Demonstrate how the individual's performance contributes to the whole organization.
    - Provide incentives for achievement: first choice on projects, opportunity for promotion, opportunity for bonus, etc.
6. *Deliver discipline.* Follow through on the consequences of deficiencies in performance.
    - Discover why performance is deficient.
    - Impose the discipline. Follow through on corrective measures.
    - Gain agreement on improved performance. Insist on a deadline.
7. *Recognize achievement.* Find ways to acknowledge good performance.
    - Deliver on promises by providing agreed-upon rewards: choice of projects, promotion, bonuses, etc.
    - Acknowledge performance to higher-ups and peers.
8. *Be a mentor.* Be available to provide assistance over time.
    - How are you doing at work?
    - Do you have any frustrations that I should know about?
    - What can I do to help to achieve your long-term goals?

- Whom would it be useful for you to know? Facilitate the introductions and follow up on the outcomes.

Action Coaching Model

Choose an individual whom you need to coach. (If you don't have someone in particular, ask someone to coach you.)

1. *Plan ahead.* Make a commitment to coach.
   - What do you want to say to the individual? Make notes on performance and suggestions for improvement.
2. *Uncover the motivational tick factor.* Discover the "why" of work.
   - Think about what excites this person—money, power, family, friends, hobbies. How can you respond to those needs in a way that leads to improved performance?
3. *Give feedback.* Let the individual know how he or she is doing.
   - Find one positive thing to say. Isolate the deficiencies. Ask the individual, "Have you considered doing this?"
4. *Get commitment.* Gain agreement and establish a time frame.
   - Make certain you gain closure: What will be done, and by when will it be done?
5. *Follow up.* Make certain you evaluate the outcome.
   - Look for opportunities to give feedback. Be vigilant for signs of improvement. When you see them, give praise. If the deadline passes with no improvement, schedule another coaching session.

VINCE LOMBARDI—THE TEACHER AS COACH

There are times in a leader's life when that leader is defined by what he or she does or does not do in a particular moment. Looking back at successful leaders, we sometimes assume that they were always good, always made the right decision, or always said the right thing. One such moment came for Vince Lombardi when he became the head coach of the Green Bay Packers. Today the success of the Lombardi Packers is legend, and so we have to peer into the history books to recall what a woeful team they were when Lombardi became their coach in 1959—the year before, they had won only a single game.[4]

THE LONG CLIMB

For Lombardi, coming to the Packers was the culmination of a long climb from Fordham University, where he had been a lineman, one of the seven blocks of granite, on a winning football team. After considering the priesthood, Lombardi eventually started his coaching career modestly—as the head coach of St. Cecilia's *basketball* team. He felt that he "wanted to be a teacher more than a coach." And teach he did: "physics, chemistry and Latin," all rigorous subjects. He was also the assistant football coach. (His basketball team posted a winning record in Lombardi's first year.)[5]

After eight years at St. Cecilia's, where he eventually became head football coach, and a successful one at that, he moved to the collegiate ranks at Fordham and later to Army as an assistant to the legendary Red Blaik. He then became an assistant coach for the New York Giants and finally, 5 long years later, moved to the Packers. While the job might not have been a prize to other coaches, it was heaven to Lombardi, and so it was with great excitement, mixed with apprehension, that he introduced himself to the team at summer camp.

QUINTESSENTIAL LOMBARDI

According to his biographer, David Maraniss, Lombardi had rehearsed over and over again what he would say to his new team. He began with the practical—taking care of the playbook and always being on time. He would keep practices short, no more than 90 minutes twice a day, as Red Blaik had done. There would be a difference, however: The practices would be tightly planned, and the players would know what they were "supposed to be doing every minute." As a result, Lombardi wanted his players on the field and ready to go at exactly the appointed hour—"prepared" and ready to learn.[6]

Then he launched into what has become known as the quintessential Lombardi lesson, which has sometimes been lost in the legend of the fiery coach's rhetoric. He spoke of how he—the coach—would "be relentless" in pushing them to try, try, and eventually succeed. His expectation for them was that they would keep in shape. He by example would do the rest—the pushing, the prodding, the yelling, and, of course, the teaching. When Lombardi finished, the room was silent until Lombardi dismissed them. Moments later, the coach pulled aside one of the players and asked how he had done. Max McGhee, the All-Pro veteran, responded, "Well, I'll tell ya, you got their attention, Coach."[7]

What Lombardi had done was put the onus of winning upon himself. He took the pressure off them as players and carried it on his own shoulders. Of course, the players would have to work hard and abide by the rules, but Lombardi would take care of the rest. He would challenge each player privately to elevate his own expectations of himself, and the entire team collectively would benefit. Sly fox that Lombardi was, he pushed and pushed, but with the tacit approval of the players, who believed in themselves enough to feel that they could succeed.

TEACHING THE SWEEP

Lombardi was first and foremost a great teacher. His greatest football lesson was the powerful motion to the strong side of the field, right into the teeth of the opposition. It became known as the Green Bay Sweep, and from this formation Lombardi devised a number of running and passing variations that would keep the other team off balance and his team in control. It was important, Lombardi said, for a team to have one play that the players felt they could run and run well; it would become, in our parlance, the "go to" play—one that would do more than gain yardage, it would instill confidence and rally the team.[8]

THE LEGEND SPEAKS

In their first year under Lombardi, the Packers finished third and Lombardi was named coach of the year.[9] In his second year, 1960, the team captured the league championship, and in his third year, 1961, the Packers took the NFL title—the first of five titles. The team capped its final two seasons under Lombardi with wins in Super Bowls I and II, games that in those days were little more than afterthoughts because it was believed that the AFL, the upstart rival conference, was not up to NFL standards. (Super Bowl III would change that perception when Joe Namath led the New York Jets to a win over the Baltimore Colts.)

Winning brought fame to Lombardi and, not surprisingly, offers to join the lecture circuit. Lombardi crafted a speech built on "seven themes."[10] All of these themes are relevant to who Lombardi is as a person; three of them tell us about him as a leader.

- *Discipline.* Speaking during the tumult of the sixties, Lombardi did not really understand the divisiveness that those times provoked. While he could be faulted for not listening to what young people at the time were rebelling against—war, conventionalism, and materialism—his words on the need for discipline are timeless. People, according to Lombardi, want to be led and will respond to and appreciate a leader who instills discipline.[11]
- *Leadership.* Educated formally by the Jesuits at Fordham and informally by Red Blaik at West Point, Lombardi had seen leadership close-up. In fact, while he was at West Point, he got to know General Douglas MacArthur when he gave MacArthur private screenings of

Army football games.[12] Lombardi said, "Leaders are made, not born. They are made by hard effort, which is the price all of us must pay to achieve any goal that is worthwhile." Leaders need to balance "mental toughness and love." Toughness emerges from discipline; love emanates from loyalty and teamwork.[13]

- *Character and will.* Leadership is built upon character and will. The Jesuits taught Lombardi that character and will are linked forever in a virtuous cycle—character "superimposed on" will, and will "as character in action."[14] Lombardi concluded:

> The character . . . is man's greatest need and man's greatest safeguard, because character is higher than intellect. . . . [T]he new leadership is in sacrifice, it is in self-denial, it is in love and loyalty, it is in fearlessness, it is in humility, and it is in the perfectly disciplined will.[15]

RELEVANT LEGEND

The question arises as to whether Lombardi has any relevance in today's world. The answer is, of course![16] His strength of character and his determined spirit are timeless, but for those of us looking at leadership communications, in his ability to teach and to coach (and with Lombardi they blend together), his example stands the test of time.

Leadership Communications Lessons

Teach, teach, teach. Teach people what they need to know. Lombardi was a superb teacher not only of football but of life itself.

Coach your people. Understand what makes people tick, and find ways to stimulate that inner desire. Lombardi knew how to motivate his players because he understood them as men.

Be firm in your convictions. Set expectations. Lombardi was clear about what he wanted his players to do. He was firm and cut little slack.

Show some humanity. Reveal the inner you. While he was famous for his fiery oratory and brusqueness, Lombardi was really a softie, a man who was not afraid to cry in public and who truly would do anything for players he loved.

Be seen as the leader. Be seen as the one in charge. On the field and off it, there was no mistaking that Lombardi was the leader, and his players rallied to him.

Live your message. Lombardi's ability to inspire comes not simply from words but from his ability to challenge his players to do their individual best and to challenge the team to do its collective best.

HARVEY PENICK—LESSONS FROM A PRO

When you think of leadership communications, chances are you don't think of golf. After all, golf, even in its competitive form, is chiefly a solitary game—one course, one player. Communications are chiefly internal; players and caddies are allowed to converse, and players of course speak to one another, but the game itself revolves around finding the shortest and best way to put the ball into the hole using nothing more than variously fashioned clubs, all derived from an ancient game that Scottish shepherds once played.

Well, there is an exception—the communication that occurs between a player and his or her coach. Plenty is said during coaching sessions, and in fact you can make the case that the lessons imparted on the golf range or in the clubhouse must be the most enduring, since player and coach are not allowed to converse during a match. The player must rely on lessons reiterated, reinforced, and remembered. One master of such teaching is Harvey Penick, a golf teacher for more than 70 years and a best-selling author as an octogenarian and even nonagenarian. His lessons were simple, straightforward, and down to earth. In his own unique way, Penick was a leader who was able to communicate with a directness that was as effective as it was heartfelt.

GETTING THE WORD OUT

Harvey Penick was a coach at the University of Texas as well as being club pro at the Austin Country Club in Texas. Along the way, he nurtured the careers of many a great player: Tom Kite, Ben Crenshaw, Mickey Wright, and many others. He himself had played collegiate golf and had flirted with the professional game. But watching (and hearing) Sam Snead shape his shots so purely and accurately made Penick realize that if he were to remain in golf, his place was in shaping the talents of others.[17] Along the way, Penick kept notes on what he told his players, and over the years the range and volume of his notes grew. It was his son, Tinsley, also a club pro, who urged him to publish.[18]

And what happened next tells you all you need to know about Harvey Penick. Bud Shrake, a respected sportswriter and novelist with a pedigree that included *Sports Illustrated*, teamed with Penick to do a book. The story goes that Shrake informed Penick that "his share" from the book deal would be $85,000. Harvey was aghast: "Bud, I don't think I can raise that kind of money."[19] What this story says about Penick is this: He was humble (a publisher wants to *pay* me!), and he was a teacher (he wanted to share the lessons he had learned himself and imparted to his pupils over a long lifetime of teaching a game he loved). The first tome, *Harvey Penick's Little Red Book,* became one of the best-selling sports books of all time and led to a series of subsequent books, television appearances, a video, and eventual worldwide recognition.

LESSONS FROM THE GAME

Simplicity is something Penick strove for always. Golf is a game of feel: *Feel* the grip, *feel* the club head, *feel* the swing. Most students respond to the simplicity, but Penick recalls the example of the woman who became flustered because he would not add more technical advice. But that was not his style.[20] "Playing golf you learn a form of meditation . . . you learn to focus on the game and clean your mind of worrisome thoughts."[21]

Penick was earnest about his teaching and prayed before beginning one of his teaching clinics; his reason was that "few professions have as much influence on people as the golf pro," and so he wanted the help of the Almighty in this endeavor.[22] At the same time, Penick was perpetually humble about his role in the game, referring to himself as a "grown caddie still studying golf."[23] About his own teaching style, Penick uses the tools of all successful teachers—"images, parables and metaphors."[24] In this way, he could make his pupils see both physically and metaphysically how they could improve their game.

TRIBUTE TO TEACHER

Penick's students who have gone on to excel in the professional game are themselves legends. Tom Kite and Ben Crenshaw were two of his favorites. Kite won the 1992 U.S. Open and gave his trophy to his tutor to hold.[25] And most movingly, Ben Crenshaw won the 1996 Masters shortly after Penick died. "I could definitely feel him with me. I had a fifteenth club in the bag. The fifteenth club was Harvey."[26]

Shortly before the 1995 Ryder Cup matches between the best American and best European golfers, Penick's son, Tinsley, summed up his father's life in a kind of elegy delivered to the players on the eve of the match. Some of the players knew Penick personally; all of them knew him in some way, if only through the lessons imparted in his books. In his talk, Tinsley spoke of his father's commitment to differences: Each player has his own unique style, and he would not try to change it. And he mentioned Harvey's sense of professionalism, never speaking ill of fellow pros.[27]

KEEP ON LEARNING

Tinsley also revealed what might be the secret of Harvey's coaching—he never stopped learning. As a coach at the University of Texas, Harvey made it a point to find out "the methods and teaching techniques" of the person who had taught the player. "My dad gained a lot of knowledge from these experiences."[28] And somehow it is fitting that a man who seemingly devoted himself to a game was in reality devoting himself to helping generations of men and women, young and old, find a better way to play the ultimate game—life itself.

Leadership Communications Lessons

Teach, teach, teach. We all need someone to show us how. Penick showed how the mechanics of an age-old game, coupled with its traditions, make for a pretty good life.

Coach your people. Find what out how the individual learns. When you discover this factor, you can coach the person to success.

Uphold honor. You can cheat in life, as you can cheat in golf. Upholding the honor system is righteous.

Be courteous. Rudeness has no place in life. Penick taught his players to be courteous to everyone. Courtesy will repay itself many times over.

Show some humility. Life is a humbling experience, as is golf. Penick preached graciousness toward opponents in moments of victory as well as acknowledgement when someone beats you.

Live your message. Consistency in thought, word, and action reinforces the coach's methods. Harvey Penick's life was a model of following through on messages he taught to others.

CHAPTER 11

> Change requires even more communication than routine activities. Top leaders need to know what's happening in the field. . . . Local units need role models to learn from the experience of their peers. . . . Change can be chaotic without a way to communicate what's happening everywhere.
>
> *Rosabeth Moss Kanter*

MAKING CERTAIN THE MESSAGE STICKS

EVERY DAY PEOPLE THROUGHOUT THE WORLD communicate with one another. These communications occur in ballrooms, boardrooms, back rooms, and even backyards.

Consider a parent who has a long talk with a teenage child about the dangers of smoking. The teen listens attentively and asks questions. Parent and child begin a dialogue with a free exchange of opinions. The teen even agrees with the parent that smoking is bad for you. Two days later the kid comes home reeking of stale cigarette smoke. What the heck happened?

You were clear in your explanation. You described the dangers of smoking and its consequences. You answered the kid's questions. What the heck did you do wrong?

As a presenter, you did fine. As a parent, you failed to gain agreement and discuss the consequences of failure. The relationship between parent and child is not the same as that between presenter and audience, but there is a parallel. As the presenter, you are the expert, "the parent of the information." The audience receives your message; it is "the child of the information." Unless some kind of transformation, or change, occurs, the message will go in one ear and out the other. You as the parent need to give the audience something to remember and something upon which to act. In short, you need to lead.

As the parent, you need to gain the child's agreement to stop smoking and list the consequences of failure to do so. As a leader, you need to gain agreement from your audience and imply the consequences, good and bad, that can occur when the people in the audience follow your message.

Successful leaders are those who take information and give it meaning, or knowledge, that others can use. *When this occurs, the message sticks* (see Figure 11-1). Whether it is Jack Welch at G.E., Colin Powell and George C. Marshall with the Army, or Vince Lombardi with his teams, a leader makes sure that people understand what the leader is saying and, better yet, understand what they need to do with the information once they have it. Ensuring the viability of a message begins with an understanding of what the leader said.

FIGURE 11-1 Making Certain the Message Sticks

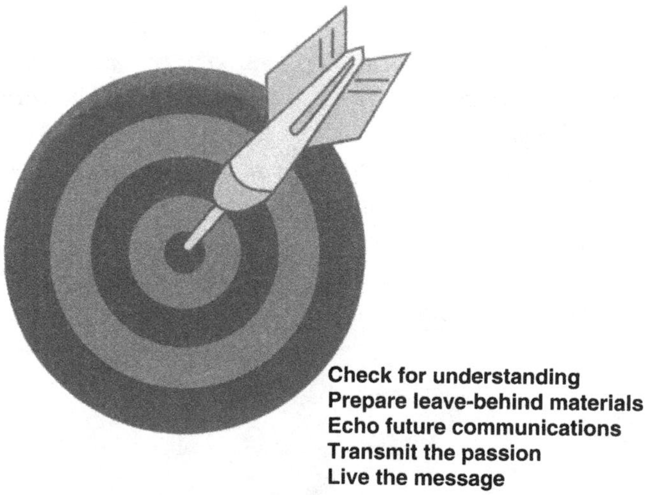

Check for understanding
Prepare leave-behind materials
Echo future communications
Transmit the passion
Live the message

CHECK FOR UNDERSTANDING

The focus of this book has been on the active process of communicating—speaking, writing, delivering, and planning. However, while it is true that communications is an active process, it is also true that much of communications involves the leader's pausing to check for understanding. Leadership communications is a two-way process, and leaders must *listen* to what their people are saying. It is not enough to deliver the message; it is also important to determine how people are receiving it. Furthermore, communications involves retaining the message, with the implication that something is done with the information received.

Two groups that have had some success in demonstrating how leaders can be more attentive are the military and the medical community. The U.S. Army has a tradition of the brief-back, asking a subordinate to put in his or her own words what the commander has just said. This is a simple method that has enormous implications. Asking the soldier to put the orders into his or her own words accomplishes two things: One, it confirms the soldier's understanding of the original order, and two, it affirms what the soldier will do as a result of the order, specifically *how* he or she will execute the order. The brief-back can work in situations large and small. For example, a master sergeant who is responsible for maintenance on an Apache helicopter can give the orders of the day regarding what the crew is to do in the way of maintaining and repairing the chopper. To ensure that everyone understands, the master sergeant may ask one or two of the crew members to repeat what was said. Likewise, during a live-fire training exercise, a junior officer may be asked by the colonel to interpret the orders and say what the platoon will do. In both instances, the communications are critical; mistakes in helicopter maintenance or a live-fire exercise can be fatal. Both situations require absolute clarity, and it is up to the leaders, those giving the orders, to ensure that everyone understands her or his role.

Physicians, likewise, check their patient's understanding when they do a patient history or begin a diagnosis. They ask questions of the patient to make certain they understand what the patient is experiencing, e.g., pain when, where, and for how long? Likewise, after they have made a diagnosis and prescribed either a therapy or a pharmaceutical or both, doctors explain the implications and lay out the course of action. Once upon a time doctors skimped on the explanation of the therapy because their options may have been limited and the nurse would always fill in the details. Today many physicians adopt a consultative approach, not only involving the patient in the decision making about available therapies, but also answering the patient's questions. They also ensure that they or their nurses can follow up on the details when questions arise.

Both of these situations are classic examples of checking for understanding. Leaders need to adopt similar approaches. Here are some suggestions.

- *Implement the "brief-back."* Much of communications involves asking people whether they understood what was said. Rather than settling for a noncommittal head nod, ask people to tell you what you have told them and what they will do as a result. This is a technique that Colin Powell made use of throughout his army career. For example, if you give a briefing on reducing absenteeism, ask your hearers for a synopsis of your message and what they will do in response to it. As with coaching, insist on specifics and timelines. Gain agreement and follow up on the specifics. By asking for the interpretation of the message, you ensure understanding. And if you don't hear what you want to hear, repeat your message and clarify it until the person understands. Ensuring understanding is a leadership responsibility.
- *Designate an information source.* Leaders need to deliver the message and keep reiterating it. They also should be available for follow-up questions. However, while communications is a paramount responsibility, leaders do not need to be available 24/7. They can, and should, designate a go-to source for follow-up information. Not only does this free up the leader's time, but it also distributes ownership of the communications process. Other people become involved and add their knowledge and experience. This makes for a much more robust communications process, one that is not dependent upon a single individual, but rather utilizes a cadre of well-informed individuals.
- *Delegate responsibility.* Ownership of the communications process needs to involve a delegation of responsibility to an individual or a team. The leader needs to give that individual or team the authority to solve problems that may arise from communications. No longer does the individual or team need to come back to the leader for permission on every decision; people can make decisions for themselves. When responsibility is intertwined with communications, the entire organization benefits by being both better informed and better able to deal with its own issues. As an army man, General Marshall always insisted on his officers taking responsibility. He insisted that his generals make decisions and live by them.
- *Invent communication loops.* Too much of organizational communications is restricted to functional channels: The boss sends out a memo or transmits an email. Often it is confined to a single medium, such as a video or a brochure. These are fine and serve a purpose, but leaders need to be flexible. Sometimes it is appropriate to go outside the

channels, to talk to people at different levels, in different functions, or even outside of the company. At the same time, most communications is one-on-one. Talk to people. Be willing to create communications that people want. For example, if you are looking for suggestions, create an email box. If you are looking for creativity, stage a pizza party. Invite people to come; the price of admission is a suggestion or a new idea. On the other hand, if there is a breakdown in communications, look for ways to get individuals or teams together. Maybe the best way is a meeting, or maybe it's a coffee outside of the office. Be willing to experiment. There is no single right way to facilitate good communications; the only limit is the power of the leader's imagination. And if that is lacking, ask people to find ways to encourage communication among themselves. This is often the best way to get people to work together.

- *Stay in the loop.* Communications is not a "cut and run" action step. It's an ongoing, circular process that is renewed and regenerated by the creation, cycling, and recycling of key leadership messages. Leaders need to stay engaged in the process, something that Winston Churchill did in his War Cabinet and Rudy Giuliani did with his city administrators. This means asking people what is going on and following up on the progress of a message. Do people understand what needs to be done? Do they understand their responsibilities? Have I communicated clearly and frequently? Communications by a leader is a discipline. The more engaged the leader becomes in the communications process, the greater the opportunity to increase levels of trust and achieve results.

LISTEN. LISTEN. LISTEN.

Depending upon the situation, one, two, or all of these methods may be applicable. The most important check of all, however, lies with the leader. The leader must be willing to listen. And listening can be difficult, especially when the leader has heard the complaint or situation before. In addition, many leaders are busy; they have a million things on their to-do list. Listening to others is rarely an action item. But in the long run, it may be the most important action step of all.

There are additional things that leaders can do to ensure that their message echoes beyond their physical presence.

PREPARE LEAVE-BEHIND MATERIALS

Mother Teresa collected some of her thinking into books of prayers. Colin Powell and Rudy Giuliani wrote books reflecting their leadership values.

Harvey Penick collected his thoughts in a series of small books. Rosabeth Moss Kanter is a prolific author on the impact of change on management and culture. In their writings, as well as their television or video appearances, these leaders are extending their message, increasing the likelihood of its being understood.

Your presentation is composed of words and possibly images. Most important, it contains you. Your challenge is to leave a little bit of yourself behind as a means of furthering your message. Make a copy of your presentation and offer it to the audience. Or, if that is not possible, post your presentation on a web site so that others who did not hear it can access it.

ECHO THE MESSAGE IN FUTURE COMMUNICATIONS

Keep the lines of communication open. You have spent a good deal of time preparing for your presentation. You should get something in return for your investment. Position yourself as an expert and strive to reappear periodically. This is a good tactic for sales presenters, but it is also useful for anyone who believes in what she or he does and wants to communicate a point of view. Shelly Lazarus has positioned herself as an eloquent spokesperson for the advertising industry as well as for the role of women in senior management. She speaks frequently to the media and to public audiences about her views, and as a result she has established herself as a credible source. In addition, she serves as a positive role model for the people in her organization as someone who lives by the values she espouses.

TRANSMIT THE PASSION

Be passionate about your communications. Watching Oprah Winfrey, you get the sense that she cares very deeply about what she does. As a communicator on television and in her publication, Oprah finds lessons that she believes will help viewers and readers live more satisfied lives. Jack Welch was passionate about his companies, and in particular about the people in them. Passion is evident in the prose of Peter Drucker, who has been preaching insights into management for more than seven decades.

People need to see that you care about what you are doing and what you are communicating. You communicate passion through both the intensity of your delivery and the consistency of your effort. When people see you delivering a message over and over again, and doing it convincingly, they will get the idea that what you are saying is important and they'd better pay attention.

IS THE MESSAGE STICKING?

How do you know when the message is getting through? It's getting through when the intent of the message is fulfilled! Sometimes it's pretty simple to tell this. For example, if you are the leader of a customer service department and your call to action specifies that people answer the phone by the second ring, you know that the message is getting through if people do this. If you are involved with an organizational transformation that involves behavioral change, that change will come slowly, possibly taking years.

As with all calls to action, however, the leader must ensure that people have the tools and resources they need in order to perform. If you are asking service technicians to fix a vehicle the first time it comes into the repair shop, but you do not provide the right tools, then you are not following through. Likewise, if an organizational transformation requires employees to take more responsibility or exert front-line leadership, and your organizational hierarchy prevents any sharing of authority, nothing will happen.

Rich Teerlink is candid about the challenges he and his team faced throughout Harley-Davidson's organizational transformation.[1] His leadership team tied communications to the business process and by so doing was able to gauge the results of communications in terms of the implementation and outcome of business objectives. Again and again, there were snags over a variety of different issues, including organizational systems, cultural values, and especially compensation plans. The leadership had to persevere and to use communications to drive the transformation home. Communications at Harley was not simply telling people what to do, but, very importantly, asking them for their ideas and creating a culture of learning in which best practices could be shared among groups. Change is never easy. What can assist the process and give it the impetus to succeed is a leader who is willing to communicate the goals and to listen to other ideas as the organization moves slowly and steadily onward.

LIVE THE MESSAGE BY EXAMPLE

As a leader-communicator, it is imperative that you live your message, i.e., that you walk the talk. What can happen when leaders fail to perform in accordance with their words can be disastrous. The sexual abuse scandal that has swept through the Roman Catholic Church is a sad example of what can happen when the values of the organization do not match the actions of its members. Although cases of priestly pedophilia had been well documented for decades, the Catholic hierarchy, chiefly the bishops, took no public action. Rather than turn the predatory priests over to the authorities, they simply transferred them from parish to parish, enabling these disturbed adults to continue their molestations. They extended this same veil of protection to homosexual priests who had abused teenage boys. The crisis came to a head in the Boston archdiocese in early 2002, when it became public knowledge that Cardinal Joseph Bernard Law had been a prime mover in protecting some of the most heinous of these pedophiles. Law's actions demonstrated that the Church was more concerned with protecting its own than in ministering to its victims. Only after repeated badgering from the media did Law and other members of the Catholic hierarchy acknowledge how hurtful they had been to the victims of abuse. Law ultimately resigned under great pressure.

Similarly, we have witnessed another spectacular fall—that of the celebrity CEOs who placed their own well-being above the well-being of their employees and their shareholders. To be sure, the overwhelming majority of CEOs are decent and trustworthy, but the examples of John Rigas at Adelphia, Dennis Kozlowski at Tyco, and Bernie Ebbers at WorldCom cast a negative light on all business executives. Their excessive greed cost shareholders billions.

These negative examples, however, did have positive outcomes as a result of the news coverage of the scandals. A more informed Catholic laity insisted on zero tolerance for abusers. A more informed investment community insisted on stricter standards of corporate governance. The effectiveness of a leader depends upon the trust of those who follow. Leadership communications reinforces that bond on a regular and frequent basis. So what can you do to ensure that you live your message?

- As an executive, you must conduct yourself for the good of the organization and make choices that are right for employees, for suppliers, and for shareholders.
- As a professional (e.g., physician, attorney, or accountant), you must embody the principles of your trade and treat people fairly and honestly.
- As a teacher or coach, you must set the rules and enforce them for everyone for whom you are responsible.
- As a parent, you must live for your children, doing what you can to promote their physical, mental, and spiritual development.

You can think of many more examples for yourself, but what it comes down to is this: Walk the talk. Lead by example.

Communications Planner: Making Certain that the Message Sticks

You want the audience to remember you and your message. The ways to ensure that you and your message live on are as varied as your imagination. Here are some ideas to get you started.

1. Look for opportunities to speak to the audience again. Follow up in a week to see how your presentation was received. If it was received well, offer to keep in touch.
2. Develop ways to keep in contact with the audience after you leave.
   - Develop your collateral materials, e.g., brochures or mailers.
   - Keep your web site active.
   - Email new information to your key clients every 6 weeks or so.
3. Make a list of leaders that you admire. They could be historical figures, or they could be people that you have known—teachers, doctors, or bosses. Consider these questions:
   - What makes these people leaders?
   - How do they lead with their words (e.g., communications)?
   - How do they lead by example?
   - What leadership traits of these leaders would you like to emulate?
4. Read biographies of leaders. Look for examples of how they used their communications, including presentations, to get their message across.
   - Julius Caesar wrote history and was an accomplished orator.
   - Franklin Roosevelt calmed a worried nation with his fireside chats.
   - Martin Luther King used rhetoric and stories from the Bible to inspire.
5. Create your own definition of leadership. How would you communicate that message to others?

ROSABETH MOSS KANTER—DOYENNE OF CHANGE

It may be a first for a professor who holds a prestigious chair at the Harvard Business School, but for Rosabeth Moss Kanter, it was a logical step—to synthesize her message into a rap song. Kanter has been writing, teaching, and consulting on change for more than two decades. "Why not take this [rap music] and turn it to a positive social purpose—to reclaim this genre from the gutter and elevate it to something that can inspire?"[2]

Kanter sees parallels between hip-hop and the corporate world. "I began to realize that the messages about the culture of business were just as good reaching down into the community. Like the line [in the song] that says, 'Don't get trapped in old divisions on a patch of tiny turf.' I had in mind both the turf battles that go on within bureaucracies and gangs on the street.' "[3]

CHARTING CHANGE

Through her 15 books and more than 100 articles, Kanter has been charting bureaucratic machinations and internecine corporate wars since the 1970s, when American businesses were hierarchical and those at the top ruled with the mindset of "my way or the highway." Today the landscape of American business is global, and the hierarchical systems that worked so well in a command-and-control economy are seen as dysfunctional. Organizations operating within this landscape need to evolve new models, new ways to adapt to change. And that's where Kanter comes in.

> Change is hard work. It takes time. We talk about "bold strokes" versus "long marches." Bold strokes are when leaders issue edicts—to open or close a department, say. But building and creating things of value—that takes long marches . . . and a lot of people volunteering to be followers.[4]

Her book *The Change Masters* was published in 1983, just as American businesses were on the verge of reawakening from a slump and trying to navigate the new challenges of global competition. In this book, Kanter proclaims a theme that is really a cornerstone of her work: the need to use what is at hand, chiefly people. As she writes,

> The issue is to create the conditions that enable companies to take advantage of the good ideas which already exist, by taking better advantage of the talents of their people. By encouraging innovation and entrepreneurship at all levels, by building an environment in which more people feel included, involved and empowered to take initiative, companies as well as individuals can be masters of change instead of its victims.[5]

PROLIFIC WRITER

Kanter is a strong essayist. As a former editor of the *Harvard Business Review*, she knows how to make a point succinctly so that readers, who are probably busy managers, can grasp the basics quickly. In the preface to *On the Frontiers of Management*, she calls the collection of her articles "an agenda for managerial work." She continues, "Taken together, [the articles] reinforce a single, timeless message: the importance of providing the tools and conditions that liberate people to use their brainpower to make a difference in a world of constant challenge and change." [6]

In her essay "A Walk on the Soft Side," Kanter addresses the inherent difficulties that managers have in dealing with the people side of business. Communications is essential, but in a cross-cultural environment—or today in alliances across companies—open communications can be a genuine challenge, one that leaders as communicators must address. "Leaders still need to listen, carefully, and they need to open the channels for others to talk, listen, contribute, and reflect." Such communications opens the door to organizational learning, allowing people throughout the enterprise to share best practices.[7]

In this same article, Kanter speaks of American managers' predisposition to "self-disclosure"—something that their counterparts in Asia and Europe do not have. Open communications thus raises the stakes for leaders: It discloses their shortcomings along with their successes.[8] Yet it is only through collaboration, involving communications, that change can occur. As Kanter writes in another essay, "[T]he best way to lead change is to create conditions that make change natural." Managers in organizations where change is part of the culture "release the potential of their people to create the future." [9]

Kanter's message of empowerment through change, enabling people to think and do for themselves as they turn change into an ally, has earned her many honors—she is a best-selling author, and she has valued consulting relationships, honorary degrees, and multiple leadership awards as well as recognition outside her realm. The *Times* of London named her "one of the 50 most powerful women in the world." [10] As a result, Kanter is an extraordinary leadership communicator, one who lives her message through her writing and teaching as well as consulting for both for-profit and not-for-profit enterprises.

E-FRONTIERS

Since Kanter is someone who has concentrated on organizational change, it was only a matter of time before she would explore the revolutions wrought by the Internet. When her book on the topic, *E-Volve! Succeeding in the Digital Culture of Tomorrow,* appeared in 2001, the bloom was already off the trend and *dot.coms* had become another word for "out of work" or, worse, for an elaborate con game. Even Kanter, a veteran trend observer, was surprised: "I've lived through many cycles of enthusiasm for something that gets excessive, swings too far, and all of a sudden is trashed, and then finally it gets incorporated appropriately . . . but I have never lived through a cycle where things turned on their heads so fast."[11]

While critical of some dot.com excesses, Kanter believes "*E-volve!* has enduring lessons about change, and it points the way toward key elements of how you run your company differently because it is on the Web, or simply because other companies are."[12]

Like her other works, *E-volve!* provides case studies of successful e-enterprises, coupled with survey research. From her studies she has distilled several lessons. One is the nature of e-culture itself. She does not mince words: "E-culture is not lipstick on a bulldog; it is a fundamentally different way of life . . . not just new wardrobe [casual clothes] . . . or a little redecoration."[13] Under her "requirements of change," Kanter cites the need for improvisation, the need for partnership networking, and the use of "customer power" as an agent of community building. She redefines "competition for talent" as an avenue for "empowerment" as well as providing a means for employees to learn to do for themselves and to be compensated financially as well as through the values of being part of a larger community.[14]

QUALITIES OF CHANGE AGENTS

It is in the people part that Kanter returns to her roots as a change agent. Citing the "star performers" in her book, those men and women who not only have adapted to e-culture but are adapting it, she posits "seven qualities of the mind" that are necessary in order to "e-volve."[15]

All of these qualities are timeless. "Curiosity and imagination," "communication," and "sensitivity to the range of human needs" are qualities that are familiar to many. What is different is the need for managers to be "cosmopolitan" and to possess a "grasp of complexity" in order to divine a new culture that takes "conflicting points of view into account." In points six and seven, Kanter gets to the heart of what it means to be a manager in today's world. Successful managers will "work with other people as resources not as subordinates" and "lead through the power of their ideas and strength of their voices" rather through position and rank.[16] In short, as Kanter says in an interview, "So my ultimate message is that we need leaders who react to change with curiosity, not denial. We need leaders who empower people—empower them to do the work better, to rethink how the system is designed . . . and who make value choices to use technology to benefit rather than to isolate and dehumanize people."[17]

MAKING CERTAIN THAT THE MESSAGE HITS HOME

According to Kanter, there are four keys that ensure understanding: "simplicity, consistency, repetition, and demonstration." Simplicity emerges from a "clear but simple message that is meaningful [as well as] understandable and motivational." Consistency occurs when "all communications and all actions tend to reinforce the same message." Repetition is necessary "because people never believe it the first, or even the second and third time." Demonstration comes when leaders "[u]se stories and examples from within the company to make the message tangible and concrete. People remember stories."

Leaders owe it to their people to keep their messages fresh. "If the basic message—such as mission, vision, values—still fits, then make sure it is communicated in terms that will capture people's attention as well as their imaginations." Again, stories are a good way to reinforce the basic message. When circumstances change, leaders must alter their messages. "[D]o a relevance check to see if the message still fits the circumstances. . . . If [it does] not, look for a better way to understand and communicate the challenges facing the organization and the actions required."

When it comes to addressing bad news, such as a corporate governance crisis, Kanter is direct. "Face the facts, and face the music. Communicate to all constituencies right away—otherwise any messages sound defensive and reactive. Identify actions to solve the problem, and announce them, even if they won't start right away. Then keep communicating, with frequent updates on revelations and progress." Keeping things quiet is not a viable strategy: "As we all know, cover-ups or silence often have worse repercussions than the original sin."

REACHING TO THE NEXT GENERATION

As for the hip-hop scene, Kanter has discovered a new audience. After she plays the song for Harvard alumni and business conferences, she says, "People really go crazy. Parents want to play it for their kids. And the kids themselves, they look at me with new respect."[18] Self-esteem aside, what Kanter is really doing is serving notice to those in the next generation that if they expect to succeed, they, too, must continue to learn and to innovate—in other words, to change.

Leadership Communications Lessons

Advocate for change. Change is an uncomfortable process. Throughout her life's work, Kanter has nudged, cajoled, and pushed organizations to find better ways of changing in order to find better ways to function and succeed.

Draw analogies. Find parallels with other businesses. Kanter has consulted and studied a great many organizations in the course of her career, and she draws lessons from each that she shares in her writings.

Share the learning. Leadership is about doing for others. As a teacher, Kanter shares her expertise with her students. She is also active in community affairs, from which her CD rap project emerged.

Live your message. In her work, Kanter has been consistent and constant in her messages about learning new ways to adapt to a rapidly evolving workplace in order to create a better workplace.

Note: The phrase "Doyenne of Change" is not original and has been attributed to Dr. Kanter previously. The author is grateful for its creation because it perfectly captures the essence of Kanter's work.

I've been an orator really, basically, all of my life. Since I was three and a half, I've been coming up in the church speaking. . . . I've spoken at every church in Nashville at some point in my life. You sort of get known for that. Other people were known for singing. I was known for talking.

Oprah Winfrey

LEADER AS STORYTELLER

THE ATMOSPHERE IN THE ROOM WAS TENSE. For the men in the room, what would happen next could mean a pat on the back on the way up the ladder, or a kick in the backside on the way down. It was an army briefing room. The man to be briefed was a legend, a soldier's soldier, General Creighton Abrams. For one young man in the room, a major, it was a chance to glimpse up close the legendary tank commander who had helped rescue the 101st Airborne at Bastogne during the Battle of the Bulge. The intervening years had not mellowed the old soldier; he was now commander of all forces in Vietnam. One by one the more senior officers stood up and made their briefings. There was no reaction from the general. Finally it was time for the major. He stood up, strode to the front of the room, and itemized unit strengths and weaknesses battalion by battalion. He did it without notes; he had only a pointer and some charts. When he finished, Abrams grunted and left the room.

Another soldier followed him out and returned minutes later with a big smile. "Abe's happy," he said. The major asked how he could tell. "For one thing, he wanted to know, who's that young major?"

The major was one that all of America would know two decades later: Colin Powell.[1]

That's a great story about an American hero!

Now imagine that a leader who was recounting this event simply stood up and said, "Once upon a time a young soldier gave a briefing to a general and made a positive impression."

True, but bor—ing! By the second line, members of the audience would be checking voicemail with their cell phones, answering email on their PDAs, or catnapping. They would not be engaged. Why? Because a clinical rendition omits *context* and *character*. It is from those two elements that good stories emerge.

Context and character reverberate throughout the communications of effective leadership communicators. Rosabeth Moss Kanter includes many stories from the front lines of change; if you just read the stories from her many books over the past two decades, you can get a good sense of the change that American management has experienced in recent times. Colin Powell is a good stump speaker, filling his speeches with stories from his life as well as stories of people he has met along the way. Harvey Penick's coaching method, which is reflected in his books, uses stories to illustrate points about the game of golf, as well as points about life in general. Mother Teresa told stories about the work in her mission to interviewers as well as to famous and not-so-famous people as a means of encouraging people to help the poor, not only in India but in their own communities.

Through storytelling, leaders can frame a current experience through the prism of context and character—their own or someone else's. Stories can be used to uplift the spirit, to caution the unwise, to provide insight into experiences, and even to laugh at a situation. Leaders who learn to tell stories are leaders who are innately aware of the human condition, an insight that prepares them to lead others (see Figure 12-1).

THE POWER OF A STORY

From our earliest days, we are told stories, or parables, about the rewards of being a good child and the dangers of being a bad one. *Grimm's Fairy Tales* are classic examples of the consequences of poor decision making. Little Red

FIGURE 12-1 Leader as Storyteller

Power of Story

Cautionary Tale
Reassurance
Inspirational Messages
Determination
Reflection
Humorous Anecdote
Kindness to Strangers
Courage and Vision

Riding Hood, for example, discovers the error of befriending strangers at her own considerable peril.

In the Middle Ages, storytellers and troubadours traveled from village to village, spinning yarns about lords and ladies, about star-crossed lovers and dishonorable dastards. What is Chaucer's *Canterbury Tales* if not a series of fables about human adventures and misadventures told by a group of pilgrims on their way to visit a religious shrine?

To read Peter Drucker is to experience the scope of history in its broadest sense. Part historian and part social commentator, Drucker links history with management in a way that puts management into context as a human endeavor—that is, as something that has been going on for quite some time—and to draw parallels with the way the people who came before us dealt with the challenges brought on by economic, social, political, and technological change.

Stories are fundamental to human character. In fact, they serve as frameworks for our character. They illustrate behavior in ways that only stories can because they transport the listener away from the current situation to learn about another similar situation. This separateness creates distance, which ideally will enable the listener to draw a lesson from the story that he or she can apply to his or her own work situation. And it is for this reason that storytelling is so compelling for today's leaders.

Let's examine eight different types of stories and how leaders may use them in the business situation.

THE CAUTIONARY TALE

Cautionary stories are endemic to business. Because they lack effective communication skills, many people in business tell, or direct, instead of showing by pointing at cautionary examples.

Lessons drawn from business history are always effective. One favorite is the tale of the Xerox executives who were shown the first version of the graphical user interface (GUI), featuring mouse commands. Curiously, their wives joined them for the presentation. The story goes that the senior managers saw no need for icons or pull-down menus. Their wives, however, many of whom had been secretaries, instinctively liked the computer interface. Their intuition did not prevail, and management passed up the development. Later, young Steve Jobs, on a tour of Xerox Parc in Palo Alto, saw the GUI, instantly recognized its applicability, and used the interface for Apple Computer products. Stories such as this illustrate the peril of ignoring the future for the comfort of the past. Willingness to take risks is essential.

REASSURANCE

A counterpoint to risk taking is reassurance. You need to make people feel comfortable. Baseball manager Joe Torre learned all about reassurance as a young man in basic training during the Cuban missile crisis in 1962. He was put in charge of some 50 recruits, and rumors of possible war were swirling around. Things were very tense, and the guys asked Joe if there would be a war. To which the young man replied, "Don't worry, we're not going to war." As Torre puts it with the wisdom of hindsight, "What did I have to lose by reassuring them?"[2] In other words, worry about what you can control, and forget about what you cannot control.

INSPIRATIONAL MESSAGES

The stock in trade of leaders is the human-interest story, the one that takes the listener from the valley of despair to the heights of redemption. While many may scoff at the triteness of these stories, it is not the story itself that is trite. What is trite is the way in which the speaker uses the story to manipulate emotion. If used appropriately and with honesty, stories of redemption truly do inspire.

The story of Oprah Winfrey is an inspiration in itself. There is a misperception that celebrities, once they make it, are on easy street. Oprah's ups and downs are living proof that every step in life can be a challenge. Oprah was born poor and black. She became a television newscaster at 19, but failed as an anchorwoman at 22. She hit her stride in talk television, first in Baltimore, then in Chicago, and then nationwide. She made it on the big screen with an Oscar nomination for *The Color Purple,* but flopped at the box office with *Beloved.* Her touch in the media business has been golden, but from time to time she has been the target of gossipy negative stories in the popular press. And through it all she has battled her weight, up and down. Once she said that she had lost 550 pounds over the course of her many diets. Over and over Oprah has persevered and continues to succeed on her own terms, the very model of self-inspiration.[3]

DETERMINATION

Everyone loves a story about the hero who is willing to pursue his or her goals even against the toughest of odds. Playing professional sports is among the most difficult pursuits. One of the hardest of these is the PGA tour. Thousands try to make it, but few have the stamina, the game, and the mental will to succeed.

Tom Kite, a noted golfer and a student of Harvey Penick, was a successful amateur. When he announced to his father that he was going to turn pro, his father was not pleased.

"Tom," he said, "for every 100 men who try the tour, 99 will fail."

"Dad," Tom replied, "I sure feel sorry for those other 99 because I intend to make it."[4]

And make it he did. At one point in his career, Kite was the biggest money winner of all time. He later became captain of the Ryder Cup, the first of Harvey Penick's students to do so. (Ben Crenshaw was the second.) Money aside, it is Kite's gritty determination that illuminates this story.

Another sort of determination can be found in quarterback Tom Brady. At each stage of his football career, he has overcome obstacles that would have felled a lesser quarterback. In his senior season, he seemed to be overshadowed by a younger, flashier player; despite some ups and downs, he persevered and led Michigan to an overtime victory in the Orange Bowl. In the pros, he was in the shadow of a $100 million quarterback; it did not appear that he would ever play until an injury felled Drew Bledsoe. And despite being a second-year quarterback with negligible playing time, Brady led the team to the Super Bowl, a game in which he was selected as Most Valuable Player. At every step, Brady persevered—sometimes against injury; other times against experience (Bledsoe) or inexperience (his own). His determination, coupled with his hard work and vocal team spirit, drove him forward.

One more example of determination is the career of Robert Redford. He could have been content to be a glamorous movie star—he had the looks and the box office appeal. Instead, he chose to extend himself as an actor and selected the roles he would play with that in mind. He also migrated to directing. Offscreen, he devoted his energies to environmental causes, freedom of speech, and, of course, the Sundance Institute, where artists can pursue their visions temporarily free of commercial pressures.

REFLECTION

This type of story is a voyage of self-discovery for the teller. The outcome is the leader's self-knowledge, i.e., "what I learned about myself and what I hope others will learn from this." Katherine Graham's autobiography, *Personal Story,* is such a case. Graham was shy and introverted and took to reflection naturally. When she became publisher of the *Washington Post,* she forced herself to come out of her shell and appear on the public stage. Her book is her attempt to gain perspective on her career, to tell more about her husband, Phil's, ultimately fatal battle with manic depression, and, as she writes, "to arrive at some understanding of how people are formed by the way they grow up and further molded by the way they spend their days." [5] Sounds like a pretty strong self-assessment. Ultimately, the reflection story not only leads to self-discovery for the one who tells it, but also contributes to heightened self-awareness on the part of the reader or listener.

HUMOROUS ANECDOTE

Stories don't necessarily need to have a moral, but it's good if they do. Yet that does not mean that stories must be dark. Quite the contrary: An exercise of wit can often evoke more wisdom.

Promoter Bill Veeck was a legendary storyteller as well as a one-man band of practical jokes. A favorite trick was to stab himself in the leg with an ice pick (his wooden leg, the one with a built-in ashtray). Only a man with Veeck's whimsy could turn a war injury into a prop for a joke. It was that sense of fun that inspired him to dream up ways to make coming out to the ballpark as much fun as going to the circus. Sports columnist Jim Murray once wrote of Veeck, "His mind was 71, but his heart was 12." [6]

Jokes, too, can illuminate and elucidate. Choose them carefully, however, particularly if you are not familiar with the audience. Make certain that the humor is either self-deprecating or else directed at a universal target of ridicule—bureaucracy, used car salesmen, the I.R.S., politicians, or Hollywood types.

For example, a Hollywood producer comes home early one morning to find his wife waiting for him. She's in a foul mood and demands an explanation. The producer explains that he had been entertaining a lovely leading lady who invited him back to her place. Then, the producer continued, "one thing led to another." The wife was not placated. "Don't lie to me. You've been out playing poker with the boys." [7]

KINDNESS TO STRANGERS

Compassion is a vital element of leadership. Leaders can talk about it until they are blue in the face, but one story can say more than all the lectures.

Mother Teresa had a rich treasure trove of stories, many of which make profound moral points. For example, she tells the story of the young child of 3 whom she encountered on the street. Seeing that the little girl was hungry, Mother Teresa gave her bread. "Eat, eat the bread. You are hungry." The girl did so very slowly. "I am afraid. When the bread will be finished, I will be hungry again." [8] When you hear a story like that, you cannot fail to be moved, first by the human need that exists in our world, and then by the inhumanity of a world that allows a child to starve. Telling stories like that enabled Mother Teresa to rally people to her cause, not simply as contributors, but as doers, people who would help others in their own communities.

COURAGE AND VISION

Much has been written about Winston Churchill as visionary and statesman, and with good reason. But often it is good to go back to the great man's own words to gain perspective on who he was as a man. Despite periodic bouts of what he called the "black dog" (depression), Churchill remained basically an optimist—so much so that it became infectious. But he was not so naïve as to assume that others would be as optimistic, so he tried to will them to be so. Here is an excerpt from a memo he sent in late May 1940, arguably Britain's most troubled hour:

> In these dark days the Prime Minister would be grateful if all his colleagues in the Government, as well as high officials, would maintain a high morale in their circles; not minimizing the gravity of events, but showing confidence in our ability and inflexible resolve, to continue the war till we have broken the will of the enemy to bring all of Europe under his domination.[9]

At the time Churchill dictated that note, most of Europe was under the heel of the Nazis. France had nearly fallen, and Russia was still allied with Germany. The United States would not enter the war for another 18 months. And here is Churchill, as courageous, righteous, and resolved as he would ever be in his life, calling on his nation's leadership to buck up and persevere in the face of all odds.

ACTING OUT STORIES

Storytelling also can take the form of play-acting. Trainers do this very well when they create role-plays and simulations. In role-plays, participants are asked to play roles related to work situations. For example, one participant may play an irate customer, and the other play the customer service representative. In another situation, participants may act out a performance appraisal. In training, it is often insightful to have participants step out of their current roles and assume different roles. In this way, direct reports will get to play at being supervisors, and bosses will assume the role of subordinates. These role-plays, if done correctly, can lead to insights that employees can take back to their workplace and use to function more effectively, as well as more humanely.

Simulations are more elaborate role-plays. They typically involve longer, more detailed play-acting based on an established storyline, usually a case study. Various participants assume the role of members of the organization, such as vice president of finance, vice president of marketing, director of engineering, or middle management functionaries. Simulations can last up to a day, or longer. They may even involve réplays if the facilitator provides additional variables that may affect the outcome. Both role-plays and simulations, however, are nothing more than elaborate story-telling exercises. They involve multiple players, as opposed to a single storyteller, but they are stories nonetheless.

IMPORTANCE OF TELLING STORIES

Stories are important to us. From the days of our tribal ancestors, we have been sharing tales, shaping fables, and writing plays about the human condition. Why? Because these stories, with their rich context and stylized character, cast a window of light into our souls. And from that experience we learn more about who we are and who we might become. Leadership that is rooted in story and guided in story is leadership that is centered in the human condition, which ultimately is where it belongs.

Communications Planner: Telling Stories with a Leadership Point of View

The ability to tell stories is a good leadership attribute. Abraham Lincoln used his storytelling abilities, honed as a country lawyer in Illinois, to make his points as artfully as he could. Stories can be powerful ways to bring people together.

1. Identify the stories in your organization. What obstacles did your company overcome as it became what it is today? Specify the context and character of each.
2. Identify the legends in your organization. Why are they legends? What things did they accomplish? What leadership lessons can you draw from their example?
3. If your organization has been around for more than 5 years, make a practice of inviting veterans in your company to spend time with newcomers. Ask them to share stories of the old days so that new people can get a sense of time, place, and culture.

4. If your organization is a brand-new venture, make a practice of inviting members of the organization to share stories from their past experiences. Some of these accounts may prove insightful; others may not. By encouraging people to share stories, you are trying to gain insight into what worked, what didn't, and why it did or didn't.
5. Use stories as vision tools. Invite the group to imagine the future of the team, the department, or the organization. Choose a date at some point in the future—1 year, 2 years, 5 years. Ask these questions to get people thinking and to create a visionary narrative:
   - What will the new organization be like? Be as descriptive as possible.
   - How will you be able to judge its success?
   - What individuals (or teams) will others want to tell stories about? Why? (*Be certain to ask someone to write the stories. Save them for future reference.*)

OPRAH WINFREY—LIFE AS A STORY

Amid the plethora of afternoon programs ranging from steamy soaps to shock-talk TV, there is a voice apart. It is one of clarity born of focus, conviction steeled by hard times, heart born of compassion, and natural ebullience that bubbles up frequently. It is Oprah. With Oprah, what you see is what you get. The woman is as genuine as the Mississippi hardscrabble from which she comes. She is inordinately rich and very powerful. And the key to her success and influence is simple—her ability to communicate and connect with people in a way that makes her seem accessible as well as intuitive. When Oprah speaks, people listen. Better yet from a business perspective, they buy. She is a communicator par excellence.

BUSINESS SCOPE

Oprah is more than a television personality; she is the doyenne of a self-created media empire. However, she says, "I don't think of myself as a businesswoman,"[10] and she has turned down invitations to serve on corporate boards such as those of AT&T, Ralph Lauren, and Intel. She has even kept a personal cache of $50 million in cash, not for a sense of wealth, but from a sense of fear—a personal "bag-lady fund."[11] It is a sentiment that many who were born to poverty feel even when they accumulate a great deal of wealth.

But Oprah isn't just about wealth for herself. She sits at the helm of a billion-dollar enterprise, Harpo, Inc. (Oprah spelled backwards). The anchor is *The Oprah Winfrey Show,* with a daily viewership of 22 million in the United States alone, not to mention the other 106 countries in which it airs. It has been the number one daytime show for 16 consecutive years. *O, The Oprah Magazine,* which Oprah describes as a "personal growth manual," is considered the "most successful startup ever" in magazine publishing, with revenues topping $140 million in 2001 and a paid subscriber base of 2.5 million. Her company also produces hit TV movies such as *Tuesdays with Morrie* and has a stake in Oxygen Media, described as "a cable TV company for women." She also ventures on the self-help circuit, speaking to audiences live.[12] Oprah is also an accomplished actress. She received an Oscar nomination for her role in Steven Spielberg's adaptation of *The Color Purple.* Another film, *Beloved*, was a critical hit, but was unsuccessful at the box office.

She has resisted taking her company public. "If I lost control of the business, I'd lose myself—or at least the ability to be myself. Owning myself is a way to be myself." [13] That's not a bad assessment of someone who has made a business of self-disclosure, both her own and that of her guests. She does, however, know how to make strategic alliances—with King World for distribution of her show and with Hearst Publications for her magazine. Oprah has also delegated the business operations to the president of Harpo, Jeff Jacobs, who has a 10 percent stake in the business. "He's a piranha—and that's a good thing for me to have," she says, in deference to the cutthroat world of multimedia entertainment.[14]

SELF-REVELATION AS A MEANS OF CONNECTION

Oprah has also collaborated with fitness guru Bob Greene to write a couple of books on fitness. Frequently the subject of barbs from comedians as well as commentators, Oprah has battled her weight all of her life. Her up-and-down struggle has been chronicled as much by her as by others, and her willingness to share her weaknesses (along with her triumphs) rings with authenticity.

Oprah has the capacity to crusade for issues in which she believes strongly. In 1992 she produced a documentary on abuse within families that was broadcast simultaneously on CBS, NBC, and PBS. She followed this broadcast by covering the topic on her own show, including a segment in which a young woman confronted her abusive stepfather during the program's taping. She continued speaking out on the topic, including traveling to Capitol Hill to testify. Only later did she come to the realization that she was not the one to blame for being abused as a child. The sharing of this intensely private revelation is an example of how she injects herself into her communications as a means of helping others come to grips with their own personal demons.[15] A year later, the

National Child Protection Act was enacted. She was present when President Bill Clinton signed the bill, which was also known as "Oprah's Law."[16]

Oprah is naturally empathetic and uses her own experiences to draw others out. While other hosts use topics like this to shock, Oprah uses them to raise awareness and perhaps begin a healing process — not only for her guests, but for her viewers. She does, however, admit to mistakes, recalling from the past a live show on adultery that resulted in the transgressing husband's confessing to his wife that his girlfriend was pregnant. Seeing the shock on the wife's face moved Oprah to tears herself. Still, the show crossed the line, and she did not wish to repeat the experience: "You should not have to come on television and be publicly shamed and humiliated."[17]

Oprah is more philosophical about her role. "I'm a black woman—I own the show, I own the studio . . . [and this] speaks volumes about the possibility of what a black person can do, a black female can do."[18] Oprah features successful men and woman of color where appropriate as a matter of inclusiveness. "[T]he point about breaking down racial barriers is to show that we're more alike than we're different, that all feelings, all pain, all joys, all sorrows, bear no color. The reason I've been successful is because I focus on the commonality."[19]

WORDS OF WISDOM

For Oprah, giving advice is second nature. In a way, her life is her message. Her achievements, tempered by her infectious sense of humor, give her stature; people want to listen to what she has to say. Here is a sampling from *Oprah Winfrey Speaks:*[20]

On Herself

> More than anything else, I would call myself a truth seeker. I'm always looking for truth and its value in my life. (p. 130)
>
> Power is strength over time. (p. 105)
>
> Gut is what got me to where I am today. (p. 113)
>
> I'm a person who lives my life with great passion, and I think that comes across on camera. (p. 37)

On the Future

> When I look at the future it's so bright I burn my eyes. (p. 173)
>
> I believe that you tend to create your own blessings. You have to prepare yourself so that when opportunity comes, you're ready for it. (p. 167)

On Her Fame

> I've developed a great respect for fish. I'll tell ya, because I've lived my life in a fishbowl. (p. 73)

On Her Impact

> I feel that my show is a ministry; we just don't take up a collection. And I feel that it is a teaching tool, without preaching to people about it. (p. 126)
>
> People have told me their lives have changed because of me. I take away from this the sense that I'm on the right track. (p. 170)

THE POWER OF HER INFLUENCE

An indication of Oprah's influence was evident in her decision to cease doing her monthly "Oprah's Book Club" in the spring of 2002. When she started the club in 1996, publishers claimed that her endorsement could boost sales by as much as one million copies. Over the years, that figure fell to 600,000—still a considerable amount by any measure.[21] This kind of influence is indicative of the way Oprah connects; her audiences trust her instincts because they find echoes of those instincts in themselves. (In early 2003, Oprah announced that she would bring back the book club.)

Oprah has announced that she will cease production of her show at the completion of the 2005–2006 season, after 20 years of doing the show. While she may be leaving one stage, it is unlikely that she will be leaving the arena completely. As one with the ability to connect so intimately with so many people, she is likely to continue using her communication gifts to extend her reach as she seeks to educate, entertain, and enrich those who hear her message.

Leadership Communications Lessons

Communicate in multiple ways. Oprah disseminates her messages in multiple forms of media—as talk show host, actress, author, magazine publisher, and producer. Each of her projects resonates with her credo and values.

Make a stand. Oprah keeps her image consistent with her values. She is direct, honest, and genuine.

Delegate to complement. Oprah is a shrewd businesswoman as well as one who knows how to delegate to people she trusts; in particular, she delegates the financial dealings of her enterprise.

Take a stand. Oprah has used her public platform to champion causes such as abused children and poverty-stricken parents. She also created a book club, which ran for 6 years, to champion authors and books that she thought were valuable for her listeners to know about.

Live your message. To paraphrase Marshall McLuhan, "Oprah is the message." What you see on television and through her multiple communications channels is her. She has not forgotten her roots, nor has she failed to capitalize on the opportunities that she has created with her talent, skills, and hard-earned financial muscle.

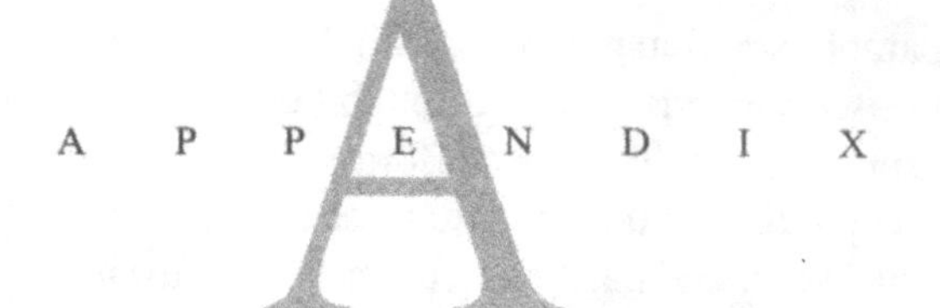

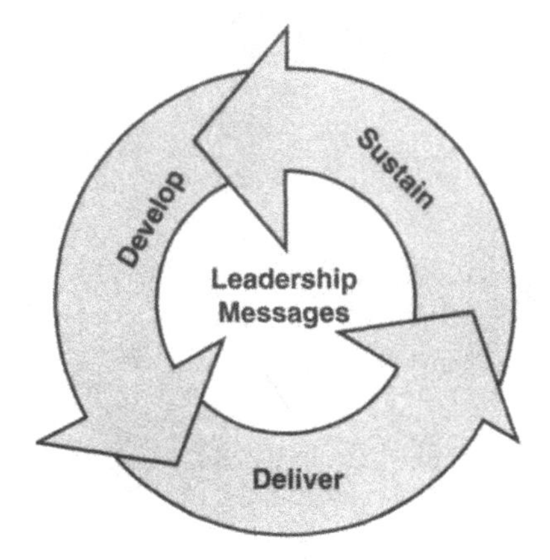

PUTTING IT ALL TOGETHER

Parts I, II, and III demonstrate how to develop, deliver, and sustain the leadership message through words and actions. This section adds some ideas for implementation: as a leader, as a speaker, and as a communications planner. It includes

- *Summary Notes*—the basics of leadership communications
- *Action Steps*—what you can do to develop leadership communications
- *Leadership Communications Action Planner*—an implementation plan for putting leadership communications into the workplace

Use the information contained in this appendix and throughout the book to improve your effectiveness as a communicator and as a leader.

SUMMARY NOTES

> In the modern world of business it is useless to be a creative original thinker unless you can also sell what you create. Management cannot be expected to recognize a good idea unless it is presented to them by a good salesman.
>
> *David Ogilvy*

WHAT LEADERS COMMUNICATE

Leadership communications are those messages from a leader that are rooted in the values and culture of an organization and are of significant importance to key stakeholders, e.g., employees, customers, strategic partners, shareholders, and the media. These messages affect the vision, mission, and transformation of an organization. The chief purpose of a leadership message is to build trust between the leader and his or her constituency. Some traits of leadership communications are as follows:

- *Significance.* These messages are about big issues that affect the present and future of the organization (e.g., people, performance, products, and services).

- *Values*. These messages reflect the organization's vision, mission, and culture.
- *Consistency*. These messages continually exemplify the organization's stated values and behaviors.
- *Cadence*. These messages occur with regularity and frequency.

WHY LEADERS COMMUNICATE

Leadership messages involve specific challenges; very often, they are tactical in nature. The messages may be designed to do one or more of the following:

- Affirm the organizational vision.
- Drive transformational initiatives, e.g., *change*.
- Issue a call to action.
- Reinforce organizational capability.
- Create an environment in which motivation can occur.
- Promote a product or service (and affirm its link to the organization's vision, mission, and values).

ACTION STEPS

1. *Set clear, credible targets.* Tell your people where you want to take the organization, whether it be a project team or an entire company. Be specific. Do not overpromise or underpromise. Steve Jobs, CEO of Apple Computer, uses his vision statements to keep people thinking about the future as well as keeping them focused on new products.
2. *Gain commitment from key stakeholders.* Engage the hearts and minds of your people. Excite them with the possibilities, and then ask for their commitment. Get your people to commit to what they will do and when and how they will do it. Lieutenant General Peter Pace of the U.S. Marines once reported to six different people. Pace strove to keep all his superiors fully informed. When disagreements arose, Pace spoke his mind, but he never went behind any of his superiors' backs. He did not always get the commitments he would have liked, but he felt that his transparent communications style served him, his superiors, and the 92,000 Marines under his command well enough.[1]
3. *Coach, coach, coach.* So much of leadership is about accomplishing results through others. People can succeed only if they have the tools and resources they need—as well as your personal involvement. And always provide plenty of feedback. Many senior leaders make it a habit to coach their direct reports regularly, giving both praise and advice on improvement, rather than waiting until the annual performance review.

4. *Be out front.* As the project or the enterprise moves forward, or even backward, make certain that you are front and center, helping to steer. See and be seen—as well as heard. In the wake of two aircraft catastrophes in New York (one on 9/11 and the other in Queens six weeks later) Don Carty, CEO of American Airlines, made himself visible. Even though his company was under siege, he was out front, taking the heat and providing a strong leadership example. Eighteen months later, Carty was forced to resign after failing to tell the unions about the existence of an exclusive pension fund for senior managers that would be untouched in the event the airline had to declare bankruptcy.
5. *Issue calls to action.* Do you need to change direction in the face of unforeseen circumstances? Or do you need to spur the team along? Speak up and ask for people's support. Telling people what needs to be done and by whom is not micromanagement; it's leadership! Football coaches excel at this: Let's run our game plan, get our points, and go home with a victory—pure and simple.
6. *Emphasize that communications is for everyone.* It's not just leaders who need to communicate. Employees need to foster communications skills peer to peer as well as up and down the organizational ladder. If only leaders speak, the organization as a whole is silent. Teams, departments, and even entire organizations that emphasize communications seem to have a greater sense of purpose and unity. Why? Because people take the time to keep one another informed and thus know what's going on.
7. *Live the message.* Communications cannot succeed on the basis of words alone. It must be reinforced constantly with actions that, like the words, stem from the culture and values of the organization. Leaders who use words to support their actions and behaviors are those who activate, energize, excite, and enthuse their followers to achieve inspired results.

LEADERSHIP COMMUNICATIONS ACTION PLANNER

What is the vision of your organization? *(Where are you going?)*
What is the mission of your organization? *(How will you get there?)*
What is the leadership communications goal of your organization? *(How will communications support the vision and mission?)*
What is the communications climate within your organization? *(Are people receptive to messages from their leaders?)* Using interviews, focus groups, and surveys, you must discover the following:

- How well leaders communicate
- How well followers understand what the leaders communicate
- How employees perceive senior leadership and the organization as a whole
- The organizational understanding of vision, mission, and values
- Any roadblocks to leadership communications (e.g., postmerger integration, a new management team, declining performance levels, or low morale)

What are your leadership communications strategies? *(How will you use communications to support organizational aims?)*

What are your leadership communications objectives? *(What do you want people to know?)*

Select and target your audiences appropriately. Looking at the following table, consider the audiences you will select for your next key leadership message.

- Will everyone receive the same message?
- Will you set up an advance briefing for key influencers?
- How will you adjust the content?
- What outcomes do you expect from each audience?

It is important to use all available channels to communicate key messages. Use this table to help you think of your key stakeholder.

Audience	Organizational	Editorial	Marketing	Web
Hourly employees				
Management employees				
Senior management				
Shareholders				
Media				
Suppliers				
Customers				

Use the following questions to assess the impact of communication:

- Which media channel aroused the most interest?
- How did leadership communications change employees' perceptions of the significant issues?
- How have the communications improved the level of trust between leader and employees?

What is the impact of your leadership communications plan? Measure results according to the following criteria:

- Who received the message?
- When did they receive it?
- How did they receive it (channel and medium)?
- What did they think of it (reaction)?
- What action did they take as a result of receiving the message?
- What behavioral changes resulted from the message?

Once your leadership communications plan is complete, what benefits will it deliver?

Use the following table as a monthly media planner to develop your next leadership communications initiative.

Media Channel	Jan.	Feb.	Mar.	Apr.	May	Jun.	Jul.	Aug.	Sept.	Oct.	Nov.	Dec.
Organizational												
Employee meeting												
Team meeting												
One-on-one discussion												
Email												
Editorial												
News release												

Guest editorial											
Speech											
Marketing											
Video											
Print											
Banner											
Web											
Webcast											
Webchat											
Postings											
Email											

NOTES

PROLOGUE

[1] Adapted from Ken Burns, "The Civil War," Public Television Viewers and PBS, produced by Florentine Films in association with WETA, Washington, D.C., 1990, as well as "Surrender at Appomattox, 1865," *Eyewitness—History through the Eyes of Those Who Lived It,* www.ibiscom.com, 1997. [References listed on website: Clarence Buel and Robert U. Johnson, *Battles and Leaders of the Civil War Vol. IV* (1888, reprinted ed. 1982; Ulysses S. Grant *Memoirs and Selected Letters*, Vol. I (1885, reprinted ed. 1990); James M. McPherson *Battle Cry of Freedom: The Civil War Era*, 1988.]

[2] Jay Winik, *April 1865: The Month that Saved America* (New York: Perennial, 2002), pp. 311–323 (bugle quote, p. 314).

[3] Ram Charan and Geoffrey Colvin, "Why CEOs Fail," *Fortune,* June 21, 1999.

[4] Ram Charan and Jerry Useem, "Why Companies Fail," *Fortune,* May 27, 2002.

[5] Robert Dallek, *Hail to the Chief: The Making and Unmaking of American Presidents* (New York: Hyperion, 1996), p. xx.

CHAPTER 1: WHAT IS LEADERSHIP COMMUNICATIONS?

[1] Peter Drucker, *Management: Tasks, Responsibilities, Practices* (New York: Harper Business, 1973, 1974).

[2] Winston Churchill, *The Second World War,* vol. 1, *The Gathering Storm* (New York: Houghton-Mifflin 1948), quoted in Geoffrey Best, *Churchill: A Study in Greatness* (London and New York: Hambledon & London, 2001), pp. 165–166.

[3] Geoffrey Best, *Churchill: A Study in Greatness* (London and New York: Hambledon & London, 2001), p. 187.

[4] Ibid., pp. 197–199.

[5] Eliot A. Cohen, *Supreme Command: Soldiers, Statesmen and Leadership in Wartime* (New York: Free Press, 2002), p. 124.

[6] Winston Churchill, "First Speech as Prime Minister," *Complete Speeches of Winston Churchill,* www.winstonchurchill.org/blood.htm.

[7] Ibid.

[8] Best, *Churchill,* p. 187. [Cited in *Mr Churchill in 1940* London: John Murray, 1948 p.29.]

[9] Cohen, *Supreme Command,* p. 120.

[10] Ibid., pp. 124–127.

[11] Ibid., pp. 127–128.

[12] Ibid., p. 132.

[13] Best, *Churchill.*

CHAPTER 2: WHO ARE YOU . . . AND WHY ARE YOU TALKING TO ME?

[1] Frank Lalli, "Guts, Grace and Glory," *Reader's Digest,* May 2002, pp. 94–105.

[2] All speech excerpts from "Text of Mayor Giuliani's Farewell Address," *New York Times,* Dec. 27, 2001.

[3] Rudolph W. Giuliani, *Leadership* (New York: Talk Miramax Books, 2002), pp. 3–26.

[4] Ibid.

[5] Ibid., pp. 183–195.

[6] Ibid., pp. 195–197.

[7] Ibid., pp. 149–154.

CHAPTER 3: DEVELOPING THE LEADERSHIP MESSAGE

[1] James Lardner, "Why Should Anyone Believe You?" *Business 2.0,* March 2002, pp. 42–48. This article provides background material on the issue of credibility.

[2] Four-step model inspired from points in Nick Morgan, "How Effective Leaders Communicate," *Harvard Management Communications Letter,* September 2002, synopsizing four points of a communications model (empathize, engage, educate, enlist) from James Wanless, *Intuition @ Work & at Home and at Play* (York Beach, Me.: Red Wheel/Weisner, 2002).

[3] Michael Useem, *Leading Up: How to Lead Your Boss so You Both Win* (New York: Crown Business, 2001), pp. 74–114.

[4] Ibid., pp. 212–247.

[5] Andy Raskin, "Free Advice for the Suddenly Non-Credible," *Business 2.0,* March 2002, p. 48. This article provides background material on the issue of reestablishing credibility.

[6] Paula J. Caproni, *The Practical Coach: Management Skills for Everyday Life* (Upper Saddle River, N.J.: Prentice-Hall, 2001), pp. 71–73.

[7] Ibid.

[8] Ibid.

[9] Katherine Graham, *Personal History* (New York: Vintage Books, 1997), p. 418.

[10] Ibid., entire work.

[11] Ibid., pp. 458–459.

[12] Ibid., pp. 575–576.

[13] Obituary of Katherine Graham, *The Economist,* July 21, 2001.

[14] Graham, *Personal History,* pp. 441–459.

[15] Ibid., p. 458.

[16] Ibid., p. 504.

[17] Ibid., p. 508.

CHAPTER 4: LEADERSHIP COMMUNICATIONS PLANNING

[1] The author is indebted to Peter Moorcroft, communications consultant and strategist, for his insights into active versus passive communications.

[2] The author is indebted to Steve Gill, author and performance evaluation consultant, for his insights and editing expertise in the section on organizational culture as it relates to interviews, focus groups, and surveys.

[3] Mark Mathis, *Feeding the Media Beast: An Easy Recipe for Great Publicity* (West Lafayette, Ind.: Purdue University Press, 2002), pp. 29-87.

[4] Eric Felten Books, "How to Be Your Own PR Flack," *Wall Street Journal,* Aug. 2, 2002.

[5] Pat Williams with Michael Weinreb, *Marketing Your Dreams: Business and Life Lessons from Bill Veeck, Baseball's Marketing Genius* (Champaign, Ill.: Sports Publishing, Inc., 2000), pp. 195–197.

[6] Daniel Morris, "PC Gamer Joins the U.S. Army," *PC Gamer,* July 2002.

[7] John Baldoni, "Selling the Message," *Harvard Management Communications Letter,* September 2002.

[8] John Schwartz, "As Enron Purged Its Ranks, Dissent Was Swept Away," *New York Times,* Feb. 4, 2002.

[9] PowerPoint presentation, "Leadership Lessons of Colin Powell," probably adapted from Oren Harari *The Leadership Secrets of Colin Powell* (New York: McGraw-Hill, 2002).

[10] Adapted from Mathis, *Feeding the Media Beast*, pp. 29-87.

[11] Shelly Lazarus, "The Boss: A Job and Life Intertwined," *New York Times,* May 23, 2001.

[12] Patricia Kitchen, "Engagement Ring to Brass Ring," *Newsday,* May 2, 2002.

[13] Ibid.

[14] Gerry Khermouch, "Shelly Lazarus: Guru of Growth," *Business Week,* Spring 2001.

[15] Ibid.

[16] Christine Canabou, "Shelly Lazarus," *Fast Company,* April 2002.

[17] Conor Dignam, "Stormy Reign for Queen of the Blue-Chip Brands," *Times* (London), Mar. 13, 2002.

[18] Canabou, "Shelly Lazarus."

[19] Ibid.

[20] Dignam, "Stormy Reign."

[21] Lazarus, "The Boss."

[22] Ibid.

[23] Thomas J. Neff and James M. Citrin, *Lessons from the Top: The Search for America's Best Business Leaders* (New York: Currency/Doubleday, 1999), p. 226.

[24] Ibid., pp. 226–227.

[25] Dignam, "Stormy Reign."

[26] Neff and Citrin, *Lessons from the Top,* p. 225.

[27] Ibid., pp. 225–226.

[28] Ibid., p. 225.

Quotes not footnoted are from an interview with the author.

CHAPTER 5: LEADING WITH E-COMMUNICATIONS

[1] Rosabeth Moss Kanter, *E-Volve!! Succeeding in the Digital Culture of Tomorrow* (Boston: Harvard Business School Press, 2001), p. 7.

[2] Carol Hymowitz and Matt Murray, "Management-Boss Talk: Raises and Praises or Out the Door," *Wall Street Journal,* June 21, 1999.

[3] Kanter, *E-Volve!* pp. 27–29.

[4] Deborah Fallows, "Email at Work: Few Feel Overwhelmed and Most Are Pleased with the Way Email Helps Them Do Their Jobs," *Pew Internet & American Life Project,* Dec. 8, 2002, www.pewinternet.org.

[5] Jack Beatty, *The World According to Peter Drucker* (New York: Free Press, 1998), p. 3.

[6] Ibid., pp. 49–68.

[7] Ibid., pp. 56–60.

[8] Ibid., pp. 184–185.

[9] Stuart Cranier and Gary Hamel, *The Ultimate Business Library: 50 Business Books that Made Management* (Oxford: Capstone Publishing, 1997), pp. 75–81.

[10] Peter Drucker, "Managing Oneself," *Harvard Business Review,* March-April 1999; and Beatty, *World According to Drucker,* p. 30.

[11] Peter Drucker, *Landmarks of Tomorrow: A Report on the "Post-Modern" World, 1959*, pp. 141–142, and Peter Drucker, *The Frontiers of Management*, p. 227, quoted in Beatty, *World According to Drucker,* p. 14.

[12] Beatty, *World According to Drucker,* pp. 25–26.

[13] Drucker, "Managing Oneself."

[14] Peter Drucker, *Management: Tasks, Responsibilities, Practices* (New York: Harper Business, 1973, 1974), pp. 481–493.

[15] Peter Drucker, *Concept of the Corporation,* (1945), p. 132, quoted in John Micklethwaite and Adrian Wooldridge, *The Witch Doctors: Making Sense of the Management Gurus* (New York: Times Books, 1996), p. 77.

CHAPTER 6: STRUCTURING THE STAND-UP LEADERSHIP PRESENTATION

[1] Andrea A. Lunsford and John J. Ruskiewicz, *Everything's an Argument* (Boston/New York: Bedford/St. Martin's, 1997), pp. 72–73.

[2] Ibid., pp. 84–85.

[3] Ibid., p. 83.

[4] Ibid., pp. 81–96.

[5] Peter Drucker, *Management: Tasks, Responsibilities, Practices* (New York: Harper Business, 1973, 1974), p. 487.

[6] Robert B. Cialdini, *Influence: Science and Practice,* 4th ed. (Boston: Allyn & Bacon, 2001), pp. 19ff, 55ff, 98ff, 143ff, 178ff, 203ff.

[7] Ibid., p. 20.

[8] Ibid., p. 53.

[9] Ibid., pp. 99–100.

[10] Ibid., p. 176.

[11] Ibid., pp. 200–201. Cialdini notes that while participants in the Milgram experiment thought that they were administering ever higher electric shocks, in fact they were not. The actor feigned pain in response to the seemingly higher voltages (pp. 180–181).

[12] Cialdini, *Influence,* p. 205.

[13] Interview with Al Hirschfeld, *60 Minutes* (date unknown).

[14] Carol Hymowitz and Matt Murray, "Management-Boss Talk: Raises and Praises or Out the Door," *Wall Street Journal,* June 21, 1999. Informality at meetings is also mentioned in Harris Collingwood and Diane Coutu, "Jack on Jack," *Harvard Business Review,* February 2002.

[15] Bill Keller, "The World According to Powell," *New York Times Magazine,* Nov. 25, 2001.

[16] Todd S. Purdum, "Embattled, Scrutinized, Powell Soldiers On," *New York Times,* July 25, 2002.

[17] Bob Woodward, *Bush at War* (New York: Simon & Schuster, 2002), p. 342. In this same interview, held in August 2002, President Bush gave a "tepid response" about Powell, calling him "a diplomat"—hardly the effusive praise he had given of him 2 years earlier.

[18] James Dao, "Powell Defends a First Strike as Iraq Option," *New York Times,* Sept. 8, 2002.

[19] Ibid.

[20] Robin Wright, "The Presidential Transition File: For Nominee, Power Lies in Restraint," *Los Angeles Times,* Dec. 17, 2000.

[21] Todd S. Purdum, "With Candor, Powell Charms Global MTV Audience," *New York Times,* Feb. 15, 2002.

[22] Purdum, "Embattled, Scrutinized."

[23] Colin Powell with Joseph E. Persico, *My American Journey* (New York: Ballantine Books, 1995; afterword 1996), pp. 380–381.

[24] Ibid., p. 343.

[25] Wright, "The Presidential Transition File."

[26] Keller, "The World According to Powell."

[27] Ibid.

[28] Woodward, *Bush at War,* pp. 321–352 (Powell's internationalism versus Cheney's unilateralism, p. 328). Also, comments made by author Bob Woodward in an interview with Gwen Ifill on *NewsHour with Jim Lehrer,* Nov. 19, 2002.

[29] Purdum, "Embattled, Scrutinized."

[30] Ibid.

[31] Keller, "The World According to Powell."

[32] Powell with Persico, *My American Journey,* p. 600.

[33] Keller, "The World According to Powell."

[34] Powell with Persico, *My American Journey,* p. 602.

CHAPTER 7: ASSESSING YOUR AUDIENCE

[1] The story of George Washington quelling the officers' rebellion at Newburgh, New York, was based on *The American President,* Episode 7, "The Heroic Posture," written, produced, and directed by Phillip B. Kunhardt, Jr., Phillip B. Kunhardt, III, and Peter W. Kunhardt, a co-production of Kunhardt Productions and Thirteen/WNET New York, 2000. [The series was based on Phillip B. Kunhardt, Jr., Phillip B. Kunhardt, III, and Peter W. Kunhardt, *The American President* (New York: Putnam Publishing Group, 1999).]

[2] Ibid.

[3] Pat Williams with Michael Weinreb, *Marketing Your Dreams: Business and Life Lessons from Bill Veeck, Baseball's Marketing Genius* (Champaign, Ill.: Sports Publishing, Inc., 2000), p. xiv.

[4] Bill Veeck with Ed Linn, *Veeck—As in Wreck: The Autobiography of Bill Veeck* (New York: Putnam, 1962); reprint, with a foreword by Bob Verdi (Chicago: University of Chicago Press, 2001).

[5] Ibid., pp. 11–23.

[6] Ibid., p. 7.

[7] Williams with Weinreb, *Marketing Your Dreams,* p. 173.

[8] Ibid., pp. 173–174.

[9] Ibid., pp. 171–172.

[10] Ibid., p. 161.

[11] Ibid., pp. 161–162.

[12] Ibid., pp. 152–165.

[13] Ibid., pp. 192–211.

[14] Ibid., pp. 192–211; in particular, p. 201.

[15] Ibid., p. 197.

[16] Ibid., p. 201.

[17] Ibid., p. 209.

[18] Ibid., p. 19.

CHAPTER 8: DELIVERING THE MESSAGE

[1] Stuart Crainer, *Business the Jack Welch Way: 10 Secrets of the Greatest Turnaround King* (New York: AMACOM, 1999), pp. 3–4.

[2] Thomas J. Neff and James M. Citrin, *Lessons from the Top: The Search for America's Best Business Leaders* (New York: Currency/Doubleday, 1999), p. 345.

[3] Crainer, *Business the Jack Welch Way,* pp. 10–14.

[4] Neff and Citrin, *Lessons from the Top,* p. 346.

[5] Jack Welch, "Letter to Shareholders," General Electric Annual Report, 2000.

[6] Harris Collingwood and Diane Coutu, "Jack on Jack," *Harvard Business Review,* February 2002, pp. 91–92.

[7] Jack Welch, interview by Stuart Varney (University of Michigan Business School), *CEO Exchange*, PBS, 2001.

[8] Collingwood and Coutu, "Jack on Jack," pp. 92–93.

[9] Ram Charan, "GE's Secret Weapon," sidebar in "Conquering a Culture of Indecision," *Harvard Business Review,* April 2001, p. 81.

[10] Varney interview.

[11] Charan, "GE's Secret Weapon," p. 81.

[12] Leslie Wayne and Alex Kuczynski, "Jack Welch in Unlikely Company," *New York Times,* Sept. 16, 2002.

[13] Jack Welch, "Commentary: My Dilemma—And How I Resolved It," *Wall Street Journal,* Sept. 16, 2002.

[14] Paul Solman, "Executive Excess: Part 4," *NewsHour with Jim Lehrer,* PBS, Dec. 5, 2002; www.pbs.org/newshour/bb/business/july-dec2002/ceo4_12-05.html.

[15] Ibid.

[16] Ibid.

[17] Neff and Citrin, *Lessons from the Top,* p. 346.

[18] Collingwood and Coutu, "Jack on Jack," pp. 92, 94.

[19] Ibid., p. 94.

CHAPTER 9: CONNECTING WITH PEOPLE BEYOND WORDS

[1] Lou Cannon, *President Reagan: A Role of a Lifetime* (New York: Simon & Schuster, 1991), pp. 46, 51, quoted in John Baldoni, "Effective Leadership Communications: It's More than Talk," *Harvard Management Communications Letter,* April 2002.

[2] Howard Gardner, *Frames of Mind: Theory of Multiple Intelligences* (New York: Basic Books, 1983).

[3] Pat Williams with Michael Weinreb, *Marketing Your Dreams: Business and Life Lessons from Bill Veeck, Baseball's Marketing Genius* (Champaign, Ill.: Sports Publishing, Inc., 2000), p. 173.

[4] "Mother Teresa," *Economist,* Sept. 11, 1997.

[5] Leo Seligsohn, "A Portrait of Mother Teresa in Action," review of *Mother Teresa,* a film by Ann Petri and Jeanette Petri; Richard Attenborough, narrator and consultant, *Newsday,* Nov. 28, 1986.

[6] Ibid.

[7] Ibid.

[8] "Mother Teresa."

[9] Mother Teresa, "Nobel Peace Prize Lecture," Dec. 10, 1979.

[10] Mother Teresa, *No Greater Love,* ed. Becky Benenate and Joseph Durepos, with a foreword by Thomas Moore (Novato, Calif.: New World Library, 1997, 2001), p. 179.

[11] "Mother Teresa."

[12] Laurinda Keys, "Mother Teresa's Writings Reveal Doubts about God," *Seattle Times,* Sept. 15, 2001; quotes were from *Vidayajyoti (Light of Knowledge)*, a Jesuit journal published in New Delhi, India, March 2001.

[13] Ibid.

[14] Mother Teresa, *No Greater Love,* p. 33.

[15] Ibid., p. 34.

[16] Mother Teresa, "Nobel Peace Prize Lecture."

[17] Neelesh Misra, "Shared Burden: Mother Teresa's Nuns Carry Out Work," Associated Press, *Orange County Register,* Sept. 5, 1998.

[18] Ed Cary, *George C. Marshall: Soldier and Statesman* (New York: Counterpoint Press, 1980), pp. 4–13 (Roosevelt quote, p. 13).

[19] Ibid., pp. 9–13 (Roosevelt quote, p. 9).

[20] Ibid.

[21] Robert D. Kaplan, *Warrior Politics: Why Leadership Demands a Pagan Ethos* (New York: Random House, 2001), pp. 13–14, citing Barbara Tuchman, *Stillwell and the American Experience in China* (New York: Macmillan, 1970). Also Forrest C. Pogue, *George C. Marshall: Education of a General (1880–1939)* (New York: Viking, 1963), pp. 247–262.

[22] Pogue, *George C. Marshall: Education of a General,* pp. 247–262.

[23] Cary, *George C. Marshall,* p. 274.

[24] Ibid., pp. 185–187.

[25] Ibid., pp. 402–403.

[26] Ibid., p. 559.

[27] Ibid., pp. 721–725.

[28] Ibid., pp. 537–550.

[29] George C. Marshall, "Text of the Marshall Plan Speech," June 5, 1947, www.bnt.com/marshall/speech.html.

[30] Forrest C. Pogue, *George C. Marshall: Statesman 1945–1959* (New York: Viking, 1987), pp. 506–507.

[31] Cary, *George C. Marshall,* pp. 6–7.

[32] Forrest C. Pogue, *George C. Marshall: Ordeal and Hope (1939–1942)*, with a foreword by General Omar N. Bradley (New York: Viking, 1965, 1966), pp. 114–119.

[33] Omar N. Bradley, foreword to *George C. Marshall: Ordeal and Hope (1939-1942)*, by Forrest C. Pogue (New York: Viking, 1965, 1966), p. ix.

[34] Cary, *George C. Marshall*, pp. 265–266.

CHAPTER 10: COACHING—ONE-TO-ONE LEADERSHIP COMMUNICATION

[1] Harvey Penick with Bud Shrake, *The Game for a Lifetime: More Lessons and Teachings* (New York: Simon & Schuster, 1996), pp. 159–160.

[2] Harley-Davidson shifted the discussion from values to behaviors. While people can debate values, what often matters more is behaviors, how people interact with others. Behaviors are observable and can be coached. For more insights into the issue of corporate values, refer to Rich Teerlink and Lee Ozley, *More than a Motorcycle: The Leadership Journey at Harley-Davidson* (Boston: Harvard Business School Press, 2000), pp. 153–157.

[3] Thomas J. Neff and James M. Citrin, *Lessons from the Top: The Search for America's Best Business Leaders* (New York: Currency/Doubleday, 1999), pp. 225–226.

[4] David Maraniss, *When Pride Still Mattered: A Life of Vince Lombardi* (New York: Simon & Schuster, 1999), p. 191.

[5] Ibid., pp. 67–87 (quote on "teacher" vs. "coach," p. 69).

[6] Ibid., pp. 216–217.

[7] Ibid., p. 217. Much has been written about Lombardi's motivational style. The last paragraph on page 157 of this book refers to Lombardi motivating players by raising their own personal expectations. A former player discussed the idea during an ESPN documentary on great coaches.

[8] Ibid., p. 222.

[9] Ibid., pp. 228–230.

[10] Ibid., p. 400.

[11] Ibid., pp. 404–405.

[12] Ibid., p. 145.

[13] Ibid., pp. 405–406.

[14] Ibid., p. 406.

[15] Ibid.

[16] Ibid. Maraniss raises this question about Lombardi's contemporary relevance in the Preface pp. 13-14.

[16] Harvey Penick with Bud Shrake, *Harvey Penick's Little Red Book: Lessons and Teachings from a Lifetime in Golf* (New York: Simon & Schuster, 1992), p. 109.

[17] Ibid., p. 26.

[18] Clifton Fadiman and Andre Bernard, eds., *Bartlett's Book of Anecdotes,* rev. ed. (Boston and New York: Little, Brown, 2000), p. 430, quoted in Robert T. Sommers, *Golf Anecdotes* (New York: Oxford University Press, 1995).

[19] Harvey Penick with Bud Shrake, *And If You Play Golf, You're My Friend* (New York: Simon & Schuster, 1993), pp. 65–67.

[20] Penick with Shrake, *Harvey Penick's Little Red Book,* p. 74.

[21] Penick with Shrake, *And If You Play Golf, You're My Friend,* p. 168.

[22] Penick with Shrake, *Harvey Penick's Little Red Book,* p. 73.

[23] Ibid., p. 25.

[24] Penick with Shrake, *And If You Play Golf, You're My Friend,* pp. 62–63.

[25] Penick with Shrake, *Game for a Lifetime,* p. 20.

[26] Tinsley Penick, epilogue to *The Game for a Lifetime,* by Harvey Penick with Bud Shrake (New York: Simon & Schuster, 1996), pp. 201–208.

[27] Ibid., p. 207.

CHAPTER 11: MAKING CERTAIN THE MESSAGE STICKS

[1] Rich Teerlink and Lee Ozley, *More than a Motorcycle: The Leadership Journey at Harley-Davidson* (Boston: Harvard Business School Press, 2000).
[2] James Verini, "Harvard Professor Has Some Rap," *New York Observer,* July 30, 2001, p. 21.

[3] Ibid.

[4] David O. Webber, "E-volving with Rosabeth Moss Kanter," *Health Forum Journal,* January/February 2002, pp. 10–15.

[5] Rosabeth Moss Kanter, *The Change Masters: Innovation and Entrepreneurship in the American Corporation* (New York: Simon & Schuster, 1983), p. 363.

[6] Rosabeth Moss Kanter, *On the Frontiers of Management* (Boston: Harvard Business School Press, 1997), p. xiii.

[7] Rosabeth Moss Kanter, "A Walk on the Soft Side," in *On the Frontiers of Management,* p. 165.

[8] Ibid., p. 167.

[9] Rosabeth Moss Kanter, "Introduction," in *On the Frontiers of Management,* p. 26.

[10] Rosabeth Moss Kanter, *E-volve! Succeeding in the Digital Culture of Tomorrow* (Boston: Harvard Business School Press, 2001), p. 352.

[11] Melissa Master, "Rosabeth Moss Kanter Says She Wants an Evolution," *Across the Board*, September/October 2001.

[12] Ibid.

[13] Kanter, *E-volve!* p. 230.

[14] Ibid.

[15] Ibid., p. 288.

[16] Ibid., p. 288.

[17] Webber, "E-volving with Rosabeth Moss Kanter," pp. 10–15.

[18] Jerry Useem, "Rapping for Managers," *Fortune,* Sept. 3, 2001.

Quotes not footnoted are from an interview with the author.

CHAPTER 12: LEADER AS STORYTELLER

[1] Colin Powell with Joseph E. Persico, *My American Journey* (New York: Ballantine Books, 1995), pp. 131–132.

[2] Joe Torre with Henry Dreher, *Joe Torre's Ground Rules for Winners* (New York: Hyperion, 1999), p. 225.

[3] Janet Lowe, *Oprah Winfrey Speaks: Insight from the World's Most Influential Voice* (New York: Wiley, 1998).

[4] Don Wade, *"And Then Jack Said to Arnie . . .": A Collection of the Greatest True Golf Stories of All Time* (Lincolnwood, IL: NTC/Contemporary Books, 1991), p. 90.

[5] Katherine Graham, *Personal History* (New York: Vintage Books, 1997), p. 623.

[6] Pat Williams with Michael Weinreb, *Marketing Your Dreams: Business and Life Lessons from Bill Veeck, Baseball's Marketing Genius* (Champaign, Ill.: Sports Publishing, Inc., 2000), p. 66.

[7] Jacob M. Braided, *Complete Speaker's and Toastmaster's Library,* 2nd ed., rev. Glenn Van Ekern (Englewood Cliffs, N.J.: Prentice-Hall, 1992).

[8] Mother Teresa, *No Greater Love,* ed. Becky Benenate and Joseph Durepos, with a foreword by Thomas Moore (Novato, Calif.: New World Library, 1997, 2001), p. 97.

[9] Randolph Churchill and Martin Gilbert, *The Churchill War Papers,* vol. 2, p. 187, quoted in Roy Jenkins, *Churchill: A Biography* (New York: Plume, 2001), p. 610.

[10] Pamela Sellers, "The Business of Being Oprah: She Talked Her Way to the Top of Her Own Media Empire and Amassed a $1 Billion Fortune. Now She's Asking, 'What's Next?'" *Fortune,* Apr. 1, 2002, p. 50.

[11] Ibid.

[12] Ibid.

[13] Ibid.

[14] Ibid.

[15] Ginny Holbert, "Oprah Winfrey Breaks Silence on Child Abuse," *Chicago Sun-Times,* Aug. 30, 1992.

[16] Maya Jaggi, "The Power of Talk Shows Has Made Oprah Rich and Famous . . .,"

Manchester Guardian, Feb. 13, 1999.

[17] Ibid.

[18] Ibid.

[19] Ibid.

[20] Lowe, *Oprah Winfrey Speaks.*

[21] David D. Kirkpatrick, "Oprah Will Curtail 'Book Club' Picks, and Authors Weep," *New York Times*, Apr. 6, 2002, p. 1.

SUMMARY NOTES

[1] Michael Useem, *Leading Up: How to Lead Your Boss so You Both Win* (New York: Crown Business, 2001), pp. 151–180.

CITATIONS FOR CHAPTER OPENING QUOTES

PROLOGUE

Louis E. Boone, *Quotable Business* (New York: Random House, 1992), p. 59.

CHAPTER 1

Steven F. Hayward, *Churchill on Leadership: Executive Success in the Face of Adversity* [Rocklin, Calif.: Forum (Prima Publishing), 1997, 1998], p. 97.

CHAPTER 2

Rudy Giuliani, "Text of Mayor Giuliani's Farewell Address," *New York Times,* Dec. 27, 2001.

CHAPTER 3

Katherine Graham, *Personal History* (New York: Vintage Books, 1997), p. 610.

CHAPTER 4

Conor Dignam, "Stormy Reign for Queen of the Blue-Chip Brands," *Times* (London), Mar. 13, 2002.

CHAPTER 5

Peter Drucker, *Management: Tasks, Responsibilities, Practices* (New York: Harper Business, 1973, 1974), p. 487.

CHAPTER 6

Colin Powell with Joseph E. Persico, *My American Journey* (New York: Ballantine Books, 1995, afterword 1996), pp. 595–596.

CHAPTER 7

Pat Williams with Michael Weinreb, *Marketing Your Dreams: Business and Life Lessons from Bill Veeck, Baseball's Marketing Genius* (Champaign, Ill.: Sports Publishing, Inc., 2000), p. 2.

CHAPTER 8

Stuart Crainer, *Business the Jack Welch Way: 10 Secrets of the World's Greatest Turnaround King* (New York: AMACOM, 1999), p. 107.

CHAPTER 9

Mother Teresa, *No Greater Love,* ed. Becky Benenate and Joseph Durepos, with a foreword by Thomas Moore (Novato, Calif.: New World Library, 1997, 2001), p. 9.

H. A. DeWeerd, ed., *Selected Speeches and Statements of General of the Army George C. Marshall* (1945), quoted in Robert A. Fitton, *Leadership Quotations from the World's Greatest Motivators* [Boulder, Colo.: Westview Press (HarperCollins), 1997], p. 197.

CHAPTER 10

David Maraniss, *When Pride Still Mattered: A Life of Vince Lombardi* (New York: Simon & Schuster, 1999), p. 406.

Harvey Penick with Bud Shrake, *The Game for a Lifetime* (New York: Simon & Schuster, 1996), p. 115.

CHAPTER 11

Rosabeth Moss Kanter, *E-volve! Succeeding in the Digital Culture of Tomorrow* (Boston: Harvard Business School Press, 2001), p. 235.

CHAPTER 12

Janet Lowe, *Oprah Speaks: Insight from the World's Most Influential Voice* (New York: Wiley, 1998), pp. 15–16.

SUMMARY

Louis E. Boone *Quotable Business* (New York: Random House, 1992), p. 156 [David Ogilvy].

Index

About the Author

John Baldoni is a communications and leadership consultant and has worked for companies large and small, including Ford, Kellogg's, and Pfizer. He is the author of three other books on leadership as well as a frequent speaker on leadership topics. John also teaches in a management development program at the University of Michigan. Readers are welcome to visit his leadership resource website at www.johnbaldoni.com.

CREDITS

For permission to reprint, grateful acknowledgment is given to the following:

PORTIONS OF CHAPTER 1

Reprinted by permission of *Harvard Management Communication Letter*. From *Effective Leadership Communications: It's More than Talk* by John Baldoni, April 2002. Copyright 2002 by the Harvard Business School Publishing Corporation; all rights reserved.

PORTIONS OF CHAPTER 2

From *Leadership* by Rudolph Giuliani. Copyright © 2002 Rudolph Giuliani. Reprinted by permission of Talk Miramax Books/Hyperion.

The author would like to thank Sunny Mindel of Giuliani Partners for her kind assistance in securing permission to quote from Mayor Rudolph Giuliani's Farewell Address.

PORTIONS OF CHAPTER 4

Reprinted by permission of *Harvard Management Communication Letter*. From *Selling the Leadership Message* by John Baldoni, September 2002. Copyright 2002 by the Harvard Business School Publishing Corporation; all rights reserved.

PORTIONS OF CHAPTER 7

The author would like to thank Pat Williams for kind permission to quote from his book *Marketing Your Dreams: Business and Life Lessons from Bill Veeck, Baseball's Marketing Genius* by Pat Williams with Michael Weinreb, Champaign, IL: Sports Publishing, Inc., 2000.

CHAPTER 11

Certain quotations appearing in the chapter on Rosabeth Moss Kanter. Copyright 1983 by Rosabeth Moss Kanter.

Reprinted by permission of Harvard Business School Press. From *Evolve! Succeeding in the Digital Culture of Tomorrow* by Rosabeth Moss Kanter, Boston, MA: 2001, pp. xiii, 26, 164-65, 167. Copyright 2001 by the Harvard Business School Publishing Corporation; all rights reserved.

Reprinted by permission of Harvard Business School Press. From *On the Frontiers of Management* by Rosabeth Moss Kanter, Boston, MA: 1997, pp. 230, 289. Copyright 1997 by the Harvard Business School Publishing Corporation; all rights reserved.

From *The Change Masters: Innovations for Productivity in the American Corporation* by Rosabeth Moss Kanter. Reprinted by permission of Simon & Schuster Adult Publishing Group.

PORTIONS OF CHAPTER 12

Certain quotations appearing in Chapter 12, "Oprah Winfrey: Life as a Story," Janet Lowe, *Oprah Winfrey Speaks: Insights from the World's Most Influential Voice*. New York: John Wiley & Sons, 1998. This material is used with permission by John Wiley & Sons, Inc.

Note: The origins of Chapters 10 ("Leader as Coach") and 12 ("Leader as Storyteller") first appeared in essay form on the author's website at www.johnbaldoni.com.